Moral
Teachings
of Jesus

Mary Foskett

ABINGDON PRESS
Nashville

MORAL TEACHINGS OF JESUS

by Mary Foskett

ISBN 0-687-03865-0

04 05 06 07 08 09 10 11 12 13—10 9 8 7 6 5 4 3 2 1

Contents

Meet the Writer

Mary F. Foskett is the Zachary Smith Associate Professor of Religion at Wake Forest University.

In addition to her extensive experience teaching undergraduate and graduate students in both religious and theological studies, Mary enjoys lecturing and teaching in congregational settings. Her major writing is in the area of New Testament and Christian origins. Mary's previous publication includes contributions to *For All the Saints: A Calendar of Commemorations for United Methodists*.

Mary resides with her family in Winston-Salem, North Carolina.

A Word of Welcome

Welcome to MORAL TEACHINGS OF JESUS, a study of the ethical teachings of Jesus as collected in Matthew's Sermon on the Mount. As you participate in this study, you will explore

- the Sermon on the Mount and how it addresses morality;
- the distinctive interests and concerns of Matthew's Gospel and their relationship to Jesus' teachings;
- loving one's enemies as a way of fulfilling God's purpose for humankind and as a means of becoming more a child of God;
- Jesus' teachings on anger and reconciliation in order to help you integrate these lessons into daily Christian life;
- Jesus' teaching on marriage, adultery, and divorce in order to facilitate your own moral examination of these issues;
- Jesus' lessons on practicing one's piety in order to help you come to a better understanding of how to practice your own piety with spiritual integrity;
- Jesus' lessons on wealth and the accumulation of material goods in order to help you develop an ethic that is informed by the Sermon on the Mount.

This study will help you rediscover ways to live a moral life based upon Jesus' understanding of the reign of God. We invite you to look closely at Jesus' moral teachings. We pray that you will be richly blessed as you reclaim the power of these teachings to revitalize your faith and to help you create a more meaningful daily life in the contemporary world.

How to Use This Resource

We hope you enjoy participating in this study, either on your own or with a group. We offer these hints and suggestions to make your study a success.

MORAL TEACHINGS OF JESUS is a self-contained study with all the teaching/learning suggestions conveniently located on or near the main text to which they refer. They are identified with the same heading (or close abbreviation) as the heading in the main text. In addition to your Bible, all you need to have a successful group or individual study session is provided for you in this book.

Some special features are provided as well, such as the **Bible 301** activities in the teaching helps. We usually think of the "101" designation as the beginning level; these "301" designations prompt you to dig deeper. In these instances you will be invited to look up Scriptures, key words, or concepts in a Bible dictionary, commentary, or atlas. On occasion, an added book or resource is cited that may be obtained from your local library or perhaps from your pastor. Those resources are extras; your study will be enriched by these added sources of information, but it is not dependent on them.

This study is intentionally invitational. In the closing activity, you are invited to do three things: (1) to give prayerful consideration to your relationship to Jesus Christ and to make or renew your commitment, (2) to offer your own spoken prayers, and (3) to pray with and for others. We trust you will participate in these activities as you feel comfortable and that you will use them as a challenge to deepen your relationship with Jesus Christ.

Session One

The Sermon on the Mount and the Moral Teachings of Jesus

Session Focus

This session introduces you to the Sermon on the Mount as a means for examining the moral teachings of Jesus.

Session Objective

We will explore the Sermon on the Mount to see how it addresses morality.

Session Preparation

Before beginning this session, read the Sermon on the Mount from beginning to end. Write your initial responses to Jesus' teachings.

Choose from among these activities and discussion starters to plan your lesson.

Imitating Jesus ■

What does the question "What Would Jesus Do?" suggest to you about living a Christian life? What does it mean to you to say that one who is a Christian is "Christ-like"?

Imitating Jesus

The imitation of Christ is both an ancient ideal rooted in the earliest of Christian traditions and a timeless appeal that calls out to every generation of faith. Recent popular trends like WWJD ("What would Jesus do?") bracelets evidence the persistence of the Christian tenet that to be a disciple of Christ is to reflect the very person and teachings of Jesus. Millard Fuller, the founder of Habitat for Humanity, places the ethics of Jesus at the very center of his international Christian ministry. To put it simply, Christians have long held that to be a Christian is to be Christ-like. Yet, as we all undoubtedly know, the imitation of Jesus is far from simple. Not only do Christians today face a host of moral challenges that are unlike those of the first century, the teachings of Jesus are themselves often complex and multi-dimensional. Following in Jesus' footsteps therefore requires not only the willingness of one's heart but the determination to examine honestly and carefully with one's mind and soul precisely what Jesus' teachings suggest about morality.

Because of the Bible's role as a primary authority to which we turn when determining what the Christian life is and how it ought to be lived, the New Testament is an essential resource for examining the moral teachings and ethics of Jesus. It also gives us a glimpse of how early Christians turned to the example of Jesus' life and ministry for help in addressing social and moral dilemmas in their own time. For instance, the anonymous writer of First Peter uses the example of Jesus' innocent suffering to encourage readers to endure their own hardships. Paul's letters, too, draw upon Jesus' example to instruct Christians in a variety of matters, including how to respond to the question of whether or not it was permissible for believers to eat meat that had been sacrificed to idols. Yet, it may be a bit surprising to learn that in all of his letters, Paul only twice quotes specific sayings of Jesus. When Paul does, he demonstrates the confidence to interpret Jesus' instruction in light of his readers' particular needs.

In short, the New Testament writings themselves show how early Christians called upon the authority of Jesus' teachings and also interpreted them for their own contexts and communities. From the beginning, determining the nature of the Christian life required not only faithful reading and listening to Jesus' teaching and example but also faithful interpretation. Christians who find themselves doing the same today stand in a long tradition.

A Cloud of Witnesses

Of all the Scripture texts to which centuries of Christians have turned to contemplate the moral teachings of Jesus, none has been more read and studied than the Sermon on the Mount (Matthew 5–7). Spanning three chapters in Matthew's Gospel, the Sermon on the Mount is a collection of

Jesus' teachings that envisions what discipleship in the kingdom of God entails. Since earliest Christianity, it has been the subject of discipleship study, training, and moral instruction. Ancient writers like Clement of Alexandria, John Chrysostom, and Augustine wrote commentaries and sermons on the Sermon on the Mount. Centuries later, Martin Luther and other Protestant reformers also reflected extensively on Matthew 5–7. John Wesley turned again and again to the Sermon on the Mount for moral and spiritual direction. More recently, Dietrich Bonhoeffer captured the radical, all-encompassing call that he heard at the heart of Jesus' sermon in his famous book, *The Cost of Discipleship*.

Therefore, in this study you are invited to join the many witnesses who have read and contemplated Jesus' instruction in Matthew 5–7. Just as Christians throughout the ages and from all walks of life around the globe have been led to a sometimes familiar, sometimes new word from God in the sermon, so may we, together with our communities of faith, hear a message and discern a vision for our own time and place. To begin, we will consider together briefly the sermon as a whole—how it speaks to morality and some of the basic premises on which it is built. Later we will reflect on how specific moral teachings of Jesus might speak to us today. Keep in mind that this study aims to partner with you so that you may hear and see within the Sermon on the Mount a word and a vision for your own life and community of faith. It is my hope that rather than limiting or defining your interpretation of the sermon, this study will facilitate your confidence in discerning for yourselves how Jesus' moral teaching speaks today.

The Sermon on the Mount

Tell one another your initial response to Matthew 5:20 and 5:48. How have you read these verses in the past? How have they affected your response to the Sermon on the Mount as a whole?

The Sermon on the Mount

Even a quick reading of the Sermon on the Mount allows us to see why Christians throughout the ages have turned to it for spiritual and moral renewal. Unfolding over the course of three chapters in Matthew's Gospel, the sermon is often divided by editors and translators under several topical subheadings, many of which clearly speak to issues of ethical and moral significance: "Concerning Anger" (5:21-26), "Concerning Adultery" (5:27-30), "Concerning Divorce" (5:31-32), "Concerning Retaliation" (5:38-42), "Judging Others" (7:1-5), "Concerning Self-Deception" (7:21-23), among others. While many biblical scholars conclude that like its parallel in Luke 6:17-49 (the Sermon on the Plain), Matthew 5:3–7:27 is more a series of teachings that have been grouped together than a sermon proper. What we call the Sermon on the Mount is carefully crafted to move and transform us. It is Matthew's way of helping us to envision with Jesus life lived according to the rule of God.

Jesus' vision offers a vision of life in a new key, and what a radically new key it is. Just as generations of readers have turned to the Sermon on the Mount for inspiration, so have many readers been more than a little taken aback by the sermon's demands. Teachings, such as "Unless your righteousness exceeds that of the scribes and Pharisees, you will never enter the kingdom of heaven" (5:20) and "Be perfect, therefore, as your heavenly Father is perfect" (5:48), are not easy to read or appropriate. So while the sermon lends itself to moral and ethical reflection, it also gives rise to questions like, "But what if I can't be perfect? Is there a word here for me?"

Practice and Wisdom

Think of the persons you have known whose lives exemplify morality as practice and wisdom. Pair up with another person in your group and discuss why and how such persons are models of discipleship.

Morality as Practice and Wisdom

Before we address particular teachings in the Sermon on the Mount, let's think about how the sermon approaches morality. To begin, we should note that 5:3–7:27 is less concerned with listing specific injunctions and laws and much more concerned with providing principles and illustrating attitudes and perspectives by which to live. This leaves to Matthew's readers the task of discerning how to interpret and live by the sermon's lessons.

As a whole, Matthew 5–7 presents us with two ways of thinking about morality. The first presents morality as something that is active, practiced, and lived out. It is something that we *do*. In terms of Christian discipleship, morality is rooted in the imitation of Jesus' actions and teaching. As we will see in our study together, the kind of moral practice that the Sermon on the Mount demands is neither mimicry nor compulsive perfectionism. Rather, the sermon urges us to put into action a particular vision of discipleship and community. Here Matthew's vision of the kingdom of heaven is foundational for how we understand discipleship and the life of our faith community.

A second way of thinking about morality is as rooted in the Sermon on the Mount as the first. Here we may think of morality not as moralism but as wisdom. In this sense, Jesus himself not only models right moral practice, he also reveals to us the actions and attitudes that are distinctive to the kingdom of heaven. If one is to practice morality, one first needs eyes to see and ears to hear precisely what constitutes moral action, values, and beliefs according to the ruling of God. Not surprisingly then, the sermon focuses on setting before us not specific commands but paradigms that help us first to imagine the kingdom of heaven.

Thus the Sermon on the Mount brings together two dimensions of morality: practice and wisdom. Our study will focus on both. This is not to suggest that our study of the Sermon on the Mount will be either definitive or comprehensive. Indeed, as biblical scholar, Daniel Patte, suggests, faithful Christians read and interpret Scripture in a variety of ways. Since our aim is to examine the moral teachings of Jesus, we will consider especially what the Sermon on the Mount teaches us about morality as practice and wisdom. Two of the ways that Patte describes for approaching Scripture nicely mirror these very aspects of the Sermon on the Mount. The first he calls "Scripture as *Family Album*," where readers gain a sense of identity and purpose from the call to imitate Jesus and participate in the kingdom of God ways. The second way of reading Patte calls "Scripture as *Corrective Glasses*." When one reads the Bible in this way, the Word "allows believers to see their lives/experiences with the eyes of faith, discerning in the midst of evil 'what is good and acceptable and perfect' (Rom. 12.2) and what God is doing" (*The Challenge of Discipleship: A Critical Study of the Sermon on the Mount as Scripture*, Trinity Press International; page 59). In our study, we will see how the Sermon on the Mount, in calling us to imitate Jesus, enables us to envision, practice, and discern what is moral.

Bible 301 ☐

Examine the different ways in which people of faith approach the Bible in general, and the Sermon on the Mount in particular, by reading Daniel Patte, The Challenge of Discipleship: A Critical Study of the Sermon on the Mount as Scripture (Trinity Press International, 1999). Look at articles on the Sermon on the Mount in commentaries and Bible dictionaries like Interpreter's Dictionary of the Bible or Anchor Bible Dictionary.

The Ruling of God ▪

What comes to mind when you pray, "Our Father in heaven, / hallowed be your name. / Your kingdom come. / Your will be done, / on earth as it is in

Envisioning the Ruling of God

As we study the moral teachings of Jesus, we will encounter important aspects of Matthew's vision of the ruling of God. Let us begin, then, by thinking together about the heaven." What do you envision when you think of God's kingdom? What feelings and longings are stirred when you contemplate the question? Draw a picture or list words that express your thoughts and feelings and then share them with one another.

Bible 301 ☐

Explore further what the kingdom of God *means. Consult a good Bible dictionary such as* Interpreter's Dictionary of the Bible *or the* Anchor Bible Dictionary.

notion of God's ruling, or kingdom. The idea itself is rooted in Jewish belief that pre-dates the ministry of Jesus. One of the most exciting aspects of the mid-20th-century discovery of the famous Dead Sea Scrolls was their confirmation of ancient Jewish belief in a future age that would be characterized by the triumph of God over evil, injustice, and suffering. Although we cannot know for sure how common such thinking was, we do know that this kind of expectation was alive, and in varying forms, in Jewish belief.

In the Gospels of Mark and Luke, this kind of future expectation finds expression in Jesus' many references to the kingdom of God. Reflecting Jewish piety that refrains from uttering the sacred name of God, Matthew's Gospel prefers the phrase, *kingdom of heaven.* Whether called the kingdom of God or the kingdom of heaven, the meaning is the same. It signals a specific way of thinking about the order of human existence and of all creation now and in the future. Referring not so much to an entity or a place, "kingdom" language describes *a new order of being* that occurs on an individual, communal, and even cosmic level. The kingdom of heaven is an order of being that manifests the power, will, and sovereignty of God over all creation.

According to the Gospels, the kingdom of God is associated with the imminent future. Time is divided into two distinct ages—the present age that is and the new, or future, age to come. The present age is character-ized, in part, by the ongoing, conflicting activity of both good and evil. But the future is cast as a wholly different age, one that will witness the unfettered power and ruling, or kingdom (*basileia*), of God. No longer war-ring against the power of evil, God's way and judgment will be recognized by all of creation. In contrast to the present age in which we now live, the future will see the *complete realization of God's way* on earth. When Jesus teaches, "The kingdom of heaven is like treasure in a field, which someone found and hid; then in his joy he goes and sells all that he has and buys that field" (13:44), he is pointing to life that is envisioned and practiced according to God's way. As Jesus' parable says, life lived in this kind of abundance and joy is worth all that one has.

If the Gospels' focus on the kingdom of God sounds familiar, it may be because it lies at the very heart of the Lord's Prayer: "Our Father in heaven, / hallowed be your name. / Your kingdom come. / Your will be done, on earth as it is in heaven" (Matthew 6:9-10). And in Matthew's Gospel, in particular, the Lord's Prayer occurs right at the center of the Sermon on the Mount. Not only is the Sermon on the Mount built upon hope in God's kingdom and its manifestation on earth, but Jesus' earthly ministry is founded upon expectation that the Kingdom is real, approaching, and even partly present. Remember that Jesus began his earthly ministry with this urgent call: "Repent, for the kingdom of heaven has come near" (Matthew 4:17). In Matthew's story of Jesus, Jesus' preaching focuses on the nearness of the kingdom of heaven. Neither Jesus' ministry nor his preaching can be understood apart from this message.

Discipleship and the Kingdom ■

What connections do you see between discipleship and the kingdom or reign of God?

Discipleship and the Kingdom

Since discipleship is about imitating Jesus and "the Way" (Acts 9:2) that Jesus reveals, it is also very much about recognizing and following the way of the kingdom of heaven. Any examination of Jesus' moral teachings must begin with this understanding. Jesus is not concerned with morality for its own sake. Jesus seeks disciples and participants in the way of being that expresses the ruling of God in people's hearts and lives. Much of the Sermon on the Mount is aimed at helping us discern the way of the Kingdom so we can make as real as possible, even in this present age, God's way on earth "as it is in heaven" (6:10).

Now and Not Yet ▮

Have you ever caught a glimpse of the ruling of God? What would it be like to experience such a moment as an ongoing, ever-present reality? Discuss what you can do to help create such moments in your life and others.

Now and Not Yet

This brings us to another important aspect of how Jesus talks about the kingdom of heaven. In the Gospels, Jesus not only proclaims the future coming of God's kingdom, he also claims that it is *partly present*—hidden alongside all that is not of God's kingdom—but nonetheless here. In Matthew's Gospel, Jesus speaks of the weeds and wheat that, sown separately, are growing together in the present age (13:24-30). It is not until the new age fully arrives that the weeds and wheat will be separated one from the other (13:37-43). At that point, the kingdom of heaven will be fully present and fully acknowledged by all. Until then, the Kingdom is here in glimpses, made known by persons and communities in Kingdom-filled moments.

At first this sounds a bit contradictory, doesn't it? Perhaps if we call to mind an experience common to many people, this way of understanding the kingdom of God may make more sense. Every now and then, we experience in our lives a moment when everything just seems to come together in the most wonderful way, when "being" itself appears to be an abundant gift. Such an experience might occur in a major life event, like a wedding or a graduation. Oftentimes, though, this kind of experience is enjoyed in the midst of a quieter, more everyday experience, like sharing a special moment with a close friend, receiving a heartfelt embrace from a young child, or gazing upon a sunset so beautiful it takes one's breath away. In moments like these we feel deeply connected to something far bigger than ourselves alone—whether to life, to another person or group of people, to beauty itself, to creation, to God. Sometimes we even feel a pang of poignancy because we know all too well how rare such moments are.

These kinds of experiences are encounters with the sacred. They afford us a glimpse of Life with a capital L—of something beyond everyday life with a little l—of Life in a different key. Through the ages, Christians have been moved by such moments. Indeed, seeking the extraordinary, or the sacred, in the ordinary practices of everyday life is one aim of Christian contemplative tradition and spiritual direction.

Perhaps Jesus' way of speaking of the kingdom of heaven as both partly present and a future reality, as both now and not yet, makes a little more sense now. In Matthew's Gospel, when Jesus talks about the kingdom of heaven as present, in part, he is describing those ways of thinking and acting that express life lived according to God's ruling, Life with a capital L. In the future age, all will be guided by the power and ruling of God. But until then, even in the midst of evil and that which runs counter to the ways of the Kingdom, Jesus' disciples are called to live in the present with one foot in the future. The Sermon on the Mount calls us to participate, as much as is possible in this age, in the Kingdom that will be fully manifest in the next.

Two Illustrations: Matthew 5:3-16 and Matthew 5:17-48

In order to see more clearly how the Sermon on the Mount envisions this sense of the now and the not yet and the place of moral practice, let's consider briefly two well-known units in Matthew 5: the Beatitudes (verses 1-12) and the Antitheses (and their introduction, verses 17-48).

Living in the Now and Not Yet

The Beatitudes, often translated as a series of blessings ("Blessed are the poor in spirit . . ."), are a series of declarations that point both to the present and to the future. By opening his sermon in this manner, Matthew reminds his readers that Jesus' instruction is inherently oriented to both the future and the present. For those who follow Jesus, the present and the future make sense in light of each other.

The Greek word (*makarios*), often translated "blessed," actually means "happy." But Jesus is not invoking the kind of frivolity that English usage of the word *happy* commonly brings to mind. Frequently used in ancient wisdom teaching, *happy* refers to the particular disposition that comes with wise discernment. What Jesus conveys in the Beatitudes is the kind of blessing wisdom confers in the present. Those whom Jesus describes here will be rewarded when the kingdom of heaven comes in the future, but they are also partly uplifted now by the knowledge of such reward.

Yet, the focus is not simply the promise of future reward. As Jesus singles out the kinds of persons who will be rewarded, he is *showing us how to discern the attitudes, values, and desires that his followers are to exhibit.* In other words, those to whom the kingdom of heaven

Living in the Now and Not Yet

Read the information in the main text about the word *makarios* ("happy"), which means much more than a pleasant feeling. What kinds of happiness do you think come with the wisdom Jesus describes in the Beatitudes?

will belong in the future *participate in the way of the kingdom now* precisely by exemplifying what Jesus describes. The kingdom of heaven will belong to the poor in spirit because they are poor in spirit (5:3); the mourners will be comforted in the future because they mourn now (5:4); those who are hungry for righteousness will be filled in the future because now they long after righteousness (5:6); and the merciful will receive mercy because they are already merciful (5:7). In other words, the promise of the Kingdom does not function like a golden apple after which Jesus' disciples strive. The promise of the Kingdom comes to those whose striving now is in keeping with the way of the Kingdom. For these, the Kingdom will come in the future, but it is partially revealed by the way these persons already live. Happy wisdom comes with both future hope and present discernment of Kingdom ways. The persons of whom Jesus speaks are models for us of morality expressed as both practice and wisdom.

Practice Makes Perfect

Practice Makes Perfect ■

Read together Genesis 1:27. Discuss what it means to be created in the image of God. How do humans reflect God's own being?

As our study proceeds, we will consider in detail several of the lessons that appear in the section known as "the Antitheses" (Matthew 5:21-48). The designation refers to the six sayings of Jesus that begin with, "You have heard that it was said . . ." only to add, "But I say to you. . . ." Readers think of the so-called antitheses as statements of opposition or contrast. However, to impose this impression on Jesus' statements is to distort the meaning of his teaching. For oftentimes, Jesus' point is to strengthen, if not radicalize, the teaching he first cites.

The Antitheses are preceded by an introduction (5:17-20) whose statements about the "law and the prophets" are essential for understanding the general thrust of Matthew 5:20-48. Far from annulling the Jewish practice of keeping the law, or Torah (also known as the Pentateuch or the Five Books of Moses), Jesus asserts that his purpose is to fulfill Torah. He proclaims: "Do not think that I have come to abolish the law or the prophets; I have come not to abolish but to fulfill. . . . For I tell you, unless your righteousness exceeds that of the scribes and Pharisees, you will never enter the kingdom of heaven" (5:17, 20). Jesus' call to "excessive" righteousness, that is, righteousness in abundance, permeates the Antitheses. And what the Antitheses serve to illustrate is summarized in the final verse of this section, "Be perfect, therefore, as your heavenly Father is perfect" (Matthew 5:48).

At first glance, the verses that frame Matthew 5:17-48 seem to smack of a futile perfectionism. We might ask, who can possibly live up to all that? Who can be perfect? If we consider carefully Jesus' reminder that his lessons are directed to those seeking to "be children of your Father in heaven" (5:45), then the meaning of Jesus' call to be perfect becomes clearer. Disciples, or those seeking to be known as children of God, are to reflect God's own self. This is not a new premise, but one that is rooted in the biblical account of creation: "So God created humankind in his image, / in the image of God he created them" (Genesis 1:27). It is also in keeping with biblical tradition that focuses on Israel's purpose to reflect the moral holiness of God: "Speak to all the congregation of the people of Israel and say to them: You shall be holy, for I the LORD your God am holy"(Leviticus 19:2). Not only is the Sermon on the Mount's call to be perfect a call to reflect God, it is also a call to complete the very purpose of humanity. The Greek word (*telios*) that is translated "perfect" suggests not perfectionism but completion and wholeness. The call to live as children of God is a call to wholeness. Far from issuing a new and rigid demand, the sermon reminds us of our identity and purpose within the community of faith, as participants in the kingdom of heaven and as human persons. While we will soon enter into a more detailed study of Matthew 5:38-48, even this overview of Matthew 5:17-48 shows us that it is moral wisdom and practice, not a punishing perfectionism, that brings persons to wholeness. In Session Three we will consider in greater depth the nature of such human (and godly) wholeness.

Looking Ahead

We will continue our study of Jesus' moral teachings in the Sermon on the Mount over the course of six sessions. Session Two will provide a general understanding of Matthew's Gospel as the context for studying the sermon. Sessions Three through Seven will focus on specific topics that Jesus addresses in the Antitheses and subsequent portions of the Sermon on the Mount. In these sessions we will consider together how the Sermon on the Mount helps us envision the way of the kingdom of heaven and the moral practices that make real among us, even now, the Kingdom that is yet fully to come.

Closing Prayer

Have one person read aloud the Lord's Prayer in Matthew 6:9-13. After taking time to meditate in silence on this prayer, repeat the Lord's Prayer again as a group.

Session Two

The Gospel of Matthew and the Sermon on the Mount

Session Focus

This session focuses on the distinctive interests and concerns of the Gospel of Matthew as the context for examining the Sermon on the Mount.

Session Objective

We will explore how the distinctive interests and concerns of Matthew's Gospel can help us engage Jesus' teachings in the Sermon on the Mount.

Session Preparation

Before this session, make a list of the various social, cultural, political, and religious realities that shape the ethical and moral issues that confront us today. Check the newspaper or TV news shows to help with your lists.

Choose from among these activities and discussion starters to plan your lesson.

Matthew's Story

Practice listening to Matthew on his own terms. Without reading the Gospel first, recount the story of Jesus' death. Then read Matthew 27:45-56. Discuss the differences between your memory of the story, which has probably been shaped by the combined witness of all the Gospel, and Matthew's particular story.

Listening to Matthew's Story

While all four of our Gospels clearly refer to the same Jesus of Nazareth, the four portraits of Jesus that they present are far from identical. Rather, each Gospel tells its own story of Jesus and presents its own witness to Jesus' ministry and teachings. Each asks to be read on its own terms and for the sake of its distinctive testimony.

To read a single Gospel in this way is a lot like being in a fellowship of believers where each person is asked to share his or her journey of faith, one at a time, with the rest of the group. While others might want to comment on his or her story, interrupting or adding to someone's personal testimony would likely be considered inappropriate. The group would want to hear each story on its own terms.

Reading Matthew with an ear for its distinctive witness is like asking other New Testament witnesses to quiet down in order to give Matthew a hearing. Familiarity with the rest of the New Testament may cause this to feel a bit awkward. But while we cannot erase knowledge of other Gospels, we can suspend our interaction with other stories of Jesus long enough to listen, as best we can, to the testimony that Matthew provides.

Between Matthew and Luke

Read Luke 6:20-26 and Matthew 5:3-12. Compare and contrast the Scriptures. Which parts are similar? Which parts are different? Notice how Matthew used Q (*quelle*) or the material that is similar in the two Gospels. What effect and purpose does Matthew's use of Q seem to serve?

Between Matthew and Luke

Reading the Sermon on the Mount on its own terms means not imposing upon it expectations, assumptions, and language from other New Testament texts, even should another text be quite similar to it. A case in point are the Beatitudes in Luke's Sermon on the Plain (Luke 6:20-26). Take a moment to read the Beatitudes in both Luke's Gospel and Matthew's (Matthew 5:3-12). The Beatitudes in the two Gospels clearly share much in common. Both describe as "happy" (*makarios*) persons who are poor, hungry, reviled, or in mourning.

A majority of scholars suggest that what Luke and Matthew both include in their Beatitudes comes from a hypothetical (that is, undiscovered) collection of the sayings of Jesus (including parables, pronouncements, aphorisms, and so forth). Since it was ancient practice to preserve the wise sayings of a philosopher or religious teacher for his or her disciples, the suggestion is a plausible one. And because Luke and Matthew actually hold in common much tradition about Jesus that appears to have been unknown to Mark, interpreters suggest that this collection of sayings (called simply "Q" for the German *quelle*, or "source") was written early enough to have circulated widely among early followers of Jesus and to have become familiar to both Matthew and Luke.

Whether or not such a hypothesis will ever be proven, it is clear that Matthew and Luke convey similar traditions of Jesus' moral teaching when they record their versions of the Beatitudes. Yet despite their similarities, the Beatitudes in these Gospels are also quite different from one another. Matthew expands on the four sayings that he shares with Luke to proclaim happy those who are meek, merciful, pure in heart, and makers of peace. Luke, in turn, adds not more blessings, but a set of four woes to the four Beatitudes that are included in Matthew. The effect is quite charged:

> But woe to you who are rich,
>> for you have received your
>>> consolation.
> Woe to you who are full now,
>> for you will be hungry.
> Woe to you who are laughing
>> now,
>> for you will mourn and
>>> weep.
> Woe to you when all speak
> well of you, for that is what
> their ancestors did to the
> false prophets.
>> (Luke 6:24-26)

Clearly, Matthew and Luke move in two directions for the purpose of sharing the testimony distinctive to each. The differences themselves signal each Gospel's special interests.

Focusing now on Matthew, read again Matthew 5:3-12. Whereas Luke refers to "you who are poor" and "you who are full now, / for you will be hungry," Matthew refers to "the poor in spirit" and "those who hunger and thirst for righteousness." The difference in language is characteristic of the sermon's overarching purpose. For as we saw in our previous session, the sermon illustrates the attitudes and practices that express the ruling of God. What many interpreters identify as a "spiritualizing" tendency in the Beatitudes reflects this larger aim. Thus Matthew includes Beatitudes absent from Luke that help fill out the vision of the Kingdom that he wishes to impart to his readers. In contrast to Luke, he places the Lord's Prayer (additional Q tradition) in the center of the Sermon on the Mount. Again we can see how Jesus' moral teaching grows out of his message about the nearness of the kingdom of heaven.

Matthew's World and Our World ■

In what ways are the challenges facing our world different from those Matthew encountered? How are they the same? Where can you connect to the issues Matthew faced?

Matthew's World and Our World

Although each of the canonical Gospels has much to offer a study of Jesus' moral teachings, the Gospel of Matthew is an especially good place to start for churches poised at the beginning of the 21st century. The opening notes to this session suggested that you prepare for this study by making a list of the various social, cultural, political, and religious realities that shape the ethical and moral issues that confront us today. If you had time to create such a list, chances are good that it includes challenging issues like an ever-increasing religious, cultural, and ethnic pluralism; current national and international debate over crime, capital punishment, and human rights; the medical and scientific advances that have outpaced reflection on the ethics of actually implementing and applying them; the threat of war and the ongoing challenge of peacemaking; and changing sexual ethics, to name just a few. The list is potentially endless. We in the information age live in an extremely fast-paced, fast-changing, and anxiety-inducing age where many yearn for a sense of direction, meaning, justice, and order—a world in which we hope not only to discover our own place but also how to relate to one another and to other communities.

Matthew's Gospel, like much of the New Testament, was born in an age of tumult, change, and anxiety. At times, it appears to bear the mark of concerns and stresses not unlike those shouldered by our own contemporary faith communities. Although we know neither the actual identity of the Gospel's author (whom we will nonetheless continue to call Matthew) nor the location where the Gospel was composed, a consensus of interpreters assumes that the author was a Jewish follower of Jesus and places the text's composition somewhere between A.D. 80 and 90. Furthermore, scholars conclude that the Gospel most likely originated in a city that included a sizable Greek-speaking Jewish population as well as a significant number of Gentiles. While centers in both Palestine (Caesarea Maritima, Sepphoris, Tiberias) and Syria (Antioch, Damascus, Edessa) have been suggested as the location of Matthew's composition, none is certain.

What is most pertinent to this study is that the Gospel's language and themes suggest the presence of social, political, and religious dynamics befitting a pluralistic and post-war context. Written in either Palestine or Syria, Matthew's Gospel emerged in a setting shaped by a variety of social and cultural realities, including religious diversity, Roman imperialism, Hellenistic culture, and Jewish tradition and identity. Moreover, it was written in the decades immediately following the first Jewish War with Rome (A.D. 66–70), the conflict that had led to the very destruction of the Temple in Jerusalem, whose surviving Western Wall (the "wailing wall") remains a sacred site to this day.

The Aftermath of War

Composing this study where I live in the United States in the year 2003 and in the aftermath of the recent war between the United States and Iraq, Matthew's postwar context is especially striking. Many US citizens, even those who felt only a minimal connection to the war, find themselves left

The Aftermath of War

Think about the different ways the US war with Iraq has been viewed by your faith community. What issues and challenges have the war and its aftermath posed for the church? How is the church affected by the political life of a nation?

with a host of disturbing questions and uneasy answers. Is the war really over? What does peace really look like? Were there not better options we might have pursued? What has happened to the role of public dissent in the US? How has the war had an impact on the social political climate for various ethnic and religious minorities in the US and their relations with others? For Christians, what was and what is a true Christian response to the workings of war and peace? And what meaning did this war really have? The questions are not likely to dissipate anytime soon. Unless one buries one's proverbial head in the sand, the reverberations and implications of war linger long after any declaration of its conclusion.

Though we cannot know specifically how Matthew's community viewed or experienced the war of A.D. 66–70 as it unfolded, we can imagine that they did feel in some way the impact of a war waged and fought in their general region of the empire. Indeed, if Matthew composed his Gospel in Antioch, the capital of the Roman province of Syria, his community would have witnessed how Antioch served as a major military base and an economic pipeline for the Roman army laying its siege against Jerusalem.

For Jews and Jewish Christians living in the aftermath of the Jewish uprising against Rome, armed opposition against Rome could have been seen as either a brave attempt at liberation from an oppressive imperialism or a foolish and self-destructive exercise in futility. As the dominant power in the region, Rome exercised an iron fist over the territories in which earliest Christianity grew. Politically dominated, heavily taxed, sometime religiously oppressed, and always subject to the threat of Roman brutality as a form of maintaining the so-called *pax Romana*, the Jewish population and all non-citizens living in the outer reaches of the empire had plenty of reason to yearn for an alternative world order.

While the history of later rebellion against Rome indicates that the Jewish people did not relinquish all hope in political liberation and national independence, it is difficult to generalize about the Jewish response to Jerusalem's defeat. What can be said is that in the aftermath of war with an empire that regarded political and military success as a sign of divine benefaction and religious piety as a civic duty (the charge of atheism was synonymous with that of sedition), language of a "kingdom of heaven" bears political meaning.

Rome and the Kingdom of God

Matthew's Gospel advocates neither political theory nor a specific political system. It does proclaim boldly the nearness of the ruling of God and the presence of God made known not by Caesar but by Jesus/Emmanuel ("God with us," 1:23). The theme of God's presence in Jesus serves as the very framework for Matthew's Gospel. Just as the opening chapter reminds us of the meaning of Emmanuel's name, the closing verses of the book consist of Jesus' reminder to his disciples: "All authority in heaven and on earth has been given to me. . . . Remember, I am with you always, to the end of the age" (28:18, 20).

Seen in this light, Jesus' central message to "[r]epent, for the kingdom of heaven is at hand" (4:17) is a call to acknowledge not only a new and alternative order to Roman rule but the sovereignty of God over all creation, including Roman rule. To envision

Rome and the Kingdom of God ■

How does Matthew 5:3-12 pose an alternative to the values and ways of imperial rule? What are the political implications that the Gospel poses today? Is it difficult to consider the political significance of the Gospel? If so, why, and how should we respond?

with Matthew the ruling of heaven is to call into question the sovereignty of Rome. Thus while the kingdom of heaven is not a political system, it is politically important. To receive fully Jesus' radical message is to understand that the rule of Caesar is not only inferior to but counter to the ruling of God. It manifests the very evil that defines the present age. As Warren Carter suggests, Matthew's account of Jesus' future return depicts a completely new order. For the kingdom of heaven that defines the future age to come is signaled by "Jesus' arrival, judgment (25:31-45), a new creation (19:28), and the end of all unjust practices as God's sovereignty or empire is established in a heaven and earth marked by health, wholeness, and plenty (28:18)" (*Matthew and Empire: Initial Explorations;* Trinity Press International, 2001; page 86). As Carter puts it, "Jesus' return is 'lights out' time for Rome" (page 88).

While hope in the coming rule of God is politically significant at any time, in the aftermath of war, such hopes are especially poignant. Matthew's Gospel clearly remembers the events of A.D. 66–70 (22:1-14) and the destruction of the Jerusalem Temple. Looking back on a catastrophe for which Matthew seems to hold both Roman and Jewish leadership responsible, Matthew also looks to the future. Taking stock of the fallibility of all human institutions, groups, and persons, the Gospel has a sometimes severe, sometimes compassionate view of the present age. Though not necessarily owing to a postwar context, Matthew's perspective is reminiscent of the more circumspect view people tend to express after, but sadly not before, engaging in violent conflict. As we study the Sermon on the Mount, we will keep in mind the significance that a postwar perspective might bring to bear on how Matthew recounts the moral teachings of Jesus.

A Changing Judaism ▆

Why do you think the war with Rome would affect the symbols of land, Temple, and Torah and thus contribute to a changing Judaism? How would life be different in the US if it were occupied by a foreign army? How do you think it would affect the practice of religion?

A Changing Judaism

Being no more monolithic than any great religious tradition, ancient Judaism varied in its practices and beliefs. Even so, the symbols that were key to every expression of Jewish faith, practice, and identity were those of the land (as in the land promised to Abraham; Genesis 12:1-3), the Temple, and Torah (Genesis–Deuteronomy; also called the Pentateuch or the Five Books of Moses).

The war with Rome changed the contours and shape of ancient Judaism. Its impact was enormous. Rome's continued occupation of the Land had been solidified and now the Temple had been destroyed. Thus Jewish identity, practice, and theology, even Judaism's place in the larger Greco-Roman world, had to be renegotiated.

It is in this context that the Torah, a sacred text and symbol that no war could destroy and that no empire could occupy, took center stage as a source of Jewish identity, faith, and practice. The early rabbis, Pharisees, and scribes who most promoted Torah study and practice became critically important to the ongoing life and survival of Judaism. They emerged as the founders of what would later become known as rabbinic Judaism. They were not alone in striving to preserve and reinvigorate Judaism. Several movements, including the Jewish renewal movement that eventually became known as early Christianity, sought to represent and revive Judaism in the wake of the Temple's destruction.

Matthew's story of Jesus emerged in this very period. Thus the way he narrates the

Bible 301 ☐

Learn more about Matthew and his Gospel. Read the "Introduction" to Daniel J. Harrington's, The Gospel of Matthew (Sacra Pagina Series, The Liturgical Press, 1991).

Examine more closely the political implications of Matthew's Gospel. See Warren Carter, Matthew and Empire: Initial Explorations (Trinity Press International, 2001).

Politics and Polemics ■

Discuss the political issues within your denomination or faith community and the way persons on either side of an issue talk about the other. What can we learn from Matthew's Gospel about the constructive and destructive uses of religious polemic?

Gospel is intertwined with the social, political, and religious dynamics of its late first-century context. Its somewhat ambivalent view of Gentiles and its ongoing intra-Jewish debate with early rabbinical tradition (represented in debates between Jesus and his disciples and the scribe and Pharisees) reflect a changing Judaism. As biblical scholar Daniel J. Harrington notes, "Matthew's Gospel should be read as one of several Jewish responses to the destruction of the Jerusalem Temple. . . . The Matthean community still existed within the framework of Judaism but in tension with other Jewish groups—especially the early rabbinic movement" (*The Gospel of Matthew*, Sacra Pagina Series, Volume 1; The Liturgical Press, 1991; page 17).

Politics and Polemics

The changes facing Judaism are key to understanding Matthew's portrayal of Jesus' relationship to Jewish tradition and leadership. Matthew's Gospel highlights and probably intensifies whatever tension existed between Jesus and the scribes and Pharisees. This is because in many ways Matthew seems to share much in common with early rabbinic Judaism, making the differences between them all the more significant. As many Christians know firsthand, groups within a common denomination finding themselves on different sides of a religious debate all too often turn to bitter, sometimes destructive, rhetoric in an attempt to win the day.

Like the scribes and Pharisees, Matthew was committed to renewing and sustaining Judaism and Jewish tradition, including reverence for Torah. Both encouraged Torah observance by all Jews, and both were committed to the ethical and moral dimensions of such practice, but Matthew read Torah as key to understanding the ministry, teachings, and story of Jesus. In addition, he regarded the ministry, teachings, and story of Jesus as key to interpreting Torah. Matthew's way of reinterpreting Scripture and the story of Jesus in light of one another was similar to what we see in the Dead Sea Scrolls. The Jewish sect associated with the scrolls also interpreted events central to the life and faith of their community in terms of Scripture, and vice versa. Matthew's overall approach to Jewish tradition, then, was not unique, even in Judaism, but it was one that was not shared by many scribes and Pharisees of his generation.

Thus when we read a passage in Matthew that heightens the tension between Jesus and the religious leaders, it is important to bear in mind that Matthew does so, in part, to further distinguish his vision of Jewish renewal from others. Like all polemic, such rhetoric can sometimes be abrasive, even ugly. It also tends to make use of a familiar menu of accusations.

Think of political campaigns. Not only is it not unusual to find the most stinging rhetoric being used against candidates who are more alike than different, there are stock accusations to which candidates running for office are subject. For instance, US political campaigns frequently charge opponents with "conducting politics as usual" or "pandering to special interests." Voters speak out against "power-hungry" or "money-hungry" politicians (as opposed to public servants). Even the words *political* and *politics* alone can summon to mind negative images about a candidate.

In antiquity, representatives of rival philosophical or religious groups also charged one another with stock accusations. Charges of hypocrisy, superstition, and charlatanry were common to polemical speech and writing. When we read similar accusations in Matthew, we need to place them in their proper socio-historical context and hear them as religious polemic. For far too long, Christians have not only failed to recognize the polemical aspects of Matthew's writing, they have perverted Matthew's rhetoric to falsely justify centuries of anti-Semitism.

Anti-Semitism and Christian Readers ■

Discuss the nature of Jewish-Christian relations and the reach of anti-Semitism in your faith community. Develop a plan for how you can address both. If there is a synagogue in your community, consider inviting its members to join you in building a relationship and conducting dialogue between your congregations.

Anti-Semitism and Christian Readers

Never was anti-Jewish interpretation of Matthew's Gospel more clear to me than when I heard a visitor to a Sunday school class ask, "Well, wasn't the Holocaust the Jews' own fault? After all, didn't they say in Matthew, 'His blood be on us and on our children!' [Matthew 27:25]? Didn't they bring it on themselves?"

While I was relieved to see that everyone else in the class looked as shocked as I was by the man's blatant anti-Jewish thinking, I also knew that his way of thinking has a long and sad history in Christian tradition and practice. Calling Jews "Christ killers" and "God murderers," actively feeding anti-Jewish and anti-Semitic sentiment throughout the ages, and partaking in crimes and injustices against Jewish persons and entire communities, Christians have much to account for on both a personal and institutional level. Thus it behooves us to consider carefully the problem of anti-Jewish interpretation of Matthew.

To make matters worse, the New Testament, and Matthew in particular, have been open to the charge of being anti-Jewish. And for good reason. In addition to Matthew 27:25, there are several instances in Matthew where Jewish leaders are drawn like stick figures, cast in terms of rhetorical polemic so sharp as to be incendiary: they are portrayed as hypocrites, conspirators, white-washed sepulchers, and so forth. The clearest example are "the woes" against the scribes and Pharisees in Matthew 23.

Thus some biblical scholars, both Christian and Jewish, conclude that Matthew's Gospel is anti-Jewish. Yet even more scholars identify Matthew himself as Jewish, or what we anachronistically call Jewish-Christian. Again, it is critical to consider the Gospel's historical context. Since the author of Matthew writes just as Christianity is at the cusp of becoming something distinct from Judaism, it is anachronistic to think of the Gospel of Matthew as anything but Jewish. Thus Daniel Harrington writes: "It makes little sense to call Matthew anti-Semitic or anti-Jewish. Yet it must be admitted than the text of Matthew's Gospel has anti-Semitic or anti-Jewish potential and that it has been used by anti-Semites through the ages (especially Matt 27:25) as the 'theological' justification for their evil deeds." *(The Gospel of Matthew*, Sacra Pagina Series, Volume 1; The Liturgical Press, 1991; pages 21–22) Ethical reading of Matthew by Christians today demands attention to the historical context of the Gospel and nothing less than clear repudiation of anti-Jewish interpretations and appropriations of it. To do anything short of this is to disrespect the Gospel and pervert its message.

Jesus and Judaism

Quite to the contrary of anti-Jewish readings of Matthew, the Jesus whom Matthew portrays is deeply committed to the traditions of Judaism and its renewal. Indeed, Jesus cannot be understood without knowledge of

Jewish tradition, its symbols, and its Scriptures. Over and over again Matthew stresses the continuity between Jesus and Jewish tradition and Torah by citing how the events of Jesus' life and ministry fulfill Scripture. And Jesus' own words repeatedly emphasize his Jewish identity and interests.

Recall how near to the opening of the Sermon on the Mount Jesus says: "Do not think that I have come to abolish the law or the prophets; I have come not to abolish but to fulfill. For I truly tell you, until heaven and earth pass away, not one letter, not one stroke of a letter, will pass from the law until all is accomplished" (Matthew 5:17-18). The Antitheses that follow, then, are presented as ways of bringing to fullness, or completion, the Torah itself. Thus the common Christian assumption that Jesus somehow annuls Torah is grossly mistaken. For Matthew, Jesus exemplifies the ruling of God and the confirmation and fulfillment of Torah, which is itself a gift from God (see Psalm 119).

Morality for the Real World ■

What do you see as some of the day-to-day implications of Jesus' moral instruction in Matthew 5:3-12?

Morality for the Real World

Like all early Christian memories of Jesus' life and ministry, Matthew's Gospel was written for the purpose of speaking to real people facing real challenges in real-life contexts. Therefore, when we encounter Jesus' moral teachings in the Sermon on the Mount and his vision of life lived according to the ruling of God, we will do well to remember that Matthew's purpose is not to overwhelm us with lofty idealism. To take Jesus' moral instruction seriously is to engage seriously the day-to-day implications of his teaching.

Just as we face challenges and opportunities posed by social change and growing pluralism, so did Matthew and his community. Just as we must work to hear Jesus' teachings anew in the context of war and peace, so did Matthew and his community. And just as we may ask questions about what is just and right, so did Matthew and his community. Then, as now, Christians look to Jesus' teachings for direction and guidance in an ever-changing world. As we continue our consideration of the moral teachings of Jesus, we must keep our eyes, ears, and hearts open not only to the ways in which Matthew's Gospel spoke to first-century believers, but how it might speak to 21st-century Christians as well.

Closing Prayer

Read aloud Psalm 119:33-40. Spend a few moments in silent prayer. Listen to how God may be speaking to you in the Scripture. Close by praying the Lord's Prayer.

Session Three

Loving One's Enemies

Session Focus ■

This session examines loving one's enemies as a way of fulfilling God's purpose for humankind.

Session Objective ■

We will see Jesus' call to love our enemies as a means of becoming children of God.

Session Preparation ■

Read Matthew 5:38-48. Think about persons whom you have considered to be your enemies or adversaries.

Choose from among these activities and discussion starters to plan your lesson.

Who Is My Enemy? ■

Do you find it difficult to think of having enemies? Why or why not? What does this reveal about who we are and who we want to become?

It may seem odd to begin our study of specific passages in the Sermon on the Mount in the middle of the section we have identified as the Antitheses (Matthew 5:38-48). Since this passage brings to light the overarching perspective that shapes this entire section of the sermon, it is a good place to begin.

Who Is My Enemy?

Whether we want to admit it or not, most of us have enemies, people we consider to be our adversaries, people who do not want life to go well for us, and people for whom we hope life does not go well. Sometimes we have enemies who actively seek to harm us. This is not an easy thing to think about, much less to admit to ourselves or anyone else. Our enemies reveal, if nothing else, something ugly in humankind and something ugly in ourselves. They bring up strong feelings of anger, fear, and rage, even hatred, within us. As we try to justify or manage such feelings in ourselves, we become even more inclined to think of the people who evoke these feelings as our enemies.

Sometimes our enemies are persons who have done great harm to us. Sometimes they are groups of people, or entire nations, who have threatened or hurt us and our communities. Sometimes we know them personally, even intimately, sometimes they are strangers whose faces we don't know and who are known to us only by the effects of the weapons they wield. Whatever the case, the more brutal they are, the less human our enemies seem. And they can leave us feeling dehumanized as well.

The preparation for this session invited you to complete an uncomfortable and difficult exercise. It asked you to think about your enemies, past and present, because the first step to grasping Jesus' teaching is to acknowledge the premise of his lesson—that *we have enemies.* Notice that Jesus doesn't say, "If you have any enemies. . . ." He assumes that we have them and that we know that we have them.

This little reality check keeps us from sidestepping the issue at hand, as if to say, "Well, that's really not a problem *I* have, Jesus. Thank you very much all the same." Jesus assumes that enemies are a problem for each of his hearers and that his lesson is a lesson for all those who will listen. The truth is that people, groups, and nations act as enemies to one another. We know the inhumanity that we inflict on one another in ways large and small.

Matthew's community knew about enemies. With war in recent memory, political oppression an everyday reality, and the presence of religious strife, Matthew and his community did not have to look far to find someone they might identify as an enemy. Imagine, then, the shock of hearing Jesus' lessons on retaliation and loving one's enemies for the first time: "You have heard that it was said, 'An eye for an eye and a tooth for a tooth.' But I say to you, Do not resist an evildoer" (5:38-39) and "You have heard that it was said, 'You shall love your neighbor and hate your enemy.' But I say to you, Love your enemies and pray for those who perse-cute you . . ." (5:43-44). Imagine, too, the kinds of questions that might have been heard in response: How can we possibly love our enemies? What about justice?

The Desire for Justice ■

How does our society think of justice? How can we put Jesus' teaching in conversation with our society's values? Consider a ministry that could help your congregation live out the values Jesus presents in Matthew 5:43-44.

The Desire for Justice

The concerns that often arise in response to Jesus' statements are indeed real and understandable. Many persons are especially troubled by the question of justice. Is it just to love one's enemies, especially if they have badly wronged, injured, or even killed a loved one or friend?

Yet in accordance with his vision of the kingdom of heaven, it is precisely the issue of justice that Jesus first addressed as he cited the "law of retaliation" (Exodus 21:24; Leviticus 24:20; Deuteronomy 19:21). Far from being a license for vengeance, as many Christians mistakenly assume, the legislation to which Jesus alluded was created to prevent punishment from becoming excessive. Retri-bution according to "an eye for an eye, and a tooth for a tooth" was a way of making sure that punishment would "fit the crime" and not exceed it. In other words, justice would require *only an eye* for an eye and *only a tooth* for a tooth. Nothing more. This legal per-spective was common to the ancient Near East, but its actual practice in the first century is unclear.

Thus, rather then demanding that his dis-ciples refrain from excessive vengeance, in the Sermon on the Mount Jesus calls his fol-lowers to commit themselves to excessive righteousness. His teaching here is in keep-ing with his message in Matthew 5:20: "For I tell you, unless your righteousness exceeds that of the scribes and Pharisees, you will never enter the kingdom of heaven."

Righteousness and justice are both translations of the same Greek term, *dikaiosuné*. The justice Jesus seeks is defined not by the measure of scales in the balance, but by the righteousness that expresses the ruling of God. Followers of the way of God are to relinquish the restitution to which they, in principle, are entitled. Jesus' disciples are to retaliate with righteousness, not "just" punishment.

Living Large

Living Large ■

What particularly challenges you as you read Jesus' teachings in Matthew 5:38-44? How does the idea of "living large" by practicing "abundance" in response to human need in all circumstances address the challenges of the Scripture?

Rather than encouraging revenge, Jesus issues the following antithesis: "But I say to you, Do not resist an evildoer" (5:39). Moving the focus off the one who commits wrongdoing, Jesus provides his disciples instruction for how to respond to five different circumstances. First, he instructs his hearers to turn away when someone insults them with a slap on the face ("if anyone strikes you on the right cheek," 5:39). It is as if he is saying, "Don't be provoked. Don't buy into the insult and feed the violence." Here a number of scholars assume that the term for *other* ("turn the other also," 5:39) is a misspelling of the Aramaic term for *back*. Read in this light, Jesus instructs his hearers to "turn their backs" to those who have insulted them.

Then Jesus moves to another example: "And if anyone wants to sue you and take your coat, give your cloak as well" (5:40). The example is another allusion to ancient legislation. In a section of laws addressing economic justice, Exodus 22:25-27 says:

> If you lend money to my people, to the poor among you, you shall not deal with them as a creditor; you shall not exact interest from them.

If you take your neighbor's
cloak in pawn, you shall
restore it before the sun goes
down; for it may be your
neighbor's only clothing to
use as cover; in what else
shall that person sleep? And
if your neighbor cries out to
me, I will listen, for I am
compassionate.

In Matthew 5:40, Jesus reverses the subject in the Exodus passage. Rather than addressing the one who requires a neighbor's garment as collateral, Jesus directs his words to the one whose garment is claimed. Given how this section opens with Jesus' recommendation not to "resist an evildoer," the bias in the illustration is toward the debtor-neighbor, not the lender.

In the next example, Jesus alludes to the case of a Roman soldier requiring the "assistance" of an ordinary civilian, urging that the civilian go an extra mile beyond that which is demanded (5:41). As Daniel J. Harrington suggests, "[T]he service probably consisted in carrying baggage from one place to another" (*The Gospel of Matthew*, Sacra Pagina Series, Volume 1; The Liturgical Press, 1991; page 89).

Finally, Jesus tells his followers to give to all who beg or wish to borrow from them. The illustrations' progression from coercion to request, and from oppression (the lender/debtor and the soldier/civilian) to charity, underscores the point: All is to be given in abundance. The emphasis is neither on how something is being asked nor on who is doing the asking. Rather the focus is on the one who is put in the position of responding. Each of Jesus' illustrations encourages responding with abundance. The disciple who follows Jesus' teaching is one who gives openly to the lender, the soldier, and the beggar and the one seeking a loan. No matter the circumstances, one's regard for humankind is constant. One's response reflects not so much one's circumstance but one's inner self and one's disposition to the world. Such is the wisdom and the practice of abundant living. Jesus' teaching adds new meaning to the phrase, "living large."

The call to live large is not just a word of spiritual wisdom, though it is certainly that. It is also a word of practical wisdom. The social and spiritual implications of Jesus' teachings in Matthew 5:39-42 have been a rich resource for those who stand in the tradition of Christian pacifism and nonviolent resistance. For in situations of socio-economic and political oppression, such as those assumed in the illustrations about one's coat being taken as collateral and being forced into service to a Roman soldier, direct opposition or resistance often intensifies the animosity of the powerful and makes a situation go from bad to worse. On the other hand, "living large" sometimes works to disarm an aggressor or shame an oppressor into some change. Abundant living is both a spiritual discipline and a practical collective tool for change.

The Call to Love

The Call to Love ■

Take time to write on a piece of paper the names of persons who have shown love for their enemies and prayed for their persecutors. Share stories of the examples that these models have set for us.

Jesus' instruction to express the righteousness of the kingdom of heaven intensifies as he continues, "You have heard that it was said, 'You shall love your neighbor and hate your enemy' "(5:43). The first half of his citation is clearly rooted in Leviticus 19:18 ("You shall love your neighbor as yourself . . ."), a text quoted not only by the New Testament Gospels but also by a number of Jewish writings. But the second half of the citation ("and hate your enemy") appears nowhere in Scripture. Here Jesus' reference to "what has been said" appears to refer to sentiment that is commonly *heard*.

Although merging Scripture with "common sense" might seem unusual or irreverent at first glance, you can probably think of similar instances yourself. When I was growing up, I heard the saying, "God helps those who help themselves," so frequently that I was sure it was written in the Bible. In the past two years since September 11, 2001, and in the wake of war in Afghanistan and Iraq, not a few Christians in the US have supported loving our neighbors and hating our enemies. And we have done so in the kind of unquestioning manner usually reserved only for the practice of sacred truths. So on a second look, the merging of scriptural teaching with quite secular thinking is all too easy to do. Surely we are not above the popular posture to which Jesus alludes here.

Thus what Jesus says next is as relevant for our time as ever: "But I say, Love your enemies and pray for those who persecute you . . ." (5:44). With Jesus' statement, our "neighborhood" becomes large enough to include our enemies so that enemies, too, become neighbors. The call to love our enemies and pray for our persecutors is not an easy one to hear, especially when the experience of persecution, oppression, or violence is recent and fresh. Think of how most persons living in the US felt toward their enemies following the events of September 11, 2001. *Why should we love our enemies?*

Bear in mind that Jesus is not calling for self-destruction. Think with me of the far too many situations we know of in which not only neighbors but even family act as enemies. Jesus is not asking the woman who is being beaten by her husband to stay in harm's way. He is not asking the child who is being victimized by a parent or another adult to stay silent. As in the previous section, Jesus' focus here is on the nature of *living abundantly*, a way of living that is expressed through our attitudes, prayers, and actions. The call to love our enemies and pray for our persecutors is determinative of our disposition to the world and toward one another. The practice of loving and praying for our enemies does not mean that one has to be a victim, nor is it dependent on being victimized. Rather it is rooted in the wisdom to which Jesus points in his next statement, a wisdom that restores a human face to both our enemies and ourselves.

Generous Righteousness ■

Read Leviticus 19:2-18. What does this Scripture say to you about God's character? about God's purpose for humanity?

Generous Righteousness

The reason why Jesus calls his followers to love their enemies is explained in Matthew 5:45. Jesus says, "Love your enemies and pray for those who persecute you, so that you may be children of your Father in heaven; for he makes his sun rise on the evil and the good, and sends rain on the righteous and on the unrighteous" (5:44-45). The lesson is stunning. It not only reminds us of who we are called to be—children of God—but it reminds us of the nature of our God.

Jesus' illustration is devastatingly simple. For in its simplicity and clarity, it disarms any counter argument we might want to present. The sun *does rise* and the rain *does fall* on all humankind and on all creation. God's blessings are given to all of us, without partiality and without prejudice.

The lesson also reminds us that our God is a creator God who blesses all creation.

And, more to the point, it reminds us of whom we were created to be. Jesus' citation of Leviticus 19:18 serves as a summary statement for Leviticus 19:2-18: "You shall love your neighbor as yourself: I am the LORD." The entire section begins with the Lord telling Moses, "Speak to all the congregation of Israel and say to them: You shall be holy, for I the LORD your God am holy" (Leviticus 19:2).

The whole thrust of the Leviticus 19:2-18 passage is to remind Israel that they are called to be a holy people, to reflect in their being and doing the very image of God who is holy and who created them in the first place.

Thus Jesus' instruction to love our enemies and pray for our persecutors is a call to return to our very purpose. The great offense of the adage, "You shall love your neighbor and hate your enemy," is not simply that it falls short of God's purpose for humanity but that it perverts what Leviticus 19:2-18 teaches about the very essence of the Holy One. To be children of this God is to embody the excessive righteousness of the way of God. It is to want what is good for all of God's creation and it is to pray for both the just and unjust, the righteous and the evildoer. God sends blessing upon us all, without partiality and with great grace.

No wonder, then, that it is Matthew who recounts Jesus' parable of the workers in the vineyard. As the landowner says to his workers who resent that they are paid the same wages as the workers who arrived only late in the day: "Am I not allowed to do what I choose with what belongs to me? Or are you envious because I am generous" (Matthew 20:15). It is a *generous righteousness* that forms the foundation of Jesus' moral teaching.

Read the parable of the workers in the vineyard (Matthew 20:1-16). Why do you think we are so concerned about what everyone else is getting? Discuss what you are learning from this parable and Matthew 5:45. What does it say to you about the "generous righteousness" of Jesus' teachings about morality?

We All Have Faces ■

We All Have Faces

Scholars debate the extent to which Jesus' illustrations refer to relationships beyond interpersonal encounters. Through the ages, Christians have interpreted Matthew 5:38-48 as applicable both to personal circumstances, community concerns, and national and international relations. No matter the context, one effect of Jesus' instruction is constant. Just as perpetrating evil and injustice dehumanizes both the oppressor and the oppressed, loving and praying for our enemies puts a human face on both our enemies and us.

Accounts of soldiers returning from combat and persons convicted of committing violent crime underscore how distancing ourselves from the humanity of others makes it easier to perpetrate violence. In turn, violence itself is often experienced as dehumanizing not only for victims but sometimes for those who commit such acts. When we pray for each other, we perceive one another as more real and more human. And that can be, in some situations, a first step in reversing the spiral of violence.

I once knew an elderly man whose adult son had been senselessly murdered years before. In sharing with me the story of his son's tragic death, the man told me of how he had petitioned the court to request that his son's murderer be given a life sentence instead of being put to death by the state. Stunned, I asked the man how he'd been able to do that for his son's murderer. I will never forget his response. He said, "I didn't do it because of what he'd done. I did it because of who I am, a child of God, and who he is, a human being." It was then that I understood Matthew 5:43-45 for the first time.

Weeds and Wheat Together

One of Matthew's distinctive emphases emerges in the parables in chapter 13 that are themselves unique to his Gospel. The parables of the weeds among the wheat (13:24-30; 36-43) and the catch of fish (13:47-50) point to how, in the present age, the evil and the righteous "grow together" (13:30). While Matthew looks to the future coming of the ruling of heaven when the evil and the righteous will be judged, he recognizes that such judgment belongs only to God and that in the present age, all of humanity receives God's blessings and all of humanity is tied together.

Matthew's wisdom is startlingly relevant for today. We live in a world that seems to be getting smaller and smaller all the time. Our global reality reminds us that we are "all in this together." Leaving God's judgment to God is a good word for our world, where the lines between the good and the evil are not always nearly as clear as we would like them to be. As we acknowledge God's blessing on all creation, how we practice morality ought to depend less on our circumstances and more on who we hope to be and become as God's own children.

Becoming More Human

Our study of Jesus' teaching on retaliation and loving our enemies would not be complete without giving some thought to the biblical foundation for both Jesus' lesson in Matthew and the levitical precedent that he cites. The call to love our enemies and neighbors and the reminder to strive to be children of God direct us back to the story of Creation. We are again reminded that the biblical account of Creation includes the astounding claim that humanity was created in the image of God (Genesis 1:27). From the beginning, humanity's purpose was to reflect God's own being. It is hard to imagine a better summary statement for the kind of moral wisdom and practice Jesus is calling for in the Sermon on the Mount.

This perspective is foundational for understanding all the passages that we will examine in our study together. Rather than annulling or overriding Torah, then, Jesus here is going to the root of Torah and presenting what he understands to be the fullness of its meaning. In this sense (and others!), Jesus' instruction is truly radical. (Remember how your math teacher called square roots "radicals"?)

Looking back at Genesis 1:27, Leviticus 19:2-18, and Matthew 5:45, Jesus' instruction to "be perfect, therefore, as your heavenly Father is perfect" (Matthew 5:48) is a reminder that humans are called not only to reflect God's way and God's being, but to become more human by doing so. What at first seems like the most unnatural instruction is instead, in essence, an urgent invitation *to return to the humanity for which we were created.* The more we become children of God, the more human we are.

The call to retaliate with righteousness and to love our enemies and pray for our persecutors is a call to live abundantly in a way that brings us back to ourselves. Here again we can see that the real focus on Jesus' instruction is on the wisdom, disposition, and practice of his followers, not on the circumstances in which they find themselves. Acknowledging that persons are persecuted and that they do have enemies, Jesus is not glossing over the real difficulty and suffering that his hearers experience. Like all Wisdom teaching, he urges his disciples to let who they are and who God is determine how they will live.

Closing Prayer ■

Read aloud Leviticus 19:1-18. Pray silently about how God may be speaking to you in this Scripture. Close by praying together our Lord's Prayer.

Session Four

Anger and Reconciliation

Session Focus

This session explores Jesus' teaching on anger and reconciliation.

Session Objective

This session can help us integrate into our own lives Jesus' lessons on anger and reconciliation.

Session Preparation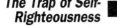

Read Matthew 5:21-26.

Choose from among these activities and discussion starters to plan your lesson.

Children of God

We each have a way of viewing human nature. In Romans 5:14, Paul describes Adam as "a type of the one who was to come." To reflect on the "theological anthropology" that you bring to this study, discuss whether you believe the kingdom of God calls us to a "new humanity" or restores us to an old one. How does your response have an impact on your relationship to others and to the world?

The Trap of Self-Righteousness

Discuss how we talk about persons who have been convicted

Children of God

Having examined Jesus' lesson on loving our enemies and praying for our persecutors, we can see how one overarching purpose of Jesus' sermon is to call us to be children of God. Jesus' moral teaching is an invitation to return to the humanity that we were intended to embody. Very much in keeping with Torah, the vision of humanity that Jesus sets before us is of personhood that reflects God's own being.

This emphasis on becoming children of God constitutes the theological anthropology of the kingdom of heaven. It expresses personhood that is lived in accordance with the way of God. As we continue our exploration of Jesus' teachings in the Sermon on the Mount, keep in mind this particular dimension of Matthew 5–7. Jesus' moral instruction depends on his vision of humanity in all its intended wholeness, or perfection. His vision of humanity is firmly rooted in both biblical tradition and Jesus' profound belief in the approaching rule of God.

The Trap of Self-Righteousness

Jesus' lesson on anger follows immediately after the declaration that "unless your righteousness exceeds that of the scribes and Pharisees, you will never enter the kingdom of heaven" (Matthew 5:20). As we saw in the of violent crime. Reflect on the self-righteousness that we sometimes fall into and how it runs counter to Jesus' teaching. How can we recognize our tendencies toward self-righteousness? What can we do to avoid self-righteous judgment of others?

Bible 301 ☐

The eschaton *refers to "the last days," that is, the turning of the ages when the current age passes away and the unfettered ruling and judgment of God is established forever.*
To learn more about eschatology in the New Testament, look up the word in a good Bible dictionary such as The Interpreter's Dictionary of the Bible *(Abingdon) or the* Anchor Bible Dictionary *(Doubleday).*

previous session, the way of the Kingdom is one of excessive, or abundant, righteousness. The righteousness that Jesus urges his listeners to adopt is one brimming with generosity and love for the whole human "neighborhood."

If Jesus' statement about the scribes and Pharisees is, in part, a rhetorical dig at them, then the series of theses/antitheses that follows is a rhetorical trap for his disciples. As in this lesson on anger, Jesus opens with a standard moral teaching: "You have heard that it was said to those of ancient times, 'You shall not murder'; and 'whoever murders shall be liable to judgment' " (5:21). Citing first the prohibition against murder in Exodus 20:13 and Deuteronomy 5:17 and then tradition probably owing to Exodus 21:12-14, Leviticus 24:17, and Numbers 35:16, Jesus voices moral injunctions most likely well known to Matthew's audience. They are certainly standards assumed by us.

Offered on the heels of the demand for righteousness, these opening lines are, by comparison, easy on the ears. If you happened to suck in your breath upon reading Matthew 5:17-20, you may have breathed a sigh of relief when you came to Matthew 5:21. Fortunately, most of us can say that we have not committed murder. An understandable first response to Jesus' thesis might be, "Oh, this isn't so bad, not too demanding."

Lest we become too smug or impressed by our righteousness, Jesus quickly counters his thesis with a sweeping antithesis: "But I say to you that if you are angry with a brother or sister, you will be liable to judgment. . ." (5:22). While many can say that they have not murdered anyone, I doubt any of us can so distance ourselves from Jesus' counter premise. For Jesus' statement concerns anyone with whom one is angry, not just members of one's congregation or family. Who among us has not been, or is not now, angry with *someone*? With one swift rhetorical move, Jesus moves us beyond the trap of self-righteousness, leaving us somewhat embarrassed and exposed. Fortunately, we are left open not only to judgment but to his Kingdom teaching as well.

Leveling the Playing Field

How do you respond to the way Jesus levels the field? Have your group share responses.

Leveling the Playing Field

By the time we get to 5:22, Matthew has leveled the playing field (if not his readers!). The lines between evildoers and do-gooders quickly begin to blur, and the categories begin to shift. As you know, this entire section, Matthew 5:17-48, begins with seemingly clear lines drawn but concludes with an emphasis on God's generosity toward all humanity. In order to enable us to envision humanity ordered according to the way of God, we must first come to terms with how we regard ourselves and one another in the everyday world in which we live. Jesus' thesis/antithesis reminds us that despite our efforts to rank ourselves above others, especially when it comes to morality, we are all much more alike than different. When we point the finger at others, we find it pointing back to ourselves. In some sense, Jesus' allusion to the "scribes and Pharisees" (5:20) is a rhetorical set-up. They are we and we are they, persons of less than abundant righteousness.

Anger and Murder

Form teams of two or three and talk about a "murder story" drawn from popular film, television, or literature. Reflect on how your selected story demonstrates the connection between

Anger and Murder

Jesus' comparison of murder and anger is much more than clever hyperbole. Anger and its many dangers was a frequent topic in ancient moral discourse. It appears in a number of vice lists in the New Testament canon anger and murder. At what point did the antagonist veer from the path Jesus set before his hearers? Where did the characters miss opportunities for reconciliation?

(1 Corinthians 4:21; Galatians 5:23; Ephesians 4:2; Colossians 3:12; 2 Timothy 2:25; Titus 3:2; 1 Peter 3:5, 15). Here in Matthew's Gospel, Jesus implies not only that anger is at the root of murder but that anger itself is somehow injuring and costly.

As in much ancient writing, Jesus' lesson links anger and speech. He augments his statements about anger and judgment with illustrations that focus on verbal manifestations of anger: "If you insult a brother or sister, you will be liable to the council; and if you say, 'You fool,' you will be liable to the hell of fire" (5:22-23). Each illustration sees an intensification of consequences. Being angry with another person makes one liable to court judgment, calling someone stupid (the Aramaic insult is *Raca!*) makes one liable to the high court of religious law, and calling someone a fool makes one liable to Gehenna (or hell fire).

The allusion to Gehenna is particularly colorful. Literally a valley outside of Jerusalem in which some of the kings of Judah had engaged in forbidden religious activities and which later came to be associated with eschatological judgment, Gehenna here appears to refer to a judgment that supercedes that of the court and the Sanhedrin (see also Matthew 5:30). Given Matthew's context, it probably refers to the Final Judgment that comes at the turning of the ages and the full manifestation of the kingdom of heaven. Thus the consequences of anger and verbal insult, if not assault, are portrayed as dire.

Anger and Injury ■

Think of common ways in which persons use verbal insults to assault one another. How does

Anger and Injury

Generations of English-speaking children have grown up with the saying, "Sticks and stones may break my bones, but names will such talk degrade another person? Why do we behave in this way to one another? Discuss ways of correcting such behavior.

never hurt me!" Adults teach children to call upon these words as a defense against the kind of hurtful speech that children hurl at one another. Though such teaching is well intended, we also know the terrible violence and injury of hate speech.

Jesus' instruction addresses the injury caused by angry and hateful speech. To harbor anger against another person is destructive. To allow such anger to reduce a person to caricature and degradation is dehumanizing. And here lies the key to what holds Jesus' illustrations together. Murder, anger, and hateful speech all hold in common a way of seeing another person as something less than a human being. Though the offenses Jesus describes certainly differ in degree, they are all rooted in the same transgression. By tying them together, Matthew forces his reader to consider the real violence of anger and verbal degradation. The righteousness that Jesus demands requires the kind of self-examination that enables us to see in ourselves the tendency to dismiss the personhood of others. We might not have murdered anyone, but most of us can probably say that we have treated someone in our lives in a dismissive and contemptible way.

Reconciliation

Reconciliation ■

Form teams of two or three. Talk about experiences of reconciliation in your own lives or in the lives of people whom you know. What moral wisdom have you drawn from such encounters? What have you learned from the persons who model reconciliation for us?

With Jesus' message about anger alone, we already have much to ponder in our hearts and minds. But just as one lesson is completed, another begins. Jesus moves to part two: "So when you are offering your gift at the altar, if you remember that your brother or sister has something against you, leave your gift there before the altar and go; first be reconciled to your brother or sister, and then come and offer your gift" (5:23-24).

Although the case is only a hypothetical one in Matthew's day, it is nonetheless pertinent. Resonating with the biblical preference for the piety of embodied righteousness over that of offerings and sacrifices ("What does the LORD require of you / but to do justice, and to love kindness, / and to walk humbly with your God?" [Micah 6:8]), Jesus' illustration is bold and dramatic. It is hard to imagine a worship situation, whether ancient or contemporary, more awkward than the one described here. Jesus' point seems to be that interrupting a worship experience to reconcile with a brother or sister is necessary to overcome the brokenness that intrudes upon proper communion with God. Just as anger, the inner disposition that lies at the root of murder, must be addressed directly, so must the disposition of the one who worships God be made right.

Again, we can see how the Sermon on the Mount brings into view for us not only the significance of human relations but also the importance of our stance to the world, to God, and to one another. The interesting twist in Jesus' illustration is that the one who is called to initiate reconciliation is not the one who has "something against" another, but the one whom "your brother or sister has something against." Unlike the hypothetical subjects in the preceding illustrations, the person in focus here is not necessarily the one on the offensive end of a breach. Rather, the subject of 5:24 is the one likely to have been on the receiving end of some kind of abuse, insult, or anger. Thus while Jesus warns his listeners about the consequences of their anger in Matthew 5:21-22, he yet puts responsibility for initiating reconciliation at the feet of the one who has been wronged.

You may well ask, Why should this be? Can you imagine the burden this places on the subject of Matthew 5:23? Hasn't the angry party been shown to be the one in the wrong? Shouldn't he or she be in the position of having to apologize and bring about some relational détente of some kind? Have you ever found yourself in a situation similar to that of the person in Matthew 5:23?

The logic of Jesus' lesson seems to be rooted in the vision of abundant righteousness that permeates the Sermon on the Mount. If we are the ones who harbor anger, we are to address our own feelings of animosity directly. If we are on the receiving end of someone else's enmity, we are to have enough generosity and wisdom to disarm the other's ill will by taking the first step to reconciliation. The way of the Kingdom allows no room for self-righteousness. The playing field remains level, no matter what side of an offense we find ourselves on.

Taking the First Step ■

How do we take the first step toward reconciliation and what would enable us to do so? Consider whether your congregation might want to sponsor workshops on reconciliation.

Taking the First Step

Like much of the Sermon on the Mount, Jesus' teaching here has long been difficult for me to grasp. As is often the case, it took someone else to open my eyes to Jesus' words. Some years ago, I found myself caught up in the middle of conflict between several people whom I considered to be important and close friends. It was awkward and painful for everyone concerned. One person had mistakenly implicated me in a hurtful exchange in which I had played no part, but there was no way of convincing her of the mistake. And little did it matter, since such a large web of accusations and hurt and missed opportunities for resolution had already been spun by all of us. It no longer mattered who was right and who was wrong, because truth to tell, we each had had a hand in whatever was right and whatever was wrong about the situation. Eventually I felt nearly numb from it all and almost resigned to the brokenness of the relationships that had once seemed strong.

The turning point came at the most unexpected time, but in very much the right place. The first Communion of a child dear to us all had brought us together once again. Everyone was polite and on good behavior, but there was yet tension in the air. We all took our seats before the service began, leaving us scattered about the congregation. When it came time to celebrate Communion, everyone who wished to participate formed two lines going up to the front of church in the manner customary of this particular congregation.

As I joined the processional line, I looked up to see that I was about to be in line just behind and beside two of the persons who had been part of this sad saga. Somehow, we had ended up coming to the Communion lines at just the same time. At first I felt awkward and distracted. But as we moved forward together, step by step, it suddenly occurred to me that this was what Communion was about, that we, each broken, each on level ground where none was above the other, were going *together* to celebrate the grace that God extends generously, equally, and without partiality. And it was a gift that we all desperately needed.

I wish I could say that I broke out of the line, reconciled with everyone concerned, and then returned to celebrate the Lord's Supper. Surely that would have been the more biblical thing to do. But I didn't. What I did experience at that moment, however, has never left me. For I realized that what was most important was not who was right and who was wrong, or how someone had been right in one way and wrong in another. What was most important was recognizing the humanity and personhood that each of us held in common and upon which God continued to give blessing and abounding love. This vision of us being the same, in need and in blessing, freed me to let go of my anger, hurt, and anxiety. And it allowed me to begin to initiate reconciliation with and among a group of hurting persons.

Only long after these events did my thoughts turn toward the Sermon on the Mount. When I read again Matthew 5:23-24, Jesus' words spoke to me anew. I heard in the summons to "first be reconciled to your brother or sister, and then come and offer your gift" (5:24) a call to initiate reconciliation and take the first step in diffusing enmity. Doing so not only acknowledges the level playing field of our common humanity, it affords us the possibility of bringing to fruition in our lives now the Kingdom's vision of our human purpose to reflect God's own benevolence and love toward us all.

Thus rather than being an undue burden, the responsibility of taking the first step toward reconciliation is gift in and of itself. For in having the wisdom to taking the first step, one practices the vision Jesus sets before us. And as we have seen, it is practice that will make us perfectly whole.

Coming to Terms ■

Matthew 5:25-26 draws on an ancient case scenario. Read it again as a group. What aspects of the illustration spark your interest, surprise, or curiosity? What are its implications for the practice of reconciliation? Does

Coming to Terms

The final illustration in Jesus' teaching on reconciliation (5:25-26) is an intensification of the first. Shifting focus to the scene of God's eschatological and Final Judgment, Jesus cites an example dependent on Roman, not Jewish, law. The scene is that of a person reconciliation mean paying our debts to one another to "the last penny," or does it involve a different kind of "coming to terms"? Which is preferable and why?

who is imprisoned for owing debts. Although Jesus makes use of illustrations drawn from oppressive Roman practices, the focus here, again, is on the disposition of the (rightly *or* wrongly) accused, not the accuser. The closing verse places the scene on an eschatological plane. Thus Jesus makes clear that the summons to initiate reconciliation is an urgent one with consequences of the greatest significance. The obvious hyperbole only accentuates the seriousness of the message.

Just as the accused person in the illustration is urged to come to terms with his or her accuser, Matthew's reader is left to come to terms with Jesus' radical teaching on anger and reconciliation. Whereas the example involves arriving at a mutual agreement to settle an alleged debt, the one who wants to follow Jesus' teaching is left to arrive, in heart and mind, at the vision Jesus sets before us. It is a vision of nothing less than the Way of God.

Re-envisioning Our World

Re-envisioning Our World

In what new ways are you being led to re-envision your community and your world? Sketch your vision, if that helps. Discuss what you are envisioning anew with your group.

As Matthew emphasizes, we can participate in the ruling of God, in part, even now. Jesus' illustrations do not present us with precise directions or propositions. They provide us with stories that are suggestive and illustrative of an alternative way and a new order of being. Jesus uses hyperbole throughout the Sermon on the Mount, but the use neither undermines nor allows us to dismiss the seriousness of the lessons we encounter here.

Instead, Jesus' illustrations encourage us to recall and ponder illustrations from situations in our own lives. They direct our attention to a reconsideration of the ways of our world and the multiple and competing values and ethics we encounter there. Jesus' lessons beg us to contemplate how we might choose values, perspectives, positions, goals, and objectives that are different from, perhaps even counter to, what we find in the everyday-ness of our lives. In short, the theses/antitheses in Jesus' sermon make us think long and hard about what we envision for our world and why. It may leave us a bit uncomfortable at first, but it can usher us into a whole new vision of the Kingdom and of what life can be.

The extent to which the Sermon on the Mount brings us to a counter-cultural vision will expand our understanding of not only the religious and philosophical implications of Jesus' moral teaching but also the social and political. One cannot take seriously Jesus' lessons without coming face to face with social and political concerns of our day. As we turn to the next session, we will see how Jesus' teaching has a direct impact not only on our vision for our personal lives but also on our vision for our larger society.

Closing Prayer ■

Read together Proverbs 15:1, 3-4. Pray silently about what these verses say to you. Close with the Lord's Prayer.

Session Five

Marriage

Different Views

After he completed his lesson on anger and reconciliation, Jesus turned his attention to another set of relationships that are closer to home. With another pairing of a thesis and antithesis, Jesus spoke to the issue of adultery. Jesus' focus on this issue gives the impression that both the practice of adultery and its consequences must have been a particularly visible concern in Matthew's day, as it is in ours. Indeed, rabbinical, Greco-Roman, and New Testament texts alike testify to the great amount of moral discourse that inquired into adultery, marriage, and divorce.

New Testament writing concerning these matters shows that there was some variation in early Christian regard for marriage and divorce. It seems that, much like today, communities of believers acting faithfully and out of goodwill came to somewhat different conclusions about the value of marriage and the appropriateness of divorce. Whereas Mark's Gospel holds an absolutist, negative view of divorce (Mark 10:2-12), Paul and Matthew allow for separation in certain circumstances (1 Corinthians 7:15; Matthew 5:32). Moreover, while Matthew and Mark view divorce as a divine concession, Paul views marriage itself as a concession and a kind of prophylactic against sexual misconduct (1 Corinthians 7:9). In short, even in earliest Christianity, people of faith pondered the

Session Focus ■

This session explores Jesus' teaching on marriage, adultery, and divorce.

Session Objective ■

Our exploration will help us develop our own moral examination of these issues.

Session Preparation ■

Read Matthew 5:27-32 and 19:3-12. Write on a piece of paper your definition of *adultery*. Compare your notes with those of others in your group.

Choose from among these activities and discussion starters to plan your lesson.

Different Views ■

Each of us brings different experiences of divorce, different theological perspectives, and a range of emotions to the topics of marriage and divorce. As of the year 2000, the divorce rate in the US was holding steady at about 50 percent. Write one sentence or phrase that expresses your understanding of what *marriage* is and then write one sentence or phrase that expresses your understanding of what *divorce* is. Discuss your definitions/phrases in small groups. Then read Matthew 5:27-32 and 19:3-12. Discuss whether Matthew's views and assumptions conform to your own. If they do, discuss in what ways.

meaning and moral complexity of marriage and divorce and sometimes drew different conclusions. It should come as no surprise, then, to find Christians today in a similar position.

With that said, it is worth mentioning that adultery is viewed in a decidedly negative light by the New Testament writings that comment on it. Although there is no uniform view of divorce and remarriage (whether after the death of a spouse or divorce), it is also fair to say that divorce is seen as something less than ideal.

The Lesson on Adultery ■

What is *lust?* How does Jesus' teaching change your understanding of adultery? What implications does it pose for how society views sexuality and personhood?

Bible 301 ☐

In this context in the Sermon on the Mount, the Greek word, soma, refers to what we might best call the "bodily self." Since ancient Jewish thought did not conceive of the body and soul apart from each other, Matthew is focusing on the downfall of the entire human person, not just the body, in Matthew 5:29-30.

The Lesson on Adultery

Focusing now on Matthew, we will see that the perspective on adultery, marriage, and divorce that emerges in his Gospel falls somewhere in the middle of the spectrum of views one finds in the New Testament. After citing the prohibition against adultery that occurs in Exodus 20:14 and Deuteronomy 5:18, Jesus adds, "But I say to you that everyone who looks at a woman with lust has already committed adultery with her in his heart" (5:28). Once again going to the root of a biblical teaching and leveling the playing field, Jesus focuses on a transgression committed even in the absence of explicit action. For Jesus, willful lusting after a woman constitutes adultery itself. Though this view is not foreign to ancient Judaism, Jesus' use of the thesis/antithesis makes his pronouncement all the more striking.

The illustrations that follow Jesus' antithesis depict the principle well. Whatever lies at the root of the transgression must be addressed directly. If lust begins with what one relishes with one's eye, then it is better to lose the eye than realize such desire only to lose one's whole self (*soma*). The significance of Jesus' reference to the right hand, in particular, is unclear and seemingly obscure. At the very least, it alludes to a clear action on the part of the subject, a concrete expression of an inner disposition and intention. Here, as before, Jesus alludes to eschatological judgment to underscore the seriousness of what is at stake: "It is better for you to lose one of your members than for your whole body to go into hell" (5:30).

Imposed Adultery

Consider again the implications of the premise "that marriages are, in fact, not easily undone. A certificate of divorce alone does not dissolve the relationship." In fact, divorced persons often experience in quite painful ways the same patterns of brokenness in their post-marital relationship that they endured in their marriage to each other. What factors make for a lasting relationship? How does Jesus' vision of "Kingdom relating" help us identify ways of strengthening, and perhaps even redefining, marriage relationships?

Jesus continues with a new thesis/antithesis that qualifies divorce, a practice that Torah allowed. Jesus' citation, "Whoever divorces his wife, let him give her a certificate of divorce," is derived from legislation occurring in Deuteronomy 24:1-3. The certificate to which Jesus alludes appears to have ensured the proper dissolution of a marriage, thereby allowing a woman who was dismissed by her husband to be free to marry another man. In short, it was issued as a means of preventing adultery.

Thus when Jesus adds the antithesis, "I say to you that anyone who divorces his wife, unless on the ground of unchasity, causes her to commit adultery; and whoever marries a divorced woman commits adultery" (5:32), he effectively nullifies the divorce certificate. The single exception he allows is not entirely clear, for the precise meaning of the Greek word, *porneia*, is difficult to translate. Most scholars agree that the term has to do with some form of sexual misconduct. The implication in this context is that unless a wife commits adultery herself, thus warranting her husband's dismissal, she is put in the position of committing adultery when her husband divorces her. The assumption is that the dismissed woman will remarry, a likely scenario, given adult women's economic and social dependence on men in antiquity.

The antithesis in Matthew 5:37 functions in a different way than the ones we have previously read. Rather than going to the root of the legal norm to which he alludes, Jesus moves the subject of discussion from the realm of legal processes to that of morality and ethics. He does not dispute the legality of issuing a divorce certificate. He addresses instead the ethical issues at stake.

Jesus clearly uses the thesis/antithesis throughout this section of the Sermon on the Mount to establish anew his particular teaching. Yet Daniel Patte reminds us that the kind of contrast Jesus draws is very much in keeping with ancient Jewish views of Torah *(The Challenge of Discipleship: A Critical Study of the Sermon on the Mount as Scripture;* Trinity Press International, 1999; page 153):

> These antitheses contrast two aspects of the commandments of Torah already distinguished in Judaism: (1) Torah as a legal system that provides civic order in society (or in the community) and is implemented by courts of law; and (2) Torah as the will of God, which claims the whole person through its moral requirements (the more demanding aspect for the individual).

Here, as throughout Matthew, it is important to bear in mind Jesus' Jewish identity and tradition.

Many Christians tend to think of the exception Jesus cites in Matthew 5:32

("except on the ground of unchastity") as justification for divorce. To take such meaning from Jesus' statement is to grasp only part of the point. Certainly we can see how adultery can serve as either the means or sign of a marriage's demise. The presupposition underlying Jesus' statement is also very important, namely, that because divorce imposes adultery on a spouse (and anyone she marries in the future), it is acceptable only when adultery has already occurred. Jesus' lesson is built upon the premise that marriages are, in fact, not easily undone. A certificate of divorce alone does not dissolve the relationship.

A Larger View ■

Write on a piece of paper some reasons why people marry. Read Matthew 19:3-12 and Genesis 1:27; 2:24. Imagine what a difference it would make to approach marriage in terms of humanity's purpose to reflect God's own self. Form teams of two or three and talk about your responses.

A Larger View: Matthew 19:3-12

The notion that marriage is not easily dissolved is confirmed in Jesus' second discussion on divorce and marriage in Matthew 19:3-12. Here Jesus addresses the issue of divorce directly after being asked by some of the Pharisees, "Is it lawful for a man to divorce his wife for any cause?" (19:3). Reflecting an ongoing debate within ancient Judaism, the focus of the question is on whether divorce is permissible in any circumstance or in only a specific circumstance, such as adultery. Instead of entering directly into current debate by laying out guidelines for divorce, Jesus cites part of Genesis 1:27 ("male and female he created them") and Genesis 2:24 ("a man leaves his father and his mother and clings to his wife, and they become one flesh"). Tying together verses from each of the two Creation stories with which Genesis opens, Jesus concludes, "Therefore what God has joined together, let no one separate" (Matthew 19:6). The implication is not only that divorce runs counter to God's intention for marriage but that in marriage the lives that are joined together become inextricably intertwined.

Intention and Concession

Intention and Concession ■

As a society, do we experience divorce as a norm, an alternative, or a concession? Discuss this with your group. Draw on examples that support your opinion. How does our collective view of divorce compare to Jesus' teaching?

In response, the Pharisees inquire about the certificate of divorce allowed by Deuteronomy 24:1. Before reiterating the statement he made on divorce and adultery in Matthew 5:32, Jesus explicitly characterizes Torah legislation on divorce as a divine concession: "It was because you were so hard-hearted that Moses allowed you to divorce your wives, but from the beginning it was not so" (19:8). Thus Jesus places two biblical texts in conversation with another, reminding us that biblical interpretation may require the sometimes-difficult negotiation of competing texts and traditions. Turning back to the Creation accounts, Jesus presents his listeners with his understanding of God's original intention for marriage.

Marriage Is Relative

Marriage Is Relative ■

Read 1 Corinthians 7:8, 32-35. List the pros and cons of single life and marriage as you see them. Talk about the list with your group. In what ways do we tend to idealize marriage or singleness? Discuss how we might promote more balanced images of both in a manner that reflects Jesus' teaching.

The disciples' response illustrates that Jesus' lesson was a hard one for them to accept: "If such is the case of a man with his wife, it is better not to marry" (19:10). This gives Jesus the opportunity to qualify marriage itself. Though Jesus' reference to "this teaching" in Matthew 19:11 is somewhat ambiguous, it becomes much clearer if we take it to mean the disciples' conclusion that "it is better not to marry." Jesus confirms, "Not everyone can accept this teaching, but only those to whom it is given," namely the celibate. Especially held in high regard are those who "have made themselves eunuchs for the sake of the kingdom of heaven" (19:12) precisely because they have done so *for the kingdom of heaven.*

Thus even as Jesus presents a view of marriage that is in keeping with his vision of the ruling of God, he also teaches that marriage is a relative value, not an absolute one. Those who are called to celibacy, especially as a means of committing themselves to the kingdom of heaven, are held in special regard. Although extended celibacy was certainly not the norm in ancient Judaism, there were some traditions within Judaism that practiced celibacy as a spiritual discipline. Another New Testament text that recommends remaining single is 1 Corinthians 7:8, 32-35. Paul holds unmarried life in high regard because, while the unmarried person is "anxious about the affairs of the Lord" (1 Corinthians 7:32, 34), the married man or woman "is anxious about the affairs of the world" that come with marriage (1 Corinthians 7:33, 34). Though he does not condemn marriage, Paul recommends the life that promotes singleness of mind and heart and complete attention to "the affairs of the Lord."

From Jesus' teaching we can conclude that in and of themselves, neither marriage nor remaining unmarried matters so much as participating in the way of the Kingdom. It is participation in the way of God that serves as the true measure of both.

A Different World ■
Share with one another responses to the sometimes vast historical, social, and cultural gap that distances our world from the biblical world. How does the example of New Testament teaching on slavery illustrate the complexity of the task of faithful biblical interpretation?

A Different World

Surely Jesus' lesson on marriage and divorce is one that we urgently need to consider. With divorce having become common in many societies today, questions about divorce and marriage abound. Following the overall thrust of the Sermon on the Mount, we ought to strive, as individuals and as communities of faith, to arrive at an ethic of marriage that both expresses the intention of

Torah and the way of God and avoids the kind of moralism and self-righteousness that the sermon consistently counters.

We probably have all been touched by divorce in one way or another. For some of us, this session may hit the closest to home and be the most difficult to take up. I wish I could hand you a neat and tidy ethic of marriage to follow, but I cannot. For one thing, Jesus' lessons do not easily translate into a set of regulations. The different views on marriage and divorce that are represented in the church today are evidence enough of that. Second, the biblical witness is rooted in a world where marriage was quite different than it is in many parts of the world today.

A major difficulty that emerges in any attempt to arrive at a "biblically based" ethic for marriage is the degree to which Matthew's world differs from our world. Just as we no longer depend on biblical views of slavery alone to argue that slavery runs counter to the ruling of God, we ought not depend on biblical images of marriage and adultery alone to address marriage and divorce today. If this sounds a bit shocking at first, let's consider together an example.

Turn again to the definitions of *adultery* you were invited to write in the Session Preparation. Chances are that you described adultery as a transgression committed by either a husband or a wife against the other. Popular culture is rife with talk, and a surplus of examples, of spouses committing adultery against each other. Until recently, men were overwhelmingly considered the more likely to be unfaithful to their spouses.

When one looks closely at the biblical definition of *adultery*, one immediately sees differences between ancient and contemporary norms for marriage. In biblical tradition, adultery involved illicit sexual relations between a married or betrothed woman and a man other than her husband or intended. As such it was a transgression that could be committed against a husband, but not a wife. Husbands could not be accused of committing adultery against their own wives, but they could be accused of committing adultery with another man's wife against her husband. In this way, it was somewhat analogous to what we would call a property crime.

Biblical legislation on marriage, in general, was overwhelmingly patriarchal. Marriage was both initiated and terminated by men, not women. Hints of some change can be detected in the New Testament. For example, Mark's discussion of divorce reflects the possibility of a wife divorcing her husband, something that was permissible according to Roman, not Jewish, law. No such possibility appears, however, on the social horizon of Matthew's Gospel.

One does not have to look very far into ancient discussions of marriage and divorce to see that they assume, in some very important ways, different social realities and contexts than those we encounter. In the many countries today, both women and men can propose marriage; and either can initiate a divorce. Adultery is often considered a transgression for which both husbands and wives are held accountable. And it is often seen as a wrong that is equally injuring to both.

Principles for an Ethic of Marriage ◼

Which of these principles is most striking to you? Write your responses and talk about them in small groups.

Principles for an Ethic of Marriage

Rather than trying to impose a false uniformity and equivalence on ancient and modern social norms, we might consider three primary principles in Jesus' teaching on marriage and divorce that speak to both Matthew's context and ours:

(1) Jesus' vision for marriage is rooted in his vision of the very humanity we were created to embody from the very beginning of creation.
(2) Divorce is a divine concession, not an ideal.
(3) A marriage is not easily dissolved.

The principles that Jesus outlines here are in keeping with teaching that we find elsewhere in the New Testament. They provide us with foundational blocks upon which we can build, in faith, an ethic for marriage in our own time and for the current day.

Marriage and Personhood

Marriage and Personhood
Read Genesis 1:27. What implications does this Scripture hold for you as you think about human relationships?

Two particular dimensions of Jesus' teaching in Matthew require further comment. Just as Jesus' vision of humanity and the way of God lies at the core of all his moral teaching, it also serves as the foundation of Jesus' teaching on marriage and divorce. Drawing on Genesis 1:27 in order to respond to the Pharisees' question about divorce, Jesus points us back to the basic premise that underlies all of the Sermon on the Mount. Not only does the Creation account observe that humanity was created male and female, it holds first that God created humankind in the divine image, in the very image of God's own self.

The biblical tradition again and again recalls this conviction about our beginnings in order to sound the call to return to our original purpose of embodying a humanity that reflects God's own being, God's justice, and God's holiness. By turning to the Creation account, Jesus fuses the divine intention for marriage with God's intention for humanity. Imagine what a difference it would make in our lives and those of our children if we would nurture our own marriages and enter into the marriage covenant with Jesus' vision in mind and heart.

Because Jesus' comments on marriage rest on his general vision for humanity, divorce emerges as a divine concession, something that falls far short of God's intention. In this way, divorce may be seen as a measure of how a marriage has failed to sustain, and has failed to be sustained by, the vision of humanity that Jesus' sermon sets before us. It is not that God's intention is for all of us to marry, but that whether we are married or not, we are to live lives that make known the way of God's kingdom. Married life and single life share in common this original intention.

Seen in this light, marriage takes on the moral obligations and ethical norms outlined in general in the Sermon on the Mount. Abundant righteousness is the measure of our humanity. Thus Jesus' lessons on anger, reconciliation, retaliation, anxiety, judgment, forgiveness, and possessions provide norms for human relations, including the relationship of marriage.

Jesus is not teaching that marriage is not an absolute good. His call to uphold and realize his view of marriage is part of a larger vision of abundant living that is patterned according to the ruling of God. This larger framework is particularly important to remember in situations where the marriage relationship falls so short of Jesus' vision for human relations that it becomes psychologically, emotionally, or physically abusive to an adult or children in the family, or both. As Session Three cautioned, Jesus' teaching here neither advocates nor defends abusive human relations. To uphold marriage as an absolute value in the face of such violence and to demand that persons turn their children over to a violent family life is to distort Jesus' own vision for humanity and to make a mockery of marriage. To denigrate personhood for the sake of either divorce or marriage is to betray the very heart of Jesus' lesson.

Beyond Contracts

Beyond Contracts ■

The experiences of children of divorce, and often remarriage, serve as a prime example of how marriage involves not just one relationship but a whole network of relationships. How do you think Jesus' teachings on abundant and generous relationships might shape the way families can envision anew their life together as a family?

Anyone who has experienced divorce, whether through the demise of his or her own marriage, that of a close friend, or that of parents, knows how painful and sad and difficult is the task of disentangling lives that were once so completely interwoven. As we all surely know, it is not only the lives of a divorcing couple but those of their children and those of their extended families that feel the impact and turmoil of separation. I think that it is here, in this larger picture, that we can grasp the meaning both of Jesus' declaration, "What God has joined together, let no one separate" (19:6), and his premise that divorce somehow imposes adultery. For what they hold in common is a sense of how difficult it is truly to dissolve a marriage and to separate lives that have been so integral to one another.

In this sense, Jesus' teaching moves beyond the legal issue that serves as the thesis of Matthew 5:31 and the center of the Pharisees' question in Matthew 19:3. Jesus' responses move the issue beyond contractual concerns. To suggest that adultery occurs even after one has willingly and legally separated from one's spouse is to highlight the degree to which marriage involves and sets into motion far more than a contract. Even after the paperwork is done, lives still revolve around one another, lines of separation blur, and attachments continue, sometimes for the benefit of children of divorce, sometimes for other reasons. A marriage may end and yet a relationship between the separating spouses may continue for years to come. We may hear, then, in Jesus' words on divorce and adultery descriptive, rather than prescriptive, language that pertains to the everyday realities that continue well beyond the legal termination of a marriage. It is not so much the punitive "if you divorce you will be committing adultery" but the more pastoral, "marriage is not so easily given to dissolution" that can also speak to us today.

Finding Our Way Today

As we strive to make how we marry and how we sustain and nurture our marriages a way of embodying the humanity for which we were created, we are in good company. For Christians throughout the ages have revisited New Testament statements on marriage and divorce many times. Arriving at an ethic for marriage is not an easy task. We can draw on the principles identified in Matthew and place them in prayerful conversation with our lives and its various contexts and with the life of our faith community. Bear in mind that the New Testament demonstrates that different communities of faith arrived at somewhat different views of marriage and divorce. With integrity and love for one another, we can express an ethic of marriage that gives voice to the good news of the Kingdom.

Finding Our Way Today

What additional principles in Jesus' teaching or other parts of the New Testament might you consider as you reflect on the ethics of marriage? Discuss these with your group.

Closing Prayer

Read together Genesis 1:26-31. Pray silently about what this Scripture says to you. Close by praying the Lord's Prayer.

Session Six

Spiritual Integrity

Session Focus ■
This session explores Jesus' lessons on practicing one's piety.

Session Objective ■
We will understand ways to practice piety with spiritual integrity.

Session Preparation ■
Read Matthew 6:1-18 and 7:21-23.

Choose from among these activities and discussion starters to plan your lesson.

Sunday Best ■
Write on a piece of paper the ways in which we "put on our Sunday best" at church. What do you see as the positive and negative motives and implications of these behaviors?

Sunday Best

When I was a child, my parents took me and my four older brothers to church every Sunday. I have many memories of getting ready to go to church. Among my favorite are the times when my mother and I (and my Barbie doll!) would wear matching dresses that my mother had sewn for us. I will never forget how proud I felt to be wearing the same outfit as my mother nor the broad smile that would light up her face as we walked into church dressed like Bobbsey twins. Neither will I ever forget all the smiles that met us on those special Sunday mornings. Over and over I would think to myself, "Look at us, everybody! *Look at us!*"

Attending church as a family was special, in part, because we went *as a family*. It was a weekly event that reinforced our sense of family and confirmed our collective public identity. It also confirmed our family's belonging to an even larger church family whose approval and recognition I valued. By an early age, then, I had become aware of some of the public and social dimensions of church attendance.

Of course the social aspect of church participation became even more evident to me during my early adult years. My circle of friends often included persons whom I had met at church, and much of my social life centered on church ministries and related activities. The church also became a politically important part of my life as I became involved in the community advocacy that was part of our church's ministry. With each of these experiences, church involvement became, for me, increasingly public and increasingly busy.

When I was a child, "putting on my Sunday best" meant dressing nicely and behaving well during sometimes long services of worship. As an adult, it came to mean meeting my church responsibilities and performing well in church leadership roles.

A problem developed, however, when at one point I began to feel as though my experience of church had been reduced to fulfilling a host of public duties and performing them well enough to earn the praise of my fellow congregants, neighbors, and friends.

A benevolent view of the situation would have held that I'd simply "burned out" from taking on too many church responsibilities (something many of us may have experienced at some point). But I knew that I had lost my way in another sense, too. I had become so focused on what I thought I was expected to do and whether others noticed how hard I was working that I forgot why and for what reason I was doing what I was doing in the first place. I soon had to rethink what church was all about.

A Lesson for Us

List activities for which persons in your congregation regularly volunteer. Chances are that some will be more behind-the-scenes than others. What can we learn from such activities and from the examples set by the persons who do them?

A Lesson for Us

At face value, Jesus' teaching on almsgiving, prayer, and fasting (Matthew 6:1-18) looks to be a fairly straightforward denunciation of public and religious self-promotion. The thrust of each lesson is stated clearly enough: "Beware of practicing your piety before others in order to be seen by them;

for then you have no reward from your Father in heaven" (6:1).

In response, many readers zero in on the references to synagogues (6:2) and hypocrites (6:2, 5, 16) and conjure images of the scribes and Pharisees whom Matthew frequently portrays in a negative light (for reasons we discussed in Session Two). As you know, the religious leaders are characters in the Gospel with whom Matthew's readers are encouraged not to identify. As such, they are also figures over which readers too often and too easily assume superiority. Our long history of Christian anti-Jewish interpretation of Matthew only intensifies this interpretive effect. In short, readers tend to take in Jesus' lessons only after placing a pretty far and safe distance between themselves and the targets of his criticism.

In Matthew's day and time, the practices of charity ("almsgiving"), private prayer, and fasting were regularly assumed by not only the religious elite but by all Jewish adherents, Jesus' lesson, then, is clearly aimed at the everyday practices of everyday people of faith. His teaching would not have been necessary if public displays of piety had not been a common enough occurrence to warrant comment. Thus the safe distance we want to assume is not in keeping with the text.

To grasp the thrust of Jesus' lesson, it may help to call to mind the everyday acts of piety that we and members of our congregations regularly practice. Whether it be charitable giving that goes beyond the regular Sunday offering, support of specific ministry or mission projects, praying for members of our community, cleaning up the clothes closet, preparing the elements for the Communion, or taking care of floral arrangements, the individual activities that we take on as expressions of our personal devotion and piety are, in many ways, analogous to the illustrations in Matthew 6:1-18. When we consider examples that come closer to home, we are more likely to find ourselves, rather than others, standing uncomfortably at the center of Jesus' lesson.

Being Seen

Being Seen

Many churches struggle with issues pertaining to church growth, public reputation, and community visibility. Drawing on Jesus' illustrations, discuss the relative significance of such concerns. What aspects of congregational life and mission ought to be public? What ought not be public, and why?

Because our communities of faith are *communities*, what we do and how we behave as members of our congregations are often inherently public acts. Having been called into communion by our deepest needs, hopes, and convictions, we are not wrong when we are mindful of how and whether we are being faithful to the calling that brings us together. After all, it is not the social and communal dimension of ecclesial life that Jesus assails in Matthew 6:1-18. What he condemns is the public display of spiritual practices that do not at all have to be public. In short, Jesus opposes the act of turning piety into performance. Being visible is part of congregational life, but it is not its aim.

Spiritual Integrity

Spiritual Integrity

In small groups, discuss the everyday values, obstacles, and distractions that get in the way of spiritual integrity. In what ways can you confront and over-come such challenges?

Jesus' opposition to an ostentatious spirituality is not just a lesson in humility. It is not only that we are to avoid the kind of religious hypocrisy and display (6:2, 5, 16) whose *only* reward is high visibility and public praise ("Truly I tell you, they have received their reward" [6:2, 5, 16]). What Jesus also points to in his fairly comic illustrations ("do not sound a trumpet before you. . . . And whenever you fast, do not look dismal" [6:2, 16]) is the importance of developing spiritual lives that are rooted in one's relationship to God. Acts of piety that transpire beyond the view of the public eye imply more than just personal integrity. The behind-closed-doors, just-between-us kind of imagery that Jesus invokes assumes an intimate relationship with a God who "sees in secret" what we do "in secret" (6:4, 6, 18). We are to cultivate in our relationship to God the kind of intimacy and integrity that is itself a reward.

It is "the Father who sees in secret" (6:4, 6, 18) who will recognize the genuine piety of a person whose charity does not call attention to itself. Likewise, fasting that is unseen by others will be seen and acknowledged by God. Charity, prayer, and fasting are not spectator sports. The focus of Jesus' lesson, then, is not only spiritual integrity and singleness of heart but intimacy with God.

A Relational Piety ■

Discuss how our relationships to God, self, and one another have an impact on and shape one another. How do all of these relationships function together as a kind of "package deal"?

A Relational Piety

Although Jesus teaches against a piety motivated by social status, he is clearly not advocating a piety of isolation. For the thrust of the Sermon on the Mount as a whole is intensely relational. The moral lessons Jesus provides have everything to do with establishing and nurturing interpersonal and communal relationships that make known the ruling of God in our midst. Whether on anger and reconciliation, loving one's enemies, withholding judgment, or keeping one's word, the teachings of Jesus demonstrate that how we relate to others is an essential dimension of Christian discipleship.

In keeping with this, Matthew 6:1-18 emphasizes that the social aspects of the Sermon on the Mount are not concerned with social status but with building social relations that reflect the love, abundant generosity, and justice of God. The foundation for doing so is the relationship we cultivate with God in the "secret" places of our hearts and minds as well as in the privacy of where we communicate with God in prayer. Thus the piety that Jesus teaches is a relational one, wherein our interactions with one another and the world reflect our identity as children of God and our communion with God.

"Let Your Kingdom Come"

Together imagine and envision the Kingdom. What does the way of God look like? What do you see when you envision God's will being "done on earth as it is in heaven"? Draw or write about what you envision.

Bible 301 ☐

The Eighteen Benedictions, or Amidah (from the Hebrew root meaning "stand up"), is a Jewish prayer recited three times daily. Though much longer than the Lord's Prayer, it is similar in language and content to the prayer Jesus taught his disciples. The continuity between the two prayers is underscored by the practice of some early Christian communities who recited the Lord's Prayer three times a day in lieu of the traditional Eighteen Benedictions.

"Let Your Kingdom Come"

At the core of Matthew 6:1-18 lies the Lord's Prayer, the heart of the Sermon on the Mount. Jesus provides his followers a model prayer that stands in stark contrast to the spectacle and verbosity that some persons make of prayer. It is concise and to the point. Since "your Father knows what you need before you ask him" (6:8), its aim appears to be that of bringing before the heart and mind of the one who prays the essential needs and longings of God's children. In this regard, although the prayer is clearly just that—a prayer of supplication—it also functions, in part, like a confession of faith. For Jesus makes clear that it is not God who needs reminding of what persons need. We are the ones who continually need to keep before us God's vision of life and of what we truly need. As Matthew's readers pray and meditate upon the Lord's Prayer, we confess anew our understanding of and our belief in what we most require.

As many scholars note, the language and style of the prayer Jesus teaches to his disciples is in keeping with ancient Jewish tradition and is reminiscent of the Jewish *Amidah*, or Eighteen Benedictions, that was customarily recited three times daily. Some have, in fact, suggested that Matthew's community might have recited the Lord's Prayer in lieu of the standard Eighteen Benedictions. What stands apart in Jesus' prayer, though, is its thoroughly eschatological perspective. The Lord's Prayer is one that looks forward to the coming kingdom of heaven. Read without appreciation for its eschatological framework, the prayer is simply unintelligible.

Thus when we read Matthew 6:9-13, we are reminded of the centrality of Matthew's notion of the kingdom of heaven for understanding both the Sermon on the Mount and the kind of piety Jesus affirms. The reference, "Our Father in heaven," stresses the relationship between the petitioner and God. It is as God's children that we are to approach and commune with God, and it is because we are children of God that we are called to reflect in our personhood God's own being (compare Matthew 5:45-48).

The primary petition in the prayer is: "Your kingdom come. / Your will be done, on earth as it is in heaven" (6:10). Not two distinct supplications, but one, the kingdom of heaven for which the petitioner longs is defined by the ruling of God and the sovereignty of God's way on earth. All else, the prayer for sustenance (6:11), the petition for forgiveness, the request to be rescued from testing (both ongoing and eschatological) and from evil (or the evil one), follows from this starting point.

Thus the way of God is where Jesus' lesson begins and ends. Making his vision of the way of God our own is the means for participating in it. The piety of self-promotion and public display is foreign to Jesus' vision. What Jesus affirms is a piety rooted in the intimate relationship with God for which humanity was created. For in reflecting God's own being, such a relational piety will also seek the realization of God's way on earth.

Forgiveness

Forgiveness
Form teams of two or three. Discuss the following questions:

As we focus on the moral teachings of Jesus, the Lord's Prayer's petition for

Why do you think that forgiveness is so difficult and passing judgment is so easy? What do we see in ourselves when we reflect together on these everyday issues? Share stories of forgiveness that you know.

forgiveness is especially pertinent to our study. Invoking again the metaphor of indebtedness to refer to human transgression, Jesus establishes here a norm of reciprocity that is echoed later in the sermon. As when he declares, "Do not judge, so that you may not be judged. For with the judgment you make you will be judged, and the measure you give will be the measure you get" (7:2-3), the main point is not so much to establish a pat formula for explaining how God deals with God's children. Rather, the effect of Jesus' rhetoric is to expose the hypocrisy that regularly manifests itself in an all-too-common refusal to forgive and a too-little-questioned insistence on judging others. Because the language of reciprocity is strikingly severe, it is also very effective.

Perhaps even more to the point, the reciprocity that Jesus' lessons assume cleverly inverts the mirror-image relationship to God that the children of God are called to embody. In Jesus' illustrations, humanity fails to reflect God's generous righteousness; and God reflects back to humanity its own hardness of heart. The somewhat startling image of God that gazes back at us from these texts, then, is a most unflattering image of ourselves. Through a negative example, Jesus underscores the contrast between abundant righteousness and love and human resistance to it. In so doing, Jesus' lesson reminds of the radical difference between life lived according to the ruling of God and the present order of human relations. Clearly, the thrust of Jesus' teaching on both forgiveness and judgment is to call us to spiritual integrity. Exposing our everyday hypocrisy and resistance to the ruling of God is an effective teaching strategy.

Pious Estrangement

How do you define *self-deception*? How do you identify it? How can you resist it? What do you see as the hazards of self-deception with regard to spiritual integrity and growth?

Reread Matthew 7:21-23. Discuss your responses to verse 23. Are you sympathetic to those who expected the Lord to receive them into the Kingdom? Why, or why not? Discuss how we can discern for ourselves the difference between doing God's will and performing "deeds of power."

Pious Estrangement

Another passage in the Sermon on the Mount that relates to the matter of spiritual integrity is concerned less with the problem of hypocrisy and more with that of self-deception. Couched in the section of the sermon where Jesus warns about eschatological judgment (7:13-29), Matthew 7:21-23 depicts the predicament of those who, having performed pious demonstrations of great power in Jesus' name, are nonetheless denied entry into the kingdom of heaven. Despite having prophesied and cast out demons, they are called doers of lawlessness, a charge reserved for the scribes and Pharisees in Matthew 23:28.

The point of Jesus' warning is made clear in the opening and closing lines: "Not everyone who says to me, 'Lord, Lord,' will enter the kingdom of heaven, but only the one who does the will of my Father in heaven. . . . I will declare to them, 'I never knew you; go away from me, you evildoers' " (7:21, 23). Those who do "the will of my Father in heaven" are held out in sharp contrast to those whom Jesus declares strangers. The difference between them is not so much what they have done, but whether or not it was in keeping with, and motivated by, the way and will of God.

As we saw in the Lord's Prayer, Matthew sustains a steady focus on the kingdom of heaven and the will of God. Neither human activity nor even human longing for the Kingdom form the center of Matthew's concern (though they are on the horizon, to be sure). Rather everything that Jesus teaches about morality as practice and wisdom is shaped by his vision of the kingdom of heaven and the very nature of God. Whereas Jesus' teaching in 6:1-18 emphasized the intimacy of one's relationship to God, here it stresses the estrangement that exists between God and those who stand apart from the will and way of heaven: "I never knew you. . ." (7:23).

The issue that looms large over this passage is that of the problem of "evildoers" (7:23). Earlier on in the Sermon on the Mount, Jesus reveals that the theme and purpose of his teaching is to underscore the excessive righteousness that characterizes the kingdom of heaven. It is a righteousness that signals neither the nullification nor the abolishment of Torah but its very fulfillment (5:17). The sermon's aim is to illustrate what the true fulfillment of Torah looks like. Thus those who are charged with being "evildoers" are persons whose lives have not been in keeping with Torah nor, by definition, with the way of God.

Jesus' lesson ultimately functions to demonstrate the importance of the Sermon on the Mount. For it is the sermon that reveals Jesus' vision of the way of God and abundant righteousness as the true manifestation of Torah. To call Jesus, "Lord, Lord," is not enough. To do the will of the Father is the essence of Jesus' teaching and of Torah. The Sermon on the Mount is Jesus' vision of what that means.

Closing Prayer ■

Join together in silent meditation about ways to offer your best to God. Close by praying the Lord's Prayer.

Session Seven

Wealth and Accumulation

Session Focus

This session explores Jesus' lessons on wealth and the accumulation of material goods.

Session Objective

We will be able to define an ethic of wealth and accumulation informed by the Sermon on the Mount.

Session Preparation

Read Matthew 6:19-34.

Choose from among these activities and discussion starters to plan your lesson.

Getting Personal

Consider how private and important money is to you. Make a list of the people who have complete knowledge of your financial status. Why are certain people included? Who is excluded? What does this tell us about how we think about money?

Getting Personal

A quick perusal of the topics listed at the beginning of this study might suggest that our consideration of Jesus' teachings on marriage would be the most private of the matters to be explored. For some, that may yet hold to be the case. But for many of us, it is this last topic that will prove to be the most personal and private.

While chances are that we know the marital status of every member of the group, we may be hard pressed to guess correctly the annual income of even one other person around the table. The truth of the matter is, in our day and time, money—how much we have, how much we owe, how we manage it, and how we spend it—tends to be a highly private matter that we guard carefully.

This may be the case especially among church folk. For if we think of money and material wealth at all in moral and ethical terms, then we are doubly self-conscious. Of all the issues that preachers and a congregation address together, those having to do with church finances and annual giving are among those that regularly prove to be sticky. Clergy and laity alike often find their church's annual emphasis on stewardship awkward. And many churches follow strict guidelines regarding who has knowledge of which members contribute to the annual church budget and how much they give.

That most of us consider money a highly private matter only underscores how much it means to us and what it signals to others about us. Thus Matthew's inclusion of Jesus' teachings on wealth, material needs, and the accumulation of goods in the Sermon on the Mount are especially relevant to us today. In an age where "money talks" and "money is power," money is certainly a moral issue.

Where Your Heart Is ■

Read Matthew 6:19-21. Form teams of two or three. Discuss what you have treasured most in life. Are your priorities in keeping with those that Jesus presents to us? What is difficult about making Jesus' priorities our own?

Read Matthew 13:44-46. What connections do you see between these parables and the teachings of Jesus in Matthew 6:19-21?

Where Your Heart Is

Jesus' first teaching on wealth and accumulation points to the wisdom of accumulating "treasures in heaven" (6:20) rather than "treasures on earth, where moth and rust [literally "eating"] consume and where thieves break in and steal . . ." (6:19). Earthly treasures are depicted in terms of cloth and either metal or possibly food, materials of value that are both perishable and subject to theft.

Jesus' lesson is clearly a warning about the misguided valuation of temporal goods. The thrust of his lesson is aptly summarized in Matthew 6.21, "For where your treasure is, there your heart will be also" (6:20). For what one accumulates belies the direction, interests, aims, and intentions of one's will. As the parables of the hidden treasure (13:44) and the pearl of great price (13:45-46) positively illustrate, the things to which we give ourselves over say a lot about who we are. The attainment and accumulation of goods requires focus, time, and attention. Therefore what we possess shows what occupies our thoughts and reveals something of our deepest longings and values.

If we are cautioned here about "treasures on earth," then what are the imperishable and invulnerable "treasures in heaven" to which Jesus alludes? Worth all that we have (think again of the parables of the hidden treasure and the pearl of great price), Jesus is referring to his teachings on the kingdom of heaven. The kind of moral practice and wisdom that evidences participation in the Kingdom, as well as the vision of the ruling of God itself, are the things that should guide one's heart. Together such practice, wisdom and vision, is itself a treasure that can be neither destroyed nor stolen. It is life itself, life lived in a new key and in a manner that counters the values of the present order. The note that Jesus sounds here can be heard again, when in his final illustration in this section, he reminds us to "strive first for the kingdom of God and his righteousness" (6:33).

Money Matters

Following close on the heels of this opening lesson is Jesus' warning, "No one can serve two masters; . . . You cannot serve God and wealth" (6:24). His metaphorical allusion to the relationship between a master and slave makes his point unmistakably clear. We serve whatever we are enslaved to, whatever it is that owns us. Ancient philosophical and religious writers, including the apostle Paul, made frequent use of this metaphor to remind readers of the many things in life to which persons could become enslaved. Money was one of them. For persons living in the US in the 21st century, it is possibly the most visible and dominant cultural presence that seeks to own our lives and personhood.

Think of how much of our life is devoted to climbing the economic ladder, conspicuous consumption, and recreational spending.

The popularity of discount stores speaks not only to frugality but also to the norm of consumption that shapes our culture and society. Not one of us is spared from the onslaught of advertising we encounter in our daily lives. Even young children are regularly subjected to the advertising manipulations of toy companies, fast food chains, and "children's programming."

Money plays a determinative role in every dimension of our collective life. Our livelihoods, jobs, public schools, access to health care, housing, and even churches are dependent on the economic choices we make and the policies we support. In the United States and around the globe, "the market," is the financial organism and nexus of power that few of us truly understand and upon which each of us yet depends. In some sense, many of us are beholden to a master whose face we have never seen. Yet Jesus' message is clear. If money is what we serve, if it is our first priority, then God is not. Money must not usurp the place of the Kingdom as that which gives shape to all of life. Given the present circumstances in which we live, Jesus' words carry even more weight now than they did in Matthew's day.

The Basics

The Basics

Read Matthew 6:25-34. How do you respond to Jesus' teachings in this Scripture? What does the teaching say to you about providing for yourself or your family? about providing for those who are poor?

On the other hand, money does matter, as does food, drink, and clothing—those things we commonly refer to as "the basics." Certainly we need to provide the basics for our children and families. So what does Jesus mean when he speaks to these very needs and says not to worry about food, drink, and clothing? What does he mean when he urges, "Therefore do not worry, saying, 'What will we eat?' or 'What will we drink?' or 'What will we wear?'. . . Indeed your heavenly Father knows that you need all these things" (6:31-32)?

Many interpret Jesus' teaching as a statement on anxiety, as if Jesus' main focus is on how we *feel* about our most basic concrete needs and our need to have them met. Yet one only needs to consider the countless number of poor and hungry children in our communities, our nation, and our world to call such a reading into question. Surely Jesus is not so callous as to suggest that we simply say to such children, "Oh, don't worry, God will take care of you." It doesn't take long to expose the emptiness and callousness of such an interpretation, regardless of how common it is.

How is your congregation addressing the concrete needs of persons in your community? Discuss whether these programs are adequate. Can they be improved? If so, how?

Getting Real About the Kingdom

Is it difficult to ponder the social and political implications of Jesus' teaching? Why, or why not? Do you think we take these dimensions of Jesus' instruction seriously enough? Talk about your response with another person in your group.

If our first response to Matthew 6:25-34 either is a facile, "Don't worry, all will be well," or a sharp, "Come on, get real, Jesus!" we need to take the time to keep reading further and to consider the larger context of Jesus' lesson. The pivotal point in Jesus' teaching occurs in Matthew 6:33: "But strive first for the kingdom of God and his righteousness, and all these things will be given to you as well." He teaches his hearers to forgo worry in order to focus on the Kingdom.

Thus Jesus directs our attention back to the Kingdom and to the excessive righteousness that makes the Kingdom known. Rather than taking us on a flight of fantasy, Jesus is getting real here. He is challenging us to *get real about the Kingdom*. For Jesus, the Kingdom is as real as the money in our hands, the food on our plates, and the clothes on our backs. The Kingdom is all about these things, not for their own sake, but for the sake of the ruling of God.

To seek the Kingdom and its righteousness is to embody Jesus' moral teaching and his vision of the justice and generosity that makes the Kingdom known. The righteousness of the Kingdom is realized in the very generosity of the healthy eye that Jesus holds out in contrast to the self-concerned unhealthy eye (Matthew 6:22-23). It is abundant righteousness that lights up the whole body and selfish obsession that darkens it. Striving for the Kingdom is not a matter of merely assenting to a nice idea. It is a matter of setting oneself to the task of living out Jesus' vision. To do so is to take seriously the reality of the Kingdom.

Striving *first* for the Kingdom, then, assumes the establishment of new collective context for meeting basic needs. It is not that we are not to worry because anxiety is a bad feeling that reveals a lack of faith. It is that striving for the Kingdom first engenders a social reality in which these needs are met. In turn, it demonstrates genuine faith not only in Jesus' vision of the ruling of God but also in the righteousness of God's way. To strive for the Kingdom is to long for the justice of God and to reflect it in our own collective and individual lives.

Matthew is not the only New Testament writer who challenges his readers to act on what they say they believe. Another New Testament teaching is even more explicit. In his Wisdom writing, James writes: "If a brother or sister is naked and lacks daily food, and one of you says to them, 'Go in peace; keep warm and eat your fill,' and yet you do not supply their bodily needs, what is the good of that? So faith by itself, if it has no works, is dead" (James 2:15-17). Concise and to the point, James exposes warm, fuzzy feelings for the poor for what they are—warm, fuzzy feelings and little more.

How do you respond to the assertion in the following sentences: "It is not that we are not to worry because anxiety is a bad feeling that reveals a lack of faith. It is that striving for the Kingdom first engenders a social reality in which these needs are met"? How do you think striving for the Kingdom will help satisfy people's basic needs?

Social Justice and Moral Holiness

Form teams of two or three. Read Micah 6:6-8; Leviticus 19:1-18; and Matthew 25:31-46. What connections do you see between these Scriptures and Jesus' teachings in Matthew 6:19-34?

Social Justice and Moral Holiness

As we have seen throughout our study together, the way of God calls us to become more human, for the Kingdom calls us to return to our original purpose of embodying a humanity that reflects God's own being, including God's love, God's compassion, and God's holiness. Throughout the Old Testament, holiness is tied directly to social justice. Whether it is Micah calling for social justice and compassion instead of Temple sacrifices or Leviticus calling for both, the message is clear: Holiness has a moral dimension, and its evidence is social justice.

Thus, Micah writes:

"With what shall I come before the Lord,
and bow myself before God on high?
Shall I come before him with burnt offerings,
with calves a year old?
Will the LORD be pleased with thousands of rams,
with ten thousands of rivers of oil?
Shall I give my firstborn for my transgression,
the fruit of my body for the sin of my soul?"
He has told you, O mortal, what is good;
and what does the LORD require of you
but to do justice, and to love kindness,
and to walk humbly with your God?
(Micah 6:6-8)

In a similar vein, Leviticus 19:1-18, which ends with the summary statement, "You shall love your neighbor as yourself: I am the

LORD," details the norms that make for social justice, and as such, illustrate love of neighbor. These norms for righteousness include "When you reap the harvest of your land, you shall not reap to the very edges of your field, or gather the gleanings of your harvest. . . . You shall leave them for the poor and the alien" (Leviticus 19:9-10) and "You shall not defraud your neighbor, you shall not steal; and you shall not keep for yourself the wages of a laborer until morning" (Leviticus 19:13).

As we discussed earlier in our study, each directive is followed by the divine reminder: "I am the LORD your God." This validates that each is an expression of the premise with which the section opens: "The LORD spoke to Moses, saying: Speak to all the congregation of the people of Israel and say to them: You shall be holy, for I the LORD your God am holy" (Leviticus 19:1-2). Social justice is required of all the children of God. In order to reflect the image of our creator, we are to embody moral holiness through the realization of social justice. For it is for this purpose and this kind of world order for which humanity was brought into being in the first place.

It is no wonder, then, that Jesus cites Leviticus 19:18, "You shall love your neighbor as yourself," as the second greatest commandment. Even more to the point, Jesus likens it to the first and greatest commandment: "You shall love the Lord your God with all your heart, and with all your soul, and with all your mind" (Matthew 22:37-40). For on these two commandments "hang all the law and the prophets." Together they summarize the purpose of humanity and the vision that drives all of the Sermon on the Mount.

Thus when we reflect on Jesus' lessons on wealth and accumulation, we are addressing matters that are integral to his vision of the Kingdom and the way of God. Jesus' teachings on money are not add-ons, nor are they lofty ideals that we can easily dismiss as being too "idealistic." Because they have an impact directly on our notion and vision of social justice, they not only speak to a very personal part of our lives, they address the fabric of our society.

To confirm the significance of this dimension of Jesus' moral instruction throughout Matthew, we need only recall his instruction to the rich young man in Matthew 19:21: "If you wish to be perfect, go, sell your possessions, and give your money to the poor, and you will have treasure in heaven; then come, follow me." Here the reference to heavenly treasure is even more explicit than in Matthew 6:20. Heavenly treasure is the righteousness of the Kingdom that attends to the needs of the poor.

Therefore, in the detailed scene of eschatological judgment that unfolds in Matthew 25:32-46, the righteous are collectively identified as those who ministered to the concrete needs of the least:

> All the nations will be gathered
> before [the Son of Man], and he
> will separate people from one
> another as a shepherd separates
> the sheep from the goats. . . .
> Then the king will say to those at
> his right hand, "Come, you that
> are blessed by my Father, inherit
> the kingdom prepared for you
> from the foundation of the world;
> for I was hungry and you gave me
> food, I was thirsty and you gave

me something to drink, I was a stranger and you welcomed me, I was naked and you gave me clothing, I was sick and you took care of me, I was in prison and you visited me. . . . Truly I tell you, just as you did it to one of the least of these who are members of my family, you did it to me."

(25:32-40)

In language reminiscent of the Beatitudes and his teaching about not worrying about "the basics," Jesus' vision for the provision of basic needs becomes clear. When we live *first* according to the ruling of God, we meet the needs of others. Rather than expending our energies on anxiety about our own needs, we ought to be giving our lives to the work of the Kingdom: "But strive first for the kingdom of God and his righteousness, and all these things will be given to you as well" (Matthew 6:33).

Beyond the American Dream

Beyond the American Dream

Discuss the Children's Defense Fund statistics cited here. Are they a surprise to you? Why, or why not? What action can your congregation take? Consider becoming a congregation in the Children's Defense Fund's movement to Leave No Child Behind.
(See *www.childrensdefense.org*)

According to the report of the Children's Defense Fund, in the year 2001, 11.7 million American children (persons below the age of 18) lived below the poverty line. (For the most current statistics on poverty in the US and information on the movement to Leave No Child Behind, see the Children's Defense Fund Web site at *www.childrensdefense.org*.) This figure translates to 1 in 6 American children living in poverty that year. And of these millions of children, three-fourths of them belonged to working families. Something is clearly wrong here. Not everyone realizes the American dream, after all. Those of us who do realize it need to be sure to look beyond it and to reconsider the morality and righteousness of the Kingdom.

I mentioned at the opening of this session that this final part of our study could turn out to be the most personal and difficult. As much as Jesus' moral teaching has to do with interpersonal matters, it also has everything to do with the social and political lives of God's children. In other words, the Sermon on the Mount is comprehensive and challenging. It is uplifting and confrontational. Most of all, it urges us to look anew at our vision of the kingdom of God, at our purpose as children of God, and at the holiness that God has shown us and that we are to embody and reflect in our own lives and in our own time.

Closing Prayer ■

Read prayerfully Matthew 6:33. Spend some moments in silent prayer asking God to give you insights about ways to strive for the Kingdom. Close by praying the Lord's Prayer together.

"Life is much more successfully looked at from
a single window after all."
-F. Scott Fitzgerald, The Great Gatsby

CONTENTS

Acknowledgements

This book is dedicated to the late Ofra Meir, our sister and sister-in-law, who had taken part in numerous discussions before the actual writing of this book began, and passed away untimely before editing the Hebrew manuscript.

We would like to thank the editor of the this book, the indefatigably intense and knowledgeable Emanuel Lottem, who left no stone unturned, fixed, polished, checked, and even added examples of his own. He belongs to a rare breed in danger of extinction.

One of us (O. K.) would like to thank his colleagues for discussions in which much learned was before writing this book: Rafi Levine, Joseph Agassi, Yehuda Band, Yariv Kafri, and especially Joseph Oreg, who even corrected a derivation.

We would like to thank those that read the original manuscript and made significant suggestions: Alina Tal, Joshua Maor, Daniel Rosenne, Noa Meir-Leverstein, Rachel Alexander, Zvi Aloni, Moshe Pereg, Galit Kafri, and Ehud Kafri. Special thanks to Dan Weiss for the numerical calculations and figures.

Prologue

Mathematician Arnold Sommerfeld (1868–1951), one of the founding fathers of atomic theory, said about thermodynamics, the branch of physics that incorporates the concept of entropy:

> Thermodynamics is a funny subject. The first time you go through it, you don't understand it at all. The second time you go through it, you think you understand it, except for one or two small points. The third time you go through it, you know you don't understand it, but by that time you are so used to it, it doesn't bother you anymore.[1]

This is true of many more things than we would like to imagine, but it is especially true of our subject matter, namely entropy.

Entropy is a physical quantity, yet it is different from any other quantity in nature. It is definite only for systems in a state of equilibrium, and it tends to increase: in fact, entropy's tendency to increase is the source of all change in our universe.

Since the concept of entropy was first discovered during a study of the efficiency of heat engines, the law that defines entropy and its properties is called the second law of thermodynamics. (This law, as its name implies, is part of the science called thermodynamics, which deals with energy flows.) Despite its nondescript name, however, the second law is actually something of a super-law, governing nature as it does.

It is generally accepted that thermodynamics has four laws, designated by numbers, although not necessarily in order of importance, and not in order of their discovery.

1. The first law, also known as the law of conservation of energy, states that the energy in an isolated system remains constant.

2. The second law is the one with which this book is concerned, and we shall soon go back to discuss it.

3. The third law states that at the temperature of -273°C, an object is devoid of all energy (meaning that it is impossible to cool anything to a temperature lower than that).

4. There is another law, called the zero law, which deals with the meaning of thermal equality between bodies.

The second law of thermodynamics concerns the inherent uncertainty in nature, which is independent of forces. Because the nature of particles and the nature of forces are not intrinsically parts of the second law, we may conclude that any calculation basing on this law that will be made in some area of physics, will also apply to other areas as well.

The main quantity behind the second law of thermodynamics is *entropy* – which is a measure of uncertainty. The forces deployed by entropy are not as strictly determined as those described by other laws of nature. They are expressed as a tendency of changes to occur, in a manner somewhat analogous to human will. In order for entropy to increase, energy must flow; and any flow of energy that leads to change, increases entropy. This means that any action in nature – whether "natural" or man-made – increases entropy. In other words, entropy's tendency to increase is the tendency of nature, including us humans, to make energy flow.

The importance of entropy is immeasurable, yet it is a safe bet that the average educated person, who is familiar without doubt with such terms as relativity, gravity, evolution and other scientific concepts, may never have heard of it, or else misunderstands it. For even those familiar with the concept of entropy admit that while they may understand its mathematical properties, they cannot always comprehend its meaning. So what, then, is entropy? We hope that after reading this book you will understand what it is, why it is significant, and how it is reflected in everything around us.

This book has two main sections:

The first section deals with the historical development of the second law of thermodynamics, from its beginning in the early 19th century to first decades of the 20th. Here, the physical aspects of the concept of entropy will be discussed, along with the energy distributions that arise due to entropy's propensity to increase.

The second part of this book deals with the effects of entropy in communications, computers and logic (studied since the beginning of the 1940s), along with the influence entropy has had on various social phenomena.

The first section is concerned with thermodynamics, which is, in essence, the study of energy flows. Every physical entity, whatever its nature, ultimately involves energy. We consume energy in order to live and we release energy when we die. Our thoughts are energy flowing through our neurons. We put in energy to communicate and consume energy to keep warm. Since energy cannot be created (or destroyed), this means it has to come, or flow, from elsewhere. Why does energy flow, and what principles guide it? Well, the reason energy flows is this: there is a theoretical quantity that is not directly measurable, called entropy, and it tends to increase. In order for it to increase, energy must flow.

The first person who quantified this flow of energy, in 1824, was a young French aristocrat and engineer called Sadi Carnot. He understood that in order to obtain work – for example, to apply a force in order to move an object from one place to another in space – heat must flow from a hot area to a colder one. He calculated the maximum amount of work that can be obtained by transferring a given amount of energy between objects having two different temperatures, and thus laid the foundations of thermodynamics.

About forty years later, in 1865, physicist Rudolf Clausius, a fanatic Prussian nationalist, formulated the laws of thermodynamics and defined a mysterious quantity that he named "entropy." Entropy, as Clausius defined it, is the ratio between energy and temperature.

About twelve years later, in 1877, an eccentric Austrian, Ludwig Boltzmann, and an unassuming American, Josiah Willard Gibbs, derived an equation for entropy – concurrently but independently. They described entropy as the lack of information associated with a statistical system. At that point, the second law obtained some unexpected significance: it was now understood that uncertainty in nature has a tendency to increase.

At approximately the same time, Scottish estate-owner James Clerk Maxwell, an illustrious figure in the history of modern science – comparable only to Galileo, Newton, or Einstein – calculated energy distribution in gases and demonstrated how energy is distributed among the gas particles in accordance with the second law.

Some forty years have passed, the 20th century began, science found itself addressing the problem of electromagnetic radiation that is emitted by all objects, and discovered that it is determined solely by their temperature. But there was an anomaly: although the radiation equation had already been formulated by Maxwell, the intensity of the radiation as a function of temperature refused to behave according the laws of thermodynamics, as understood at the time.

This "black body radiation" problem, as it was known, was solved in 1901 by Max Planck, a German intellectual. He showed that if the energy distribution is calculated according to the second law of thermodynamics while assuming that radiation energy is quantized (that is, comes in discrete amounts), the distribution observed experimentally is the one anticipated theoretically. Planck's discovery started the quantum revolution, a storm that raged in the world of physics over the next decades. Planck's calculated energy distribution was such that Maxwell's distribution turned out to be a special case of the Planck distribution. Later on, Planck's distribution was generalized even more, and today it is known as the Bose–Einstein distribution (unfortunately, discussing it lies beyond the scope of this book).

Up to this point, entropy had been discussed in purely physical contexts. Part Two of this book discusses "logical entropy" and shows how the boundaries of entropy were expanded to include the field of signals transmission in communication. This began when, during the Second World War, an American mathematician and gadgets aficionado called Claude Shannon demonstrated that the uncertainty inherent in a data file is its entropy. What was unique here was that the entropy that Shannon calculated was purely logical: that is, it lacked any physical dimension. In the second part of our book we shall explain under what conditions physical entropy becomes logical entropy, and devote a special section to numerical files and Benford's Law, which states that the distribution of digits within a random numerical file is uneven. We shall see that this uneven distribution results from the second law.

The significance of the tendency for logical entropy to increase is manifested in a spontaneous increase of information, analogous to the spontaneous increases of ordered phenomena (life, buildings, roads, etc.) around us. Now, if the second law is indeed responsible for this creation of order, it should show up as logical distribution. We shall examine the distribution of links in networks, of wealth among people, and of answers to polls, and we shall see that calculations obtained from logical thermodynamics do in fact firm up actual rules of thumb that have been known for some time. In economics, the Pareto rule (also known as the 80:20 Law) is quite famous. In linguistics, there is Zipf's Law. These rules, which physicists classify under the general name of "power laws," are all derived from calculations made by Planck, basing on Boltzmann's work, more than a century ago.

So it seems that contrary to Einstein's famous quote that "God does not play dice with the world," logical entropy and its expression in probability distributions proves that God does, indeed, play dice, and actually plays quite fairly.

This book has three layers: historical background, intuitive explanation and formal analysis.

The historical aspect includes the biographies of the heroes of the second law – those scientists whose names are perhaps not as familiar to the general public as those of singers, actors, artists and other celebrities are, but as long as humankind aspires to know more, they will be engraved forever in science's hall of fame. Our heroes are Carnot (a Frenchman), Clausius (a Prussian), Boltzmann (an Austrian), Maxwell (a Scotsman), Planck (a German), and Gibbs and Shannon (Americans). Their biographies reveal the historical motives that informed these scientists in their various research efforts: the industrial revolution, science's golden age, and the age of information. It is important however to remember that these persons did not do their work in a vacuum, so a few brief biographical sketches of others who worked alongside them or were otherwise affiliated with their work are given at the end of this book.

The second layer in this book presents intuitive explanations, those which scientists sometimes contemptuously dismiss as "hand waving arguments." Yet these intuitive explanations represent the essence of science and the essence of culture. Of course, there is no alternative in science to formal mathematical analysis, but this has value only so long as that it quantifies the verbal explanation which consists of words, mental images and often "gut feelings" – which is the reason why they are called "intuitive." Every mathematician knows that behind his or her pure mathematical equations resides intuitive understanding, and everyone accepts that the laws under which we live are guided by intuition.

Finally, there is the third, formal layer, contained in the appendixes at the end of the book, providing mathematical derivations for readers with technical and scientific background. If you studied engineering, economics or the physical sciences, you will be able to examine these mathematical analyses directly, without having to bother with monographs on the various subjects. The derivations were chosen so that they would match the intuitive explanations in the book.

This book was written jointly by a team of husband and wife. He – a scientist in the relevant fields: thermodynamics, optics and information science. She – an educator and welfare worker, translator and editor. The process which led to this work was an ongoing dialogue between two different worlds, which, we hope, will make our book an enjoyable, educational, and enlightening experience. It is intended not only for the general public interested in the nature of things, but also for students, engineers and scientists.

Part I

Physical Entropy

Chapter 1

Entropy and the Flow of Energy
Carnot's Efficiency

Thermodynamics came into being during the industrial revolution, which began in England and then spread to Europe and America, from the mid-18th to the mid-19th century. The industrial revolution was propelled by the development of the coal-burning steam engine. Initially this engine was used only in mining, but following improvements by James Watt (between 1781 and 1788), it spread into the textile industry, agriculture and transportation. This technological revolution literally transformed society and economy, first in Europe and then all over the globe. Hitherto agricultural and commercial societies, which used water, wind and animals as sources of power, became now urban-industrial societies using the enormously more powerful steam engines. Engineering, which until then had been concerned either with the construction of buildings, bridges, and other structures, or for military purposes arms manufacturing and fortification building, was now expanding to include new applications: machines and engines for mining, metallurgy and agriculture, allowing quick and efficient production. Interestingly, until about 1840, the inventors of early technologies were actually craftsmen; only toward the latter part of the 19th century did science become involved in industry, in a partnership that still goes on today.

One result of the mechanization of agriculture was a reduction of the workforce required, leading to a flow of people from rural areas to the cities, launching the vast process of urbanization.[2]

It was only a matter of time before the steam engine was introduced into the world of transportation: first on land, then on sea. Indeed, Richard Trevithick's first steam locomotive had appeared back in 1804, but twenty-one years passed before this form of transportation came into practical use in 1825, when the first tracks for passenger-cargo trains were laid between Stockton and Darlington, two industrial centers in England. By 1829, railways were laid also in the United States and France (using steam locomotives manufactured in England).[3]

At sea, the process was more gradual and the transition from sail to steam only took place by 1865. This was mainly because, initially, the amounts of coal steamships had to carry for their engines were so huge that it made them cumbersome and inefficient.

The mechanical principles of a steam engine's operation are actually very simple: a boiler full of water is heated by burning coal, thus transforming water into steam. A valve installed in the boiler releases the steam into a chamber, where it pushes against a piston that moves and turns a wheel. This wheel, depending on how it is set up, is capable of moving trains or propelling boats. In effect, the steam pressure which drives the piston is similar to the wind pressure that drives a windmill, except that steam is controllable, hence always available – a great advantage for ships, for instance: now they were no longer depending at the mercy of the wind.

The vast possibilities opened up by the invention of the steam engine seized the imagination of Sadi Carnot, a twenty-eight-year-old French engineer, and led to one of the most exciting and important developments which paved the way to the science of thermodynamics. As Carnot wrote in a little book he published in 1824, which made him world famous, *Reflections on the Motive Power of Heat and on Machines Fitted to Develop that Power*:

Every one knows that heat can produce motion. That it possesses vast motive-power no one can doubt, in these days when the steam-engine is everywhere so well known.

To heat also are due the vast movements which take place on the earth. It causes the agitations of the atmosphere, the ascension of the clouds, the fall of rain and meteors,[1] the currents of water which employed but a small portion. Even earthquakes and volcanic eruptions are the result of heat.

From this immense reservoir we may draw the moving force necessary for our purposes. Nature, in providing us with combustibles on all sides, has given us the power to produce, at all times and in all places, heat and the impelling power which is the result of it. To develop this power, to appropriate it to our uses, is the object of heat-engines.

The study of these engines is of the greatest interest, their importance is enormous, their use is continually increasing, and they seem destined to produce a great revolution in the civilized world.

Already the steam-engine works our mines, impels our ships, excavates our ports and our rivers, forges iron, fashions wood, grinds grains, spins and weaves our cloths, transports the heaviest burdens, etc. It appears that it must someday serve as a universal motor, and be substituted for animal power, waterfalls, and air currents.

Over the first of these motors it has the advantage of economy, over the two others the inestimable advantage that it can be used at all times and places without interruption.

If, some day, the steam-engine shall be so perfected that it can be set up and supplied with fuel at small cost, it will combine all desirable qualities, and will

---

[1] In those days it was accepted, following Aristotle, that meteors were an atmospheric phenomenon.

afford to the industrial arts a range the extent of which can scarcely be predicted.

The safe and rapid navigation by steamships may be regarded an entirely new art due to the steam-engine. Already this art permitted the establishment of prompt and regular communications across the arms of the sea, and on the great rivers of the old and new continents. It has enabled us to carry the fruits of civilization over portions of the globe where they would else have been wanting for years. Steam navigation brings nearer the most distant nations. In fact, to lessen the time, the fatigues, the uncertainties, and the dangers of travel – is not this the same as greatly to shorten distances?[4]

Sadi Carnot

"Wherever there exists a difference of temperature, motive-power can be produced."
  – Sadi Carnot[5]

Sadi Nicolas Leonard Carnot, 1796-1832

Sadi Nicolas Leonard Carnot was born on June 1, 1796 in the Palace du Petit-Luxembourg in Paris. His father Lazare Carnot, a brilliant scientist in his own right, was a fascinating and highly influential figure during the time of the French

Revolution. A statesman endowed with a vast global outlook, he believed in the importance of education and was one of the first to advocate compulsory education for all. (Unfortunately, he was not successful in convincing his revolutionary colleagues.) Carnot senior deeply believed in involving intellectuals, scientists and industrialists in the policy making process and making them national leaders, and encouraged many such persons to enlist for the good of France. He strove to strengthen France from within, including the improvement of her economy, as a prerequisite to influencing all of Europe. When he took upon himself responsibility of the army in 1793, he quickly mobilized the leading scientists and industrialists of the period and applied their ideas as quickly as he could to military, education and economic affairs. Within five months of his appointment, the failing and feeble French army was transformed, and four years later it was to become the scourge of Europe. His influence on military strategy was invaluable, and his innovations, which were proven on the battlefield, changed the face of modern warfare. He believed that officers should be appointed based on qualifications rather than social status, and had no qualms about dismissing officers born to the nobility who lacked ingenuity, replacing them with more qualified individuals, even if the latter had no social standing to speak of. In keeping with his vision, it was Lazare Carnot who bestowed upon the lowly Corsican Napoleon command of the French military and supported him in his rapid rise to power. In 1794 Carnot founded the École Polytechnique, which within a few years became one of the most outstanding scientific institutions in Europe.

Before becoming involved in military and political affairs, Carnot senior had written the "Essai sur les machines en general" ("An Essay about Machines in General", 1786), describing the principles of energy involved in a falling mass, and gave the first proof that kinetic energy is lost when semi-elastic bodies collide. He was a follower of the great German scientist Gottfried Wilhelm Leibniz (1646-1716), and applied Leibniz's principles about the conservation of mechanical energy. For example, he claimed that in an imaginary perfect waterwheel, the energy embodied in the water would neither be lost nor dispersed, and its movement would be reversible (that is, if the water wheel was moved in reverse, it should become a perfect pump). Small wonder, then, that his son Sadi adopted his idea, expanded it to steam engines and opened up a new and important branch of science, as will be described below.

In 1797 Lazare Carnot was removed from power, losing his seat in the French Directorate that had been established in 1795, and was forced into exile for a short while – first to Switzerland and then to Germany. He returned in 1799, when Napoleon, now First Consul of the French First Republic, called Carnot back to France and made him Minister of War. Carnot resigned this position a year later due to difference of opinions with Napoleon, and even though he continued to fill various political positions until 1807, he found that his influence in government declined, mainly because he was one of the few individuals who opposed Napoleon's imperial aspirations. With time on his hands, he returned to devote his time to science – publishing articles on geometry and working in the scientific section of the engineering school that he had founded in 1794[6] – and to the education of his son, Sadi, who would later become one of the most brilliant scientists of all time. He had named his son after the classic Persian poet whom he much admired, Sadi of Shiraz (c. 1213 – c. 1291).

Sadi Carnot entered the École Polytechnique in 1812, when he was only sixteen. Among his teachers were the eminent Joseph-Louis Gay-Lussac, one of the discoverers of gas theory; Siméon-Denis Poisson, a founder of statistical distribution studies; and André-Marie Ampère, one of the founding fathers of electrodynamics. In 1814, upon graduation at the Polytechnique, Carnot went on to study military engineering for two years at the École du Génie in Metz.

In 1815 Napoleon returned to rule France for the Hundred Days Reign, appointing Lazare Carnot as minister of the interior. But in October of that year, following Napoleon's defeat at Waterloo, Lazare was exiled to Magdeburg, Germany, where he remained for the rest of his life.

Sadi Carnot finished his studies and became an engineer in the French army. His job consisted of inspecting fortifications, counting bricks, repairing walls, drawing up plans and writing reports which were promptly buried in archives. Carnot despised his job, not only because his reports were not given the attention he felt they deserved, but mainly because he was routinely refused promotion and granted jobs that did not befit his talents. He now realized that his name, which up until a short while ago had made sycophants beat a path to his doorstep, was now a stumbling block to his military career.

Carnot's frustration and his inability to satisfy his passion for continuing his education made him take the entrance examination required for position in the General Staff Corps in Paris in 1818. He passed the tests and on January 20, 1819 became a lieutenant. Almost immediately, though, he took a leave of absence to devote himself to his studies, which were interrupted only once, in January 1821, when he traveled to Germany to visit his father.

Carnot began to attend courses at various institutions of higher education in Paris, including the Sorbonne and the Collège de France. He plunged enthusiastically into mathematics, chemistry, technology and political economics. Besides, he was passionate about music and other fine arts, and also practiced various sports, including swimming, fencing and even ice skating, paying close attention to the theories underlying these pursuits. At that time he became intrigued with industrial issues and also studied the theory of gases. During his visit to his father in 1821, the two undoubtedly discussed the steam engine. The first engine had reached Magdeburg three years before and had greatly interested Lazare. Sadi Carnot returned to Paris full of enthusiasm and determination to develop a theory of steam engines.[7]

Carnot went deeper and deeper into the research that

would eventually lead him to the discovery of a mathematical theory of heat – the precursor of modern thermodynamics. By 1822 he had carried out his first major work: an attempt to find a mathematical expression for the work produced by one kilogram of steam. It is obvious from the style of his writing that he had intended it for publication, but it was never published, and only discovered in 1966. The publication that actually made him famous was the one in which he calculated the efficiency of the ideal steam engine – the Carnot cycle.

In 1824, at the tender age of 28, Carnot published the results of his steam engines studies in a slim volume whose title was typical of that period, almost two hundred years ago: *Réflexions sur la puissance motrice du feu et sur les machines propres à développer cette puissance* (*Reflections on the Motive Power of Fire and on the Machines Fitted to Develop this Power*). Hippolyte, his brother, who returned to Paris after their father had died in exile in 1823, helped Sadi rewrite his ideas so as to make them more accessible to the general public, more popular in style and using just the absolute minimum of basic equations; detailed calculations were supplied in footnotes. The most important part of the book was an abstract description of the ideal engine, which explained and clarified the basic principles which underlie any heat engine, of whatever mechanical structure.

Carnot's book did not gain the attention it deserved, and after it was sold out a short time after its publication in 1824, was not reprinted and for a while was extremely hard to find. Even Lord Kelvin, a great leader in the formulators of the laws of thermodynamics, had difficulty obtaining a copy. The work became known to a wider audience in 1834, after physicist Benoît Clapeyron published its analytic version, and it gained the respect it deserved only after Kelvin quoted it a number of times in 1848 and 1849. Fortunately, this work (with some additional paragraphs not included in the printed version) was saved in a printout of *The Motive Power* made by Hippolyte in 1878. What little we know about Carnot's personal life is due to his brother, who wrote about him with love and deep respect.

REFLEXIONS

SUR LA

PUISSANCE MOTRICE

DU FEU

ET

SUR LES MACHINES

PROPRES A DÉVELOPPER CETTE PUISSANCE.

PAR S. CARNOT,

ANCIEN ÉLÈVE DE L'ÉCOLE POLYTECHNIQUE.

A PARIS,

CHEZ BACHELIER, LIBRAIRE,

QUAI DES AUGUSTINS, N°. 55.

1824.

The title page of Carnot's Reflections on the Motive Power of Fire and on the Machines Fitted to Develop this Power.

Carnot continued his research. Although he never published any of it, some of his notes were preserved. Judging by what he wrote between 1824 and 1826, he was beginning to question the "caloric" theory of heat that was accepted at the time. He described in his notes details of experiments that he intended to perform in order to examine the influence of temperature on liquids. Some of these experiments were identical to those that James Prescott Joule and Lord Kelvin would carry out many years later.

Toward the end of 1826, there was a reorganization of the General Staff Corps in Paris and Carnot was recalled to full service again. He served for a year as a military engineer with the rank of captain, first in Lyon and later in Auxonne, but he was not happy in the military and felt it limited his freedom. He therefore retired completely and returned to Paris, intending to pursue his research further into the theory of heat.

Carnot, who shared his father's political views as an adamant republican, was happy with the direction in which France was moving after the July Revolution of 1830. At that time he became involved in public life, especially with the improvement of public education. He was offered a government position but declined, and with the restoration of the monarchy, returned to his scientific work.

His health, which has never been good, began to deteriorate. In the words of Hippolyte:

> His excessive application affected his health towards the end of June, 1832. Feeling temporarily better, he wrote gaily to one of his friends who had written several letters to him: "My delay this time is not without excuse. I have been sick for a long time, and in a very wearisome way. I have had an inflammation of the lungs, followed by scarlet-fever. (Perhaps you know what this horrible disease is.) I had to remain twelve days in bed, without sleep or food, without any occupation, amusing myself with leeches, with drinks, with baths, and other toys out of the same shop. This little diversion is not yet ended, for I am still very feeble."
>
> There was a relapse, then brain fever; then finally, hardly recovered from so many violent illnesses which had weakened him morally and physically, Sadi was carried off in a few hours, August 24, 1832, by an attack of cholera. Towards the last, and as if from a dark presentiment, he had given much attention to the prevailing epidemic, following its course with the attention and penetration that he gave to everything.[8]

Carnot was only thirty-six when he died of cholera. For fear of contagion, his belongings, including many of his writings, were buried with him. Aside from his book, only a handful of his writings remain.

Thus, the road leading to the science of thermodynamics, including the formulation of its second law, began with Carnot and his study of the efficiency of steam engines in 1824. It was not Carnot who formulated the second law, nor was he aware of entropy. Nevertheless, he understood intuitively – in all likelihood, following on the conversations he had had with his illustrious father – that if a machine, of any type, transferred energy from a hot place to a colder one, then the maximum amount of mechanical work that one could expect to obtain would be the amount of energy removed from the hotter object, less the amount absorbed by the colder one. Indeed, this result was identical with the solution to the problem which had intrigued Lazare Carnot: What is the maximum work that can be obtained from water that drives a turbine? The answer is that the amount of work expected cannot be greater than the energy released when the water falls down from a higher level to a lower one.

Mechanical work is defined as a force applied to an object along a given distance: this force will change the object's motion – its speed and/or its direction, namely its velocity. Moving objects can be used for various purposes: in transportation, for example, it is used to change the spatial location of an object; in a mixer, to knead dough; in the circulatory system, to transport the oxygen required for our bodily functions. Indeed, movement is a characteristic of life itself.

Therefore we can say that motion is an expression of energy. In fact, the amount of energy stored in the motion of an object is directly proportional to the product of its mass and the square of its velocity. Today we call this energy of motion "kinetic energy." The first to define the energy of a moving object, in 1689, was Gottfried Wilhelm Leibniz, a German mathematician and influential philosopher, who was also the first one (simultaneously with Newton, but independently) to develop calculus. Leibniz called this energy "*vis viva*" – Latin for "live energy."

It is not too difficult to understand intuitively that kinetic energy somehow corresponds to mechanical work, but in fact, it also corresponds to heat energy – in this case, not with respect to the object as a whole, but rather to its molecules, atoms, electrons and other particles which constitute matter. In Carnot's day, however, there was still no knowledge of the particles of the matter; Atomic theory was way in the future; also, the prevailing belief was that heat was some form of primeval liquid that, when absorbed by any material, caused it to be hot (somewhat the way an alcoholic beverage causes a warm sensation in our throats). This liquid was called *caloric* (by Antoine Lavoisier, in 1787).

There is another form of energy, one that is not linked at all to motion, which is called "potential energy." This energy is stored in an object as a result of some force that has acted (or is acting) upon it. For example, water situated up high contains more energy than water down low, because work must have been done to overcome earth's gravity in order to raise the water to a higher level. If we allow the water to flow back down, its potential energy is released and can be used to drive a waterwheel. And even though Carnot was not interested in the amount of work that could be obtained from the potential energy of a waterfall, but rather the work energy that could be extracted from a hotter object, the results that Carnot obtained (with respect to the amount of work that can be obtained when heat passes from a hotter object to a colder one) were, amazingly, similar to those obtained from the study of falling water. (It is worth noting that there are other forms of energy that have no connection to mass, for example the energy of light.)

Carnot's showed the extent of his genius in the calculation he made to find the efficiency of the process. As we shall see, this calculation is no more complicated than the trivial conclusion that he reached, presumably, intuitively. This efficiency, which is called today Carnot's efficiency, is one way of expressing the second law of thermodynamics.

So, what exactly is the second law of thermodynamics? The general answer is amazingly simple: heat tends to flow from a hotter object to a colder one. But in fact, this needs to be stated a bit more carefully: *heat will never flow spontaneously from a colder object to a warmer one, without an application of work.* Indeed, the second law is no more complicated than this simple statement, yet as we shall see, it has many facets, meanings and implications – some of them even affecting how we decide what to buy in a store.

One need not be a scientist in order to know that when we want to warm ourselves, we cuddle next to something warmer than us, or go out into the sunshine. And when our home is too warm and we want to cool it (that is, to emit energy from our home into the warmer surroundings outside), we turn on our air conditioning. Heat tends to flow from a hotter object to a colder one for the same reason that water tends to flow down. And while both phenomena are similar, there are obvious differences between them. For example, everyone understands what height is. In principle, we can measure the height of any object that we want with a ruler. But what is temperature and how do we measure that? Of course, everyone understands what a hot object is, but even though the thermometer was invented hundreds of years ago, it is still difficult to really comprehend what, exactly, is temperature. We understand temperature as a value that represents the internal energy stored in an object's particles (which makes it is similar to potential energy). But as we shall see, part of the difficulty inherent in understanding the second law and its accompanying evasive quantity, entropy, stems from the difficulty in properly understanding the concept of temperature (or, alternatively, from actually misunderstanding its nature).

Carnot's contemporaries did not know about atoms and did not comprehend the true nature of heat. In those days *caloric* was the accepted theory explaining heat: hot object was a combination of this object with caloric, somewhat analogous to a compound or an alloy. The smaller/greater the amount of caloric absorbed in the object, the colder/warmer it was. It was also believed that caloric inherently tended to flow from hotter objects to colder ones. To modern readers, the difference between this *material* called caloric and the concept of the kinetic energy of an object's particles may not be so obvious. Surely we may assume that the readers of this book are aware that Einstein showed that matter is a form of energy, and *vice versa*. In addition, even in today's terminology we can say that the concept of the caloric in relation to the steam engine is identical with the way we think of energy, and thus, Carnot's caloric and the energy of motion (that is, mechanical work) are different forms of essentially the same thing.

In Carnot's time, it was already known that gases behave according to a simple set of rules, known today as the "ideal gas laws,"[2] according to which, the product of the gas's volume and pressure is in direct proportion to its temperature. (In other words, the higher the temperature, the larger the volume and/or pressure.) This essentially means that a gas at a higher temperature has the ability do more work, since an increase in temperature represents an increase in the internal energy of the gas.

Carnot's aim was to calculate the efficiency of the steam engine, or, in other words, to find the maximum amount of mechanical work that can be expected to be produced by one kilogram of steam. The calculations that he did were amazingly simple, basing on the fact that a gas can be compressed or expanded under controlled conditions using a piston in a cylinder. The piston does work in order to compress the gas, which subsequently heats up. When the compressed gas is allowed to expand, it now produces some work and, usually, cools down. Using these facts, Carnot described a hypothetically ideal engine, what is called today the Carnot heat engine, or the Carnot cycle. Carnot's heat engine – a gas-filled cylinder – is situated between two objects that are kept at constant temperatures, one of the hotter than the other. The gas is allowed to come into contact with the hotter object and to heat up to its temperature. (Here Carnot assumed that the hotter object is infinitely large, and thus can heat up the gas without having its own temperature reduced; such an object is called a *hot infinite reservoir*.) The heated gas expands and produces work, at the same time cooling down to the temperature of the colder object. Thus, the energy of the hot gas is reduced: some of it passed on to the colder object and some used to do the work. Now we have a cold gas in contact with the colder object. In order for this gas to reach again the temperature of the hotter object, energy must be used to compress it again, and the cycle is then repeats. To summarize the process, Carnot moved energy ("caloric") from the hotter object to the colder one, and obtained work in the process. This action could be repeated *ad infinitum* in a cyclic fashion. The equation that Carnot came up with was the following:

---

[2] Originally formulated by Gay-Lussac, Carnot's teacher, and John Dalton of England.

$$\frac{W}{Q} \leq \frac{T_H - T_L}{T_H}$$

where W represents the amount of work that can be obtained from the gas, Q is the amount of energy ("caloric") that is extracted from the hotter object, T_H is the temperature of the hotter object, and T_L is the temperature of the colder object.

Because the above-mentioned inequality has important implications in the worlds of chemistry, biology, computers and even the human mind, as we shall see in due course, it would be worth our while to try to grasp the full significance of these symbols.

Let us start with the most problematic quantity – temperature. Almost all over the world, temperature is measured on a scale named after its inventor, Swedish physicist Anders Celsius (1701–1744), as indicated by the letter C. On this scale, the freezing point of pure water (at standard atmospheric pressure) is 0°C and the boiling point (under the same conditions) is 100°C. On the other hand, in the United States temperature is measured on a scale named after German scientist Daniel Gabriel Fahrenheit (1686–1736), indicated by F. The zero point in Fahrenheit's scale was the freezing point of a particular brine solution (0°F is equal to – 18°C); and the 96°F point was the "blood-heat" temperature that can be measured under the armpit of a healthy person.

The problem with these scales is twofold:

Putting into Carnot's efficiency equation temperatures measured on the Celsius scale would yield a value different from what we would obtain using the Fahrenheit scale. This would mean that efficiency is, incongruously, dependent on which scale we choose.

Since negative values may appear on both scales, using a negative value in the equation would result in an efficiency value greater than one – obviously illogical, since this would mean that the amount of work obtained is greater than the heat consumed.

These two problems can be eliminated by using a temperature scale that is "absolute." If you recall, according to the gas laws, the product of the volume and pressure of a (ideal) gas is directly proportional to its temperature. Put differently, the state that the gas is in (volume and pressure) is a product of the work needed (or "taken out" of it) to bring the gas to that state. If we cool down a gas to a temperature at which it has zero volume, this would mean that the temperature would also have to be zero. We can thus conclude that there exists some temperature such that both the pressure and the energy of a gas is zero. Now we assign some temperature scale such that its point of "zero temperature" coincides exactly with the gas's state of "zero energy" – obviously, this scale can never have any negative value. We have thus solved both problems in one stroke. Note that there is no real significance to the size of the intervals between the gradations (degrees) on the temperature scale – it is arbitrary – meaning that the value T_L/T_H becomes a pure ratio, that is, the ratio between the absolute temperatures of the hotter and colder objects.

Such a scale has indeed been defined, and it is now called the Kelvin scale. Its starting point is called absolute zero, and the gradations (derived directly from the Celsius scale, i.e., each gradation represents precisely $1/100^{th}$ of the difference between the freezing and boiling points of pure water at standard atmospheric pressure) are called kelvins; their symbol is the K. On the Kelvin scale, the freezing point of water is 273 K ($\equiv 0°$ C).

Let us return now to the Carnot heat engine. Calculating its efficiency is not merely a matter of finding the efficiency of some archaic machine, since it leads to a very important law of nature that states that *it is impossible to build any machine whose efficiency will be greater than its Carnot efficiency*. Stated differently but equivalently, the maximum efficiency possible for any machine will be Carnot's efficiency.

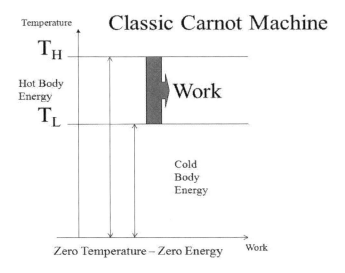

Figure 1: *An illustration of the energy and temperature in a Carnot heat engine shows its similarity to a waterfall, except that instead of differences in height, there are differences in temperature (indicative of the energy in the hotter and colder objects.) In this case, the temperature differences are fully exploited in the conversion of thermal energy into mechanical work.*

Looking at Figure 1, we see that it follows from the gas laws that absolute temperature is directly proportional to the energy stored in the gas (the product of pressure and volume is proportional to the energy of the gas). Thus, the ratio between the work that can be obtained and the energy removed from the hotter object (W/Q) is identical to the ratio between the difference in temperature between the hotter object and the colder one, and the temperature of the hotter object:

$$\frac{T_H - T_L}{T_H}$$

According to the above equation, *all* the energy of the hotter object can, in principle, be converted into work (making the efficiency equal to one) – provided that the temperature of the colder object is absolute zero.

Carnot's theorem is a generalization of the results of specific calculations made for a special case. Anyone who would like to disprove his generalization must perform an experiment which will show that it is possible to build a heat engine with efficiency higher than Carnot's. Till now, nobody has successfully built a machine whose efficiency is greater than Carnot's heat engine. It is worth noting that Carnot's theorem exhibits its profound importance precisely because the Carnot heat engine does not – and actually never will – work at its maximum efficiency. This is important because, as we shall see, in any case whose efficiency is smaller than the maximum value of Carnot's efficiency, entropy – the driving force of our universe – necessarily increases.

In order to understand the significance of Carnot's theorem, two crucial concepts must be explained, since they determine when maximum efficiency can theoretically be obtained from a Carnot heat engine. These concepts are *equilibrium* and *reversibility*.

Equilibrium is a "steady state." A system in a steady state will not show any changes when left on its own over a period of time. (Since today's accepted theories state that even the universe is not infinitely steady time-wise, it is clear that the very nature of a definition of a steady state requires reference to time.) It is also important to understand that dynamic systems, if observed macroscopically rather than microscopically, also exhibit equilibrium. A good example of this is the temperature of earth's atmosphere. The atmosphere's average temperature is almost constant: even the most alarming forecasts of the ecological catastrophe heading our way as a result of global warming predict a change of only about 2 °C from the beginning of the 20th century to the end of the 21st (a change which may, small though it appears to be, still have dire ecological consequences). Yet this stability of the atmosphere's *average* temperature does not contradict the fact that at any given moment one can find temperatures above earth's surface ranging from less than -40°C to more than 40°C, depending on location.

This example shows what thermodynamics is all about. If we observe that gas-filled cylinder in Carnot's heat engine and attempt to measure the gas's pressure or temperature at different places in it, we shall find that the measured values vary from time to time and from place to place – similar to the way that air pressure and temperature vary in the atmosphere, depending on where they are measured.

Returning to the ideal gas laws, a basic assumption is that the values of pressure and temperature are well-defined and *identical* everywhere in the cylinder. The system is assumed to be homogenous, and as we have pointed out just now, this does not necessarily occur in reality. Therefore, when Carnot calculated the efficiency of his heat engine, he understood that in basing his calculations on the gas laws he was assuming a hypothetical, theoretical equilibrium.

One of the most important properties of equilibrium is that *every system tends to reach it*. If we throw a stone into a lake, for instance, ripples form – but they will disappear in due course. The state with no ripples, in which the surface of the water is uniformly level, is its state of equilibrium. Here, the tendency to reach equilibrium seems obvious. By the same token, if we could observe the behavior of gas particles in a container, it would be similarly obvious that the "ripples" of gas atoms will tend to flow from areas of high to low concentration (pressure), until the pressure becomes uniform. And this is also exactly what happens when there are differences of temperature in a system: heat will flow from hotter area to cooler one. This tendency of a system towards equilibrium, this propensity that is so intuitively obvious, is actually the profound meaning of the second law of thermodynamics. Furthermore, it would not be an exaggeration to say the universe looks the way it does – complex, spectacular, and so full of diversity – precisely because of this property.

Let us turn now to reversibility. A change will be reversible if it can be "cancelled" in such a way that it would be impossible to observe that the change has ever happened. Picking an apple from a tree is irreversible. But taking an apple out of a basket – so long as we don't bite it – is reversible. We can return it to the same place, and there will remain no evidence to the fact that we had moved it in the first place. The moment we sink our teeth into the apple, however, we perform an action that can never be reversed to the apple's original state. Most actions in our day-to-day world are irreversible.

Interestingly, even though most actions in this world are irreversible, this fact is not a direct consequence of any of the laws of nature. On the contrary, the laws of nature *are* reversible. Gravity, for example, compels two masses to approach each other, resulting in a release of energy which can be stored – perhaps in the stretching or compression of a spring. By releasing that spring, the stored energy can force those objects apart, back to their original positions. Another common example of a reversible process is a battery cell which is used to convert stored chemical energy into electrical energy. There is nothing in the law of conservation of energy that prevents us from making electrical energy flow back through the battery, thus converting it back into chemical energy, and indeed this is what happens in rechargeable batteries.

This line of reasoning, that the laws of nature enable a perfect back-and-forth cycling of any reaction, is called the *deterministic approach*: natural forces are so precisely defined that it is possible to determine – even in a system containing an enormous number of atoms – what state that system will be in at any given time in the future, provided we know the present condition of its components and the vectors of their velocities. Moreover, if we believe in the deterministic approach, we may conclude that by reversing the direction of the velocity vectors of particles (a difficult task, of course!), the system will move backward in time to its previous state. In other words, it seems that with precise information about the state of a system at a given moment in time, it is possible to know both the system's past and future. Yet this is obviously not the case. And indeed, the second law of thermodynamics, as we shall show in detail later on, disproves this deterministic approach, proving rather that such an occurrence is impossible.

So, to restate Carnot's theorem: a *reversible* engine which is in a state of *equilibrium* during its operation will have a Carnot efficiency of

$$\frac{W}{Q} = \frac{T_H - T_L}{T_H}$$

That is, the maximum amount of work that can be produced by removing a quantity of heat Q from an object whose temperature is T_H to a colder object whose temperature is T_L, is the temperature difference divided by the temperature of the hotter object. However, if the engine is not working reversibly, the efficiency will be smaller than Carnot's efficiency.

What is the meaning of a *reversible* Carnot heat engine? A Carnot heat engine transferring an amount of heat Q from a hotter object to a colder one produces mechanical work. If we can apply that exact same amount or work that we obtained and cause the engine to transfer the exact same amount of heat, Q, back from the colder object to the hotter one, we could say that the machine is reversible. Therefore, the gas in the cylinder must be in equilibrium at all times – a practical impossibility, to say the least – otherwise the engine's efficiency will be smaller.

Viewed historically, against the background of the industrial revolution, is it is easy to understand what were Carnot's motives for calculating the efficiency of the steam engine. It is harder to understand why this problem should interest you, our readers. Even so, assuming you *are* interested, for reasons best known to yourselves, there still remains the question, why is Carnot considered by historians of science to be one of the greatest scientists of the nineteenth century?

The reason is the universality and simplicity of his findings. By revealing that the efficiency of his heat engine is dependent only on its high and low temperatures (and has nothing to do with the way it is constructed) he proved that *it is impossible to build a machine whose efficiency is greater than Carnot's efficiency, and therefore maximum efficiency attainable by any machine, whatever its construction, is its Carnot efficiency.* Furthermore, the importance of Carnot's theorem lies in the fact that it was the first formulation of the second law of thermodynamics – a law that, as we know now, guides the nature of things in our universe. This law, that can be expressed verbally in a number of ways (some of which will be stated later on), is not only immensely important, but also, considering what was known at the time, represents a tremendous intellectual achievement.

It is interesting to note that the "caloric" theory became obsolete only in 1850; nearly twenty-five years after Carnot had published his work. Scientists were persuaded that this theory was invalid mainly by a simple experiment performed by the English physicist James Prescott Joule (1818–1889). He demonstrated that when two chunks of ice were rubbed against each other, the ice melted into water. Since water was supposed to have more "caloric" than ice, it could not have come from the ice, which led to the conclusion that motion energy can be converted to "caloric". This experiment, alongside with the theories independently offered by German physicists Julius Robert von Mayer (1814–1878) and Hermann von Helmholtz (1821–1894), laid the foundations for the first law of thermodynamics, also known as the law of conservation of energy. This law states that in an isolated system, *energy may change its form, but its total amount must remain constant*. For example, if an acid and a metal are placed in a sealed isolated container, heat will be produced as a result of the chemical reaction between the acid and the metal, which produces a salt and a gas. The amount of heat released will be *exactly* the same as the energy that the molecules of the metal and acid lost during this transformation. If we wish now to change these salt and gas back to metal and acid, we must supply an input of energy which is at least equivalent to amount of the heat that was released.

A furious scandal surrounded the discovery of the law of conservation of energy: In 1847, Julius von Mayer read Joule's article on the conversion of mechanical energy into heat and claimed that he had actually preceded Joule in discovering this phenomenon. And indeed, seven years earlier, while serving as a doctor on a Dutch ship in the Indian Ocean, he began to question the nature of heat and its production (inspired by his observations that storm-whipped waves were warmer than water in a calm sea). He wrote a paper that discussed the conversion of mechanical work into heat (and *vice versa*), but it went largely unnoticed by his colleagues. He later rewrote the paper and republished it elsewhere. Joule refused to acknowledge Mayer's claim. Mayer, realizing that Joule now had the credit that should have been his by rights, threw himself out of his third-floor window and ended up hospitalized in an insane asylum.[9] Later on, Hermann von Helmholtz was also to lay a claim to the discovery of the first law of thermodynamics, since he had published in 1847 a book whose title was *On the Conservation of Force*[10] (the term *energy* was not in use at the time in its modern meaning).

Be this as it may, let us go back to Carnot and his awareness of the notion of conservation of energy: even though Carnot still used the term "caloric", the idea behind his heat engine was based on his belief that "caloric" can be converted into work, and work into "caloric". Today we can appreciate that Carnot understood the first law of thermodynamics, despite his use of a now obsolete term. In his book, *Reflections on the Motive Power of Fire*, he wrote:

> One can therefore posit a general thesis that the motive power is an unchangeable quantity in nature; that, strictly speaking, it is never created nor destroyed. In truth, it changes form; that is to say that it sometimes produces one kind of motion, sometimes another, but it is never annihilated.[11]

This is just amazing. True enough, Carnot's heat engine and Carnot's theorem were defined in terms of the "caloric" (being at the time something everyone believed in; today, we suppose, many scientists are not even familiar with this term). Yet over two centuries that have passed since, during which an amazing number of machines have been invented, and Carnot's theorem still stands firm and is still relevant.

It is no wonder that Carnot is considered one of science's greats.

The Clausius Entropy

Forty years have passed since Carnot's had written his monumental paper on the efficiency of heat engines before the scientific community finally gave him the recognition he deserved. The first to do so was Prussian nationalist and war hero Rudolph Clausius – the physicist who gave formal definition to the laws of thermodynamics. Clausius identified within Carnot's efficiency a quantity of strange and mysterious properties, and called it entropy. This new quantity was quite unusual: first, because its amount in the universe can only get larger, never smaller – it is not conserved as many other physical quantities are; and second, because entropy, through its tendency to increase, is the cause of any flow of energy.

Contrary to other forces in nature that are applied in precise and measurable ways, entropy's effects can only be predicted as tendencies. According to thermodynamics, heat *tends* to flow from a hotter object to a colder one; however, entropy neither initiates the process nor defines the length of time it takes. Rather, it seems to stimulate a propensity that can be compared in some limited ways to human will. For example, water at the top of a hill has a tendency to flow down to the valley. Will it flow? That depends. If it is contained in a concrete pool, it will stay in place. But if there is a crack in the concrete, even the smallest one, water will begin oozing its way down. And given a more substantial opportunity, it will gush down the mountain with gusto. Its entropy will increase – a truly human-like behavior – and as we shall see further, this is not an idle analogy.

Clausius's work, based entirely on his studies of Carnot's efficiency, marked the beginning of the science of thermodynamics. Yet unlike Carnot, whose work went largely unrecognized in his day, Clausius' work was immediately accepted, probably thanks to the prominent position he had already occupied in the scientific community during this golden age of science.

The significance of the discoveries and inventions which occurred during a mere twenty five years in the latter half of the 19th century cannot be overstated. In those few years, breakthroughs took place that totally changed science's concepts: in 1855, Neanderthal man was discovered; in 1856, Robert Bunsen and Gustav Robert Kirchhoff founded spectroscopy; in 1859, Charles Darwin published his book *On the Origin of Species* and started a controversy that amazingly continues to this very day; in 1861, Louis Pasteur invented pasteurization and Alfred Nobel developed dynamite; in 1864, Maxwell published his complete theory of electromagnetism, a central landmark in the history of science; in 1865, Gregor Mendel published his seminal paper on genetics (which was totally ignored!). Also in 1865, Clausius formulated the laws of thermodynamics and defined entropy and its properties. In 1869, Dmitri Mendeleev created the periodic table of the elements, Johannes Friedrich Miescher identified the DNA molecule (claiming but not proving that it was somehow connected to heredity), and Georg Cantor developed the mathematical concept of infinity. It is hard to explain why such an explosion of human genius occurred over such a short time span, and only in Europe.

Rudolph Clausius

"The entropy of the universe tends to a maximum."
— Rudolph Clausius, 1867[12]

Rudolf Clausius, 1822–1888

Rudolf Julius Emanuel Clausius was born in Koslin, Prussia (today Koszalin, Poland), the sixth son of a German school principal. As a child, he attended the school his father ran and then studied at the gymnasium (high school) in Stettin (today Szczecin, Poland). In 1840, having completed his high school studies, he entered the University of Berlin, studying mainly mathematics and physics. He graduated in 1844, and in 1847 submitted to the University of Halle his doctoral dissertation, which discussed the problem of why the sky appeared blue during the day but red at sunrise and sunset. He based his explanation on the phenomena of light reflection and refraction; however, this was later proven to be erroneous.[3]

Clausius was the first scientist who identified the entity known as entropy in Carnot's efficiency and described its macroscopic properties, and this was reason enough to earn him a place in the pantheon of science. Unfortunately, he tended to ignore the works of his contemporaries, and even when they acknowledged the significance of his insights, Clausius himself did not reciprocate in kind. His biographer, E. E. Daub, found this puzzling:

> Clausius's great legacy to physics is undoubtedly his idea of the irreversible increase in entropy, and yet we find no indication of interest in Josiah Gibbs' work on chemical equilibrium or Boltzmann's views on thermodynamics and probability, both of which were utterly dependent on his idea. It is strange that he himself showed no inclination to seek a molecular understanding of irreversible entropy or to find further applications of the idea; it is stranger yet, and even tragic, that he expressed no concern for the work of his contemporaries who were accomplishing those very tasks.[13]

Perhaps his ardent patriotism made him ignore work done outside Prussia, even to the point of dispute with Lord Kelvin on priority in the discovery of the first law of thermodynamics: Kelvin attributed it to Joule (an Englishman), while Clausius insisted that the same discovery was made by Helmholtz (a German). However, it is far more reasonable to attribute it to Carnot (a Frenchman).

---

[3] Lord Rayleigh, whom we will meet further on in connection with the thermodynamics of light, later showed that the real reason was the scattering of light according to its wavelength, a phenomenon called today the Rayleigh scattering.

In 1869, Clausius moved to Bonn. This was a period of political transformation in Germany, and it has had an enormous impact on his personal life. Bismarck, who had succeeded in uniting the northern German states into a confederation, was looking for ways and means to encourage the southern states to join in, and came to the conclusion that war with France could bring about German unity. France, for its part, was confident that it could easily defeat the new German state, and its reaction to Bismarck's provocations was just as he had expected. As it turned out, in the war that followed (1870–1871), the Germans proved far more powerful than the French had expected, and made short shrift of their enemies. Clausius, by then almost 50 years old and a well-respected scientist, still felt obliged to serve his homeland. He enlisted and was given command of an ambulance corps consisting of students from Bonn. During the war, he sustained leg injuries and remained painfully disabled for the rest of his life. For his services, he was awarded the Iron Cross. Since then, in an attempt to relieve his pain and on his doctor's advice, he used to make his way to the university on horseback.

In 1872, following the publication Maxwell's paper, *The Theory of Heat* (which will be discussed later, in connection with the Maxwell-Boltzmann distribution), a bitter controversy developed between Clausius and Scottish physicist Peter Guthrie Tait over claims of priority for this theory. Tait, best known for his physics textbook, *Treatise on Natural Philosophy*, which he wrote with Kelvin in 1860, was one of the pioneers of thermodynamics, and had written a book on the history of thermodynamics in 1865. Unfortunately, Tait too got carried away by patriotic fervor that warped his judgment and compromised his scientific integrity. Clausius was adamant that the British were claiming credit far beyond whatever they deserved for the theory of heat, and it seems that he was quite right about this.

It should be noted that in later years, Maxwell fully recognized Clausius's contribution.

In 1875, Clausius's wife died while giving birth to their sixth child. He continued teaching at the university, but his academic career suffered because he had to spend much more time taking care of his children. His brother Robert remarked that Clausius was a devoted, loving father who invested much in their education.

Clausius won many honors for his work. From 1884 to 1885, he served as Rector at Bonn University. In 1886 he remarried and had another child, but departed from this world only two years later, at the age of sixty-six.

In 1850, Clausius published his most famous paper, *On the Moving Force of Heat, and the Laws Regarding the Nature of Heat Itself Which are Deducible Therefrom*,[14] in which he discussed the mechanical theory of heat. This paper included his first version of the second law of thermodynamics. During the next fifteen years, Clausius published more than eight papers in which he attempted to formulate this law mathematically, in a more simple and general way. In 1865 he published a collection of these papers in a book entitled *The Mechanical Theory of Heat*.[15]

In 1867, Clausius moved to Würzburg. Only then did he use the term "entropy" for the "transformation equivalence" that he had described in his papers, and this was the first appearance in print of its mathematical equation (which he had actually defined in 1850):

$$S \geq \frac{Q}{T}$$

That is, the change in entropy S is equal to or greater than the ratio of heat (Q, energy added or removed) to temperature, T.[4]

---

[4] See Appendix 1-A.

Clausius explained how he came up with the word "entropy":

> If we wish to designate S by a proper name we can say of it that it is the transformation content of the body, in the same way that we say of the quantity Q that it is the heat and work content of the body. However, since I think it is better to take the names of such quantities as these, which are important for science, from the ancient languages, so that they can be introduced without change into all the modern languages, I proposed to name the magnitude S the entropy of the body, from the Greek word η τροπη [e *trope*], a transformation. I have intentionally formed the word entropy so as to be as similar as possible to the word energy, since both these quantities, which are to be known by these names, are so nearly related to each other in their physical significance that a certain similarity in their names seemed to me advantageous.[16]

Clausius did not specify why he chose the symbol "S" to represent entropy, but it is plausible to suggest that he did this in honor of Sadi Carnot.[17]

Clausius's inequality (the value Q/T is smaller than entropy) occurs in two instances:

when a process is irreversible;
when a system is not in equilibrium.

Under such conditions, the maximum value of Q/T can be S, such that

$$S \geq \frac{Q}{T}$$

or, entropy is always greater than Q/T, unless the system is in equilibrium, in which case they are equal. This inequality, now called "Clausius's inequality," is the formal expression of the second law.

Why did Clausius specify that it was *Q/T in equilibrium* that defined the system's entropy? The reason is that *Q/T* can be exactly defined only when it *is* in a state of equilibrium. When we measure some physical quantity, we prefer that the measurement be unique. That is, no matter when and where the same quantity is measured, its value should be the same. In the case of an ideal gas, the temperature at equilibrium is homogenous throughout its volume, and thus the value of *S* will be identical throughout. However, in a gas that is not in equilibrium, some areas may be hotter or cooler than others and thus *Q/T* will not be uniform throughout, and the entropy will not be well defined.

Take, for example, a sugar cube and water in a cup. Each on its own is in equilibrium, and the entropy of each can be calculated. But if we place the sugar into water and wait for a period of time, the sugar will dissolve in the water. Sugar dissolves in water spontaneously because the entropy of the solution is higher than the entropy of the sugar and the entropy of the water – indeed, this is the reason the sugar *tends* to dissolve in water. However, at this point we have no way of knowing the entropy of the solution itself, at least not until the sugar has completely and uniformly dissolved and the solution is completely homogenous. Then the system will again be in equilibrium and its entropy can be determined based on the difference in temperatures between the solution and pure water. It will be observed that the entropy did, indeed, increase.

Another, somewhat different example is the process of spontaneous separation of milk into cream, which floats on top, and skim milk beneath it. The reason this happens is that the entropies of both cream and skim milk, separately, are higher than that of whole milk. (In this industrial age, natural milk undergoes homogenization to prevent this spontaneous separation.)

Another important property of entropy is that it is additive, or as the physicists call it, "extensive." This means that the addition of the values of the same property in two different objects yields a value that is the sum of both. Weight, for example, is an extensive property: a kilogram of tomatoes and a kilogram of cucumbers placed together yield a total weight of two kilograms. On the other hand, temperature is not: if we mix water at 50 °C with water at 90 °C, we shall not end up with water at 140 °C. Thus temperature is not an extensive property.

Entropy, on the other hand, is extensive. If two boxes, A and B, are in equilibrium, and if box A has entropy S_A and box B has entropy S_B, the two boxes together will have an amount of entropy that is equal to $S_A + S_B$. This property gives entropy a physical significance that is preferable to that of temperature, because it describes a well-defined quantity, so to speak, whereas temperature is not more of a property, rather than quantity.

However, if the system under study is *not* in equilibrium, then quantity Q/T is *not* extensive. Thus, because most systems in the real world are not in equilibrium – even though they always tend toward it – it follows that in general:

$$(\frac{Q}{T})_{A+B} \neq (\frac{Q}{T})_A + (\frac{Q}{T})_B$$

That is, Q/T of A and B combined will *not* be equal to the sum of both.

As we shall see later, S can, in principle, be calculated for any well-defined system. And since every system naturally tends to reach equilibrium, the value of Q/T tends to increase over time.

And what about entropy? If it were possible to reduce its amount, that would mean that a heat engine with an efficiency greater than one could be achieved. A Carnot heat engine with an efficiency greater than one is called a perpetual motion machine (*perpetuum mobile*) of the second kind, because it violates the second law of thermodynamics. (By the same token, a machine that produces work without any energy input is called a perpetual motion machine of the first kind, because it violates the first law of thermodynamics, that is, the law of conservation of energy.) Because the laws of thermodynamics are considered proven, established and impossible to violate, this negates any possibility, ever, of creating of a perpetual motion machine of any kind. Indeed, the US Patent Office will reject out of hand any patent application involving such a machine. Although its mandate requires it to examine any and all applications, perpetual motion proposals are specifically exempt.

And so, as stated in the Carnot and Clausius inequalities, the value of Q/T cannot be reduced; it will always increase. Some think, incorrectly, that Q/T is entropy, because of its tendency to increase. However, when the system is not in equilibrium, Q/T is not uniquely defined and can be different in various locations and at various times. Entropy, on the other hand, is well defined, namely, for a given system it has a unique value.

This discussion can be summed up by saying the increase in the value of Q/T expresses nature's tendency to reach equilibrium. Heat tends to flow from a hotter object to a colder one because this action will lead to an increase in entropy. Thus, any process that increases entropy will be a spontaneous one, similar to sugar dissolving in water or cream separating from the milk. Conversely, the fact that the sugar tends to dissolve in water proves that the entropy of the system has increased. In fact, any change that occurs in nature, *even a change brought about through human intervention*, is spontaneous in the sense that if the process occurred, entropy must have increased. And if entropy increased, it was a spontaneous process.

But if nature is spontaneous, and entropy does in fact always increase, how is that lake surfaces freeze in winter, or liquid water turns to ice in a freezer?[5] There are two ways to explain why water freezes:

First, the frozen water is part of a larger system, in which the entropy did in fact increase. That is, while the entropy of the water in the freezer decreased, electricity was used to power the compressor and fan that cooled the compressed gas and circulated it to make freezers cold, and that electricity was produced from some process, at the power station, that released more heat to the surroundings than the amount of heat extracted from the water when it froze, and so on. Overall, therefore, the amount of entropy in the world has increased. Similarly, the process that causes lake surfaces to freeze was probably due to a cold wind that was driven by energy released from the sun. The energy released was greater than the heat that the lake has lost. Therefore we must be more precise and say that the entropy in a *closed* system is never

---

[5] It will be explained in the next chapter, which deals with the connection between entropy and the possible ways in which a system can be ordered, the amount of entropy in ice is smaller than that of the same amount of liquid water.

reduced. A "closed system" is one that is defined as thermally isolated from its surroundings.

Another way to address the question is to view the entire universe as a closed system that is not in equilibrium. Any subsystem can reduce its entropy, provided that entropy increased elsewhere. Thus, the entropy in the universe is always on the increase. (Some would go even further than that and say that time itself is essentially entropy: just like entropy, time increases constantly and never decreases. But we do not intend to engage in such philosophical discourse.)

Clausius's definition of entropy, despite its simplicity, does not explain entropy's meaning. Clausius never stated precisely that entropy was the amount of *uncertainty* contained in a system. This was done a few years later by two of his contemporaries, the Austrian Boltzmann and the American Gibbs.

Chapter 2

Statistical Entropy

The Boltzmann Entropy

It is unbelievable how simple and straightforward each result appears once it has been found, and how difficult, as long as the way which leads to it is unknown.
- Ludwig Boltzmann, 1894[18]

Not long after Clausius isolated entropy in Carnot's efficiency and discovered its unusual properties – nine years, to be precise – a depressive Austrian physicist by the name of Ludwig Boltzmann gave entropy its modern form, as a statistical quantity. Just as Carnot had realized – long before the three laws of thermodynamics were formulated – that energy is conserved (the first law) and that there is a temperature of absolute zero at which there is no energy in matter (the third law), so it was clear to Boltzmann that matter is made of atoms and molecules – long before this was accepted by the entire scientific community. This intuitive realization probably informed his statistical approach to entropy.

Boltzmann's expression for entropy is substantially different from Clausius's: first of all, it is a statistical expression; and second, it *cannot be directly measured*. While the Clausius entropy

42

is something tangible – defined as an actual amount of heat, divided by an actual measure of temperature – Boltzmann's expression deals with the uncertainty of a system.

In order to appreciate Boltzmann's achievement properly, it must be remembered that in the 1870s, many leading scientists did not believe in the existence of atoms and molecules in the first place. Despite an ever growing amount of persuasive, even compelling evidence, they denied their existence, even though in the very same year that Clausius defined entropy, 1865, his friend Josef Loschmidt calculated Avogadro's number, which has everything to do with atoms and molecules.[6] Nevertheless, many scientists were still inclined to think that science should deal with concrete matters, that is, things that could be observed directly. If there are atoms, then show them to us; if we cannot see them, then they do not exist. Incredibly, even Dmitri Mendeleev, the man who gave us the periodic table of the elements, subscribed to this view.

This denial of the "atomic hypothesis" was ideologically motivated. Prolific scientists such as Wilhelm Ostwald, the father of physical chemistry, or Ernst Mach, the founder of fluid mechanics (better known nowadays for the Mach unit that is called after him, which is the speed of sound in air), subscribed to a philosophy that was later dubbed "logical positivism," and viewed Boltzmann's work as useless philosophizing. And behold a paradox: despite (or perhaps because of) such an attitude, which is almost diametrically opposite to our grasp of science today as being open to new, innovative and different ideas (as long as they are in the realm of accepted scientific method), the profound scientific breakthroughs that occurred at the end of the 19th century and the beginning of the 20th were immensely grander and more significant than those of today.

Indeed, the atomic hypothesis became acceptable to the scientific community (whatever that means) only after the publication of Einstein's 1905 paper in which he explained Brownian motion in fluids (like the movement of dust particles in still air). Brownian motion is the random movement of particles

---

[6] Avogadro's number is the number of molecules of a substance whose weight, in grams, is equal to the molecular weight of that substance.

that results from collisions between them. This phenomenon was first discovered in 1828 by British biologist Robert Brown, who observed pollen particles in suspension through a microscope and noted that they moved to and fro in patterns that seemed a result of collisions between them. If the momentum of these colliding particles was greater than the effect of gravity upon them, their movement would continue for a long time because the particles tend not to sink to the bottom of the fluid's vessel, but rather stay afloat inside it. The movement of particles in fluids from a place of high concentration to a place of low concentration due to collisions is called diffusion – a measurable physical phenomenon of profound importance (i.e., diffusion is the responsible to the balance of liquids in our bodies). In a spectacular statistical calculation, Einstein derived the dependence of the diffusion coefficient in a system of colliding particles on temperature, and provided the necessary link between measurable values from fluid mechanics (such as the diffusion coefficient and temperature) and the movement of particles. With this, he finally laid to rest all arguments concerning the viability of the atomic hypothesis.

All this, however, had not yet come to pass when Boltzmann reformulated the concept of entropy and declared that a system's entropy is directly proportional to the number of possible distinguishable ways its components can be arranged (or, more precisely, to the logarithm of this number). A fierce argument broke out between Boltzmann with his supporters and those who opposed his ideas. The question was whether there was still a need for Clausius's inequality, or perhaps it was just a consequence of Boltzmann's definition. Boltzmann's desire to derive Clausius's inequality from his own definition made him interpret his entropy in a controversial manner, so that even though his mathematical expression for entropy was correct, an enormous and eternal intellectual achievement, it dragged him into controversies that continue to echo in the scientific world to this very day. We shall discuss the misunderstanding created by Boltzmann's choice of expression later.

Ludwig Boltzmann

Ludwig Eduard Boltzmann, 1844-1906

Ludwig Boltzmann was born in Vienna, Austria, on February 20, 1844, to a middle-class family. His father, a treasury official, earned a stable, comfortable living for his family. Boltzmann's early years were spent in northern Austria. In his youth, he learned piano with Anton Bruckner, then a thirty-years-old organist in the Linz cathedral, well before gaining his fame as a composer. Bruckner's career as a piano teacher to young Boltzmann came to an abrupt end one day when he put his wet overcoat on a sofa in the Boltzmann residence and irked the ire of the mistress of the house. Boltzmann, though, continued playing the piano and became quite proficient. Although his family was not known for intellectual achievements, Boltzmann himself was an unusually brilliant student. When he was fifteen his father died, and a year later his 14 years old brother passed away too (both, apparently, from tuberculosis). Boltzmann senior's death tightened the family's finances somewhat, but his pension still allowed them to live comfortably. From then on, Boltzmann's mother invested all her energy and resources in the education of her son.

In 1863, Boltzmann went to study physics at the University of Vienna. Though he was not aware of this at the time, Boltzmann found himself in an institution that, under the leadership of Josef Stefan (the discoverer of the radiation law named after him), eagerly adopted the hypothesis of the atomic theory. Stefan, who was one of Boltzmann's teachers, made him one of his protégés. At this point, Boltzmann had not as yet exhibited any special inclination toward a specific branch of physics, but immersed as he was in an environment that kept up with all new developments in this science (such as kinetic theory or electrodynamics), it no doubt influenced his final choice of direction. He presented his dissertation on the kinetic theory of gases (which combined thermodynamics with molecular theory) in 1866. In 1867 he was appointed lecturer at the university, and also worked as Stefan's research assistant of at the Erdberg Physical Institute. Stefan encouraged Boltzmann to study Maxwell's work on electrodynamics; discovering that his student could not read English, he also gave him a book on English grammar. (And indeed, Boltzmann admired Maxwell and his work, and even described him as the "greatest of theoreticians".)

While in Vienna, Loschmidt (the physicist who calculated the value of Avogadro's number) befriended young Boltzmann and became to him something of a father figure. In 1869, at the tender age of twenty-five, Boltzmann was appointed Professor of Mathematical Physics at the University of Graz in Austria, and moved to that city. By then he had already published eight scientific papers. It was an impressive appointment for him, but also a great benefit for the university, which had not been particularly notable till then in the physical sciences. The budget, however, was rather tight, and the tiny laboratory was freezing in wintertime. (In fact, August Toepler, the head of the physics department, had to lend Boltzmann a Russian fur coat so that he could keep working on his experiments in the extreme cold.) Boltzmann also gave lectures in elementary physics but not enthusiastically.[19]

In 1872 Boltzmann published a 100-page long paper which transformed him from a fairly talented physicist into an acknowledged genius. This paper, *Further Studies of the Thermal Equilibrium of Gas Molecules*,[20] dealt with the velocity distribution of gas molecules, and marked the first appearance of the expression known today as the Maxwell-Boltzmann distribution. At its core was what Boltzmann called "the minimum theorem," or what was later called the *H*-theorem (see below).

Few were able to understand his methods, and even fewer managed to read through the lengthy paper in which Boltzmann turned his back on the rigid determinism which was a hallmark of the period. His colleagues found this difficult to accept. Even Maxwell, who already in 1859 had described the distribution of the velocity of gas molecules in thermal equilibrium, wrote to his colleague, Peter Guthrie Tait, in 1873: *"By the study of Boltzmann I have been unable to understand him. He could not understand me on account of my shortness, and his length was and is an equal stumbling block to me."*[21] Rumors began to circulate that Boltzmann had done something remarkable, but no one could understand what it was, precisely, and it took some years before a few scientists engaged in an effort to fathom the depth of the issue. Surprisingly, the importance of his work was first recognized in England. In 1875, Lord Kelvin mused about Boltzmann's work while riding on a train, and wrote to a colleague: *"it is very important... The more I thought of it yesterday in the train, the surer I felt of its truth."*[22]

In May 1873 Boltzmann met Henriette von Aigentler, a nineteen-year-old student at the teachers' training college. A year earlier, this determined young woman had decided that she wanted to audit science courses at the university. Even though the administration initially refused to allow this (it was well known that women were of fickle mind, distractions to the male students and faculty, and incapable of the rational thinking required for the study of chemistry, physics or mathematics), she eventually obtained the necessary permissions, not before she presented testimonials ascertaining her proper, quiet decorum. In 1872 she began attending lectures, although was required to present her letter of permission for each course that she registered for. In 1873, after Boltzmann accepted the position of Associate Professor of Mathematics at the University of Vienna, and returned to that city, the two kept up their correspondence. In 1875 he sent her a marriage proposition by letter, and they were married in July 1876.

After the publication of the Maxwell-Boltzmann equation, Boltzmann devoted most of his energy to experimental physics. He published many papers – twelve in three years – but only by the end of these three years did he begin to delve deeper into theoretical physics. In 1877 he returned to Graz, and this time he remained there for fourteen years. In the same year, Boltzmann developed a statistical-mechanical explanation for the second law of thermodynamics, and in 1877 he published it in two papers presented to the Science Academy of Vienna.

Back in Graz, Boltzmann attempted, not without success, to reproduce the atmosphere in which he had been imbued during his early years as a scholar in Vienna. Among other things, in 1879 he carried out the research that led him to discover a fundamental relationship between radiation theory and thermodynamics, now known as the Stefan-Boltzmann law. His fame has spread by then throughout Europe, and students were coming from all over to study with him. Walter Nernst, the 1920 Nobel laureate in chemistry, fondly remembers the open atmosphere that prevailed there and Boltzmann's readiness to devote time to discuss things with his more advanced students (but only with them). To his regret, they were not numerous.

Highly respected and honored, Boltzmann nevertheless felt scientifically isolated in Graz, distant from other scientific giants of the period. As a researcher, he believed in scientific intuition regarding the result being aimed for, ignoring hardships along the way. In addition, he did not believe in the importance of scientific elegance. He used to say: "Elegance is for the tailor and the shoemaker." He published prolifically during this period. In good days, he was an unforgettable lecturer: enthusiastic, involved and attentive to his students. He devoted a lot of time to teaching, and it was important to him that his students, even if they were only medical students, even if they did not intend to devote their future careers to research, would fully understand what he was teaching them. But he wrote just as he spoke, without hesitation, without polish, and without caring about proper, clear and elegant presentation – making it difficult for his readers and listeners to understand him.

In 1885, Boltzmann's mother died at the age of 75. Although 41 years old, ten years married and a father of four, he sunk into a deep depression that was not, alas, to be his last one. In that year he published only one paper on statistical mechanics, his response to a paper by Helmholtz. From then on, Boltzmann's life was marked by instability – frequent moves from place to place and sharp mood swings.

In 1887 he was appointed President of the University of Graz. However, the administrative duties forced upon him were not to his liking, and in 1890, after long, drawn-out negotiations (as was his wont), Boltzmann, then 46, was given the Chair of Theoretical Physics at the University of Munich, in which he did not have to do experimental physics. The teaching burden was not heavy, nor were his administrative duties, and a short time after his arrival in Munich, Boltzmann derived the second law of thermodynamics from the principles of statistical mechanics and published a thick volume, Lectures on Maxwell's Theory on Electricity and Light.[23]

Meantime, the University of Vienna was looking for a way to induce him back to Austria, especially since he had received an honorary degree in England. An opportunity presented itself in 1893, when Josef Stefan died. Some of the faculty in Vienna wanted to see his position given to Ernst Mach, then in Prague, who was considered an excellent lecturer and a multi-faceted researcher. Again, Boltzmann conducted long and convoluted negotiations before finally accepting the offer; it was obvious that Vienna was willing to agree to just about anything in order to win him back. In September 1894, at the age of fifty, he returned to Vienna as a Professor of Theoretical Physics and the head of the institute where he had begun his studies thirty years earlier. One year later, in May, 1895, Mach too joined the faculty of the University of Vienna, as a professor of the history and philosophy of science. Unfortunately, since he was Boltzmann's bitter scientific rival, the relationship between them were difficult, to say the least, profoundly affecting Boltzmann's state of mind.

The heated debate between atomists and energists[7] came to a head in September 1895, during a conference organized by the German Society of Scientists in Lübeck. Boltzmann invited Wilhelm Ostwald from Leipzig to participate. These two had first met in 1887, when Ostwald was studying in Graz for a few months, and a warm relationship based on mutual respect had developed between them. But at the conference Ostwald showed himself a devout energist. In his lecture he declared that

> The actual irreversibility of natural phenomena thus proves the existence of processes that cannot be described by mechanical equations, and with this the verdict on scientific materialism settled.

Arnold Sommerfeld, who would later become a famous mathematical physicist, was present at the meeting and later described the argument that ensued between Ostwald and Boltzmann.

> The battle between Boltzmann and Ostwald resembled the battle of the bull with the supple fighter. However, this time the bull was victorious. ... The arguments of Boltzmann carried the day. We, the young

---

[7] The energists were scientists who believed in logical positivism, insisted that natural phenomena can be explained in terms of energy and refused to accept the "atomic hypothesis".

mathematicians of that time, were all on the side of Boltzmann."[24]

When the convention ended, both sides were still holding steadfastly to their respective positions, and the participants left with a deep sense of discomfort. Ostwald and his followers felt besieged, and Boltzmann had a sense of failure because he did not succeed in converting any of the energists to his views. Actually, Ostwald was correct in his claim that the mechanic equations included in Boltzmann's H-theorem (below) could not explain irreversibility in nature. On the other hand, Boltzmann was correct in his claim that matter is composed of atoms.

Upon his return to Vienna, Boltzmann found himself alone in his views against the leader of the opposition to atomism, the eminent Ernst Mach. Joseph Loschmidt, Boltzmann's old colleague, died in July 1895, the number of Mach's admirers was steadily growing, and Boltzmann felt more isolated, unappreciated and miserable than ever. At the same time, Joules Henri Poincaré published a theorem which implied that Boltzmann's intuitive insight which underlie his work on the H-theorem was erroneous, and immediately after, Ernst Zermelo published another paper that questioned the correctness of the H-theorem. Boltzmann responded to these papers, but his answers were perceived by others, for good reason, as somewhat evasive. Planck and Kelvin, too, disagreed with him. Mach's supporters began to view Boltzmann as a relic from the past, the last champion of atomism; indeed, most leading scientists in Germany and France were convinced at the time that the kinetic atomic theory had outlived its role, because it could not explain irreversibility in nature.

Maxwell died in 1879, Clausius in 1888, Stefan in 1893 and Loschmidt in 1895. In 1890 in Vienna, Boltzmann found himself surrounded by intellectual rivals, with no young physicists to support him. Some of his feelings can be gleaned in a letter he sent to the editors of the scientific journal which published his comment on a paper by Zermelo:

Since I am, so it appears, now that Maxwell, Clausius, Helmholtz, etc., are dead, the last Epigone for the view that nature can be explained mechanically rather than energetically, I would say that in the interests of science I am duty-bound to take care that at least my voice does not go unheard.[25]

In 1898 he wrote to his assistant, Felix Klein:

Just when I received your dear letter I had another neurasthenic attack, as I so often do in Vienna, although I was spared them altogether in Munich. With it came the fear that the whole *H*-curve was nonsense.[26]

This confirms the widespread supposition that Boltzmann was aware of the problematic nature of his *H*-theorem, even though this detracts nothing whatsoever from the correctness of his expression for entropy. He could not know that within three years, this expression would help Planck in his monumental discovery of the atomistic nature of electromagnetic radiation.

Boltzmann remained in Vienna, his hometown, for another six years, the time when Mach's influence was at its peak. Mach preached a science based on sensory perceptions and vehemently opposed any scientific hypothesis about things that could not be felt nor seen. Meanwhile, Boltzmann was spending more and more time defending himself and writing philosophical essays aiming to discredit Mach's outlook. But his students beat a path to Mach's lectures, and few of them did science for its own sake. Vienna's days as an important center for research in physics were just about over. During that period Boltzmann published a book called *Lectures on the Theory of Gases*,[27] which was included his own research on the kinetic theory of gases.

The unhappy Boltzmann longed for a change of place and atmosphere, but only in 1900 could he finally move to Leipzig at Ostwald's invitation, barely taking the time to say goodbye to his colleagues and friends. Despite the warm welcome he received in Leipzig, and despite his good relationship with Ostwald, he was miserable and deeply troubled by the rise of energism that Ostwald was now leading. Academically, he published very little, and whatever he did publish was a kind of blend of physics and philosophy. He was not especially interested in the work done by others around him – not even in Planck's, which was making innovative use of his treatment of entropy. Also, Boltzmann's eyesight was deteriorating and he suffered violent mood swings. Six months had barely passed, and he was already contemplating a return to Vienna. And indeed, Vienna – painfully, no longer a bastion of the physical sciences – was anxious for him to return. As always, complicated formal negotiations were required, among them the getting the Kaiser's approval, which was given on condition that Boltzmann would give his word of honor never to apply for a position outside the Austro-Hungarian Empire. These negotiations went on until 1902, while Boltzmann's mental state continued to deteriorate.

In the latter half of 1902, Boltzmann returned to find a pitiful scientific environment. The standard of teaching in physics was high, but there was not one researcher of his caliber. He got back his former chair in theoretical physics, which had remained empty since he had left a couple of years earlier. During the next few years Boltzmann was happier, especially since Mach had left the university in 1901 due to ill health. In 1903, in addition to teaching mathematical physics, Boltzmann was asked to take over Mach's course in philosophy. His philosophy lectures quickly became a hit, and the auditorium was too small for all those who wished to attend. Yet Mach's health was still good enough for him to continue his vehement attacks on atomism and on the last of its champions, namely Boltzmann. Despite a temporary improvement in Boltzmann's spirit, his health continued to bother him, and his anxiety attacks never let up.

In 1904 Boltzmann completed the publication of his last important book, *Lectures on the Principles of Mechanics*.[28]

He also visited the United States, where he had another public debate with Ostwald on atomism. For the young physicists attending the event – among them Robert Millikan, later a Nobel laureate – who were already familiar with the concept of atomism, the whole issue must have seemed archaic and hard to fathom. Regretfully, even though radioactivity had already been an established field of research for a number of years, Boltzmann did not understand that the new discoveries he learned about during his visit were about to prove atomic theory conclusively, once and for all. Despite this, however, his work continued to be criticized, and he fell again into depression. As he saw it then, his life work was about to implode despite all his efforts.

In 1905 Albert Einstein published his three papers that would change the face of physics (one of them, on the Brownian movement mentioned above, would give final proof to the atomic hypothesis). Astonishingly, even though Einstein's work was a confirmation of Boltzmann's doctrine, Boltzmann did not have an inkling about its very existence. At that point he was busy with editing his lectures on philosophy; in writing an entry on kinetic theory for the *Encyclopedia of Mathematics* that his friend Felix Klein was editing; and on preparing a volume of his popular articles from past years. Upon completion of these tasks, he sunk into melancholy. In May 1906 he resigned his teaching duties.

A month later, in June 1906, he went with his wife and three daughters to a seaside resort near Trieste, Italy, hoping to calm his nerves before the commencement of the new academic year. They stayed there for three weeks, and at first it looked as if the vacation was doing him good. But again he sunk into depression, so serious that his wife felt obliged to call for their son, who was then serving in the army. In the evening of September 5, before his son had arrived, Henriette and their daughters went down to the sea. When Boltzmann did not follow, Henriette sent their young daughter, Elsa, to fetch him. She found Boltzmann hanging from the window of their room.

Boltzmann's work was received with mixed reaction in his lifetime, and to this day there is no consensus about the merits of his legacy. Boltzmann was viewed by some of his contemporaries, and by himself, as the defender of the atomic theory of matter in an era when leading scientists in Germany (such as Ostwald and Mach) opposed it. Thus was born the widespread yet false impression that his contemporaries ignored or opposed him, and some even relate his suicide to the awful injustice done to him. The fact that he died virtually on the eve of the victory of the atomic hypothesis, thanks to the work of Einstein and Perrin,[8] adds a dramatic twist to the story.

Actually, Boltzmann's reputation as a theoretical physicist was well-established and highly regarded. Universities fought for the privilege of giving him chairs, and he won many awards and honors (though never the Nobel Prize). It seems that his suicide was due more to a deterioration of his physical and mental health than to any academic issue, even though it is possible that his doubts regarding his H-theorem also contributed to his mental distress. However, Boltzmann's place in the pantheon of great scientists is assured thanks to his statistical definition of entropy, which he proposed on his own, independently of Josiah Willard Gibbs.

In 1933, after years of neglect, a tombstone was erected on his grave in the Central Cemetery in Vienna, on which was engraved his formula:

$$S = k \log W$$

---

[8] Jean Perrin (1870–1942) was a French scientist who, in 1908, conducted experiments that proved the validity of Einstein's explanation for the Brownian motion under various conditions.

The *H*-theorem was derived from Boltzmann's wish to show that an ideal gas will increase its entropy over time as a result of collisions between its particles, in accord with Clausius's inequality. Using kinetic theory, Boltzmann calculated entropy as a function of time and gave it – for some unknown reason – the symbol *H* (in fact, *H* equals $-Q/T$). The premise for his formula was this: a system in a relatively ordered state – for example, a vessel in which all the gas molecules are concentrated in one corner – will reach, in its striving for equilibrium, a random state such that all molecules are uniformly dispersed throughout the vessel (that is, a state of higher probability and less order, compared with a state in which all the molecules are found in one corner). Thus, supposedly, the system's entropy has increased, or equivalently, its *H* function has decreased. The problem with Boltzmann's premise was that it was incorrect. There remained a probability – albeit quite low – that a random system undergoing random collisions *could* reach a more ordered state. If such a thing could take place, it would contradict the second law of thermodynamics, which says that entropy may only increases or remains the same, but may never decrease. This "paradox" can be removed, however, by introducing the concept of "microstate" (which will be explained shortly). That is, entropy is defined only in equilibrium and is determined by Ω, the number of microstates of a system. An ordered microstate is equivalent to any other microstate and, in equilibrium, all microstates have equal probabilities.

In 1877 Boltzmann published a paper in response to Josef Loschmidt's disagreement with his (Boltzmann's) statement that *H* can only decrease. In fact, Loschmidt claimed that Boltzmann's systems were reversible. In this paper, Boltzmann's famous equation for entropy, $S = k \ln \Omega$, appeared for the first time. (Actually, this is the modern formulation, slightly different from the one that Boltzmann wrote himself – the one engraved on his tombstone.) In this equation, *k* is a constant (called today the Boltzmann constant) and Ω[9] is the number of different possible

---

[9] Boltzmann used the Latin letter W; nowadays the Greek letter omega is used.

ways to arrange a system (in terms of the previous example, to place gas particles in different locations within the vessel). This number is variously referred to as the number of combinations, or configurations, or microstates. In order to understand the concept of a *microstate*, which is often confused with other quantities, we shall define the concept of *macrostate* as well, using the following example:

Let us assume a macrostate of six lots and three houses. Each lot can either have a house built on it or none. This is the system's macrostate: three lots with houses, three without. For some purposes, this description may suffice; but not when it comes to entropy, because it is concerned with microstates. There are several different possibilities for how the three houses can be distributed among the six lots, and each individual possibility is called a microstate.

For example, in one microstate, lots 1, 2, and 3 have a house each, and lots 4, 5, and 6 have none. Another microstate would have lots 1, 2, and 6 with a house, and 3, 4, and 5 without one, and so forth. In total (you can see this calculation in Appendix A-2) there are 20 different microstates. Therefore, the entropy of these lots, according to Boltzmann, is: $S = \ln 20 = 2.9957...$ (Note that in this example we set $k = 1$, as is its value in information theory, which will be discussed in Chapter 4.)

Now let us consider what the entropy would be if only one lot out of the six had a house. (In other words, the macroscopic system would have six lots, but only one with a house built on it.) Since there are now only six possible microstates, the entropy would be smaller: $S = \ln 6 = 1.7917...$ The number of states that each lot can have remains the same (two – with or without a house), but the number of the microstates has changed.

What would happen if we added another empty lot to the first system, so that it will now have a macroscopic system of seven lots with three houses? The number of microstates will be 35, and entropy will increase accordingly, to $S = \ln 35 = 3.5553...$ On the other hand, if we were to add an empty lot to the second system (the one in which only one lot has a house), the number of the microstates will be 7, and entropy will grow only slightly, to $S = \ln 7 = 1.9459...$

The above was a simple example. It was easy to calculate the number of microstates, since we assumed that all the houses were identical. But even a slight change in the macrostate will substantially complicate the entropy calculation. For instance, if the area of one house is 900 square feet, three houses will have 2,700 square feet. If however the entire information we have is that there are six lots with a total built area of 2,700 square feet, what is the number of microstates now? Or, rather, what would the entropy be now? It would be significantly higher, because there are a great many ways to build 2,700 square-feet-worth of houses on six lots. To calculate such problems, physicists generally use a technique called *Lagrange multipliers*, which enables them to find a distribution of the buildings' total area among the lots such that the number of the microstates is at a maximum (see Appendixes A-4, A-6, B-2, and B-3).

Now we can see the intuition behind Boltzmann's entropy, which was really quite simple: the greater the number of microstates, Ω, that a closed system may be found in, the greater its entropy. In equilibrium, the number of microstates is maximal, and each microstate has equal probability.

The way that Boltzmann arrived at the expression of entropy described here was long and convoluted. Physicist Abraham Pais wrote about it in his biography of Albert Einstein, *Subtle is the Lord:*

> Boltzmann's qualities as an outstanding lecturer are not reflected in his scientific papers, which are sometimes unduly long, occasionally obscure and often dense. Their main conclusions are sometimes tucked away among lengthy calculations.[29]

By the way, this is the reason we derive the Boltzmann expression in Appendix A-2 the way Planck did it, rather than the way actually used by Boltzmann.

Boltzmann's question was this: in what way is the heat in a vessel distributed among the particles of an ideal gas (an ideal gas is one in which no intermolecular forces operate between its particles.) To answer it, Boltzmann built a model of a box containing "microscopic billiard balls" that act upon each other only through elastic collisions.

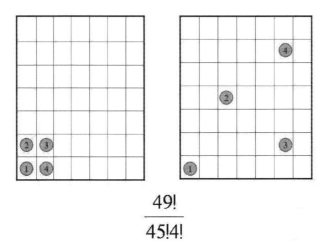

$$\frac{49!}{45!4!}$$

Figure 2: Two possible ways to arrange four balls in 49 places.

In this model we assume that there are much fewer balls than available cells (that is, there is an infinitely small chance of finding two balls in the same cell, or state). The actual arrangement of balls in the box is its microstate. The balls can be arranged in a very ordered manner (for example, concentrated in one corner and leaving the rest of the area empty, as illustrated on the left in Fig. 2), or scattered (as on the right) with no discernible order. There are many more possible disordered microstates than ordered ones, so if we were to shake the box when it is in a fairly ordered microstate, we should expect that the balls will end up in a different, less ordered microstate.

Returning to the gas in the vessel: if we could take a snapshot of the arrangement of its atoms or molecules, with exposure time that is shorter than the time necessary for an atom to move from its place, we would be observing one microstate. Taking multiple snapshots over a more extended period would provide us a number of microstates, since the gas particles are constantly changing position due to the unceasing collisions between them. Taking a series of snapshots for eternity lets us observe *all* possible microstates, because the system, theoretically, will change from one microstate to another, eventually passing through every possible one. What is important to note is that the entropy in the vessel is not influenced by the specific arrangement of the particles at any instant, but rather by the number of *all* the possible microstates, both ordered and disordered. To calculate this entropy, therefore, one must count all possible microstates.

Boltzmann got his results using kinetic theory, that is, by analyzing the dynamics of the collisions between the particles, and not by simply counting the microstates, and therefore his intuition proved incorrect. In particular, the following misconceptions must be considered:

Shaking a box in which P balls are arranged in one corner will increase the number of microstates, and therefore will increase entropy. This is a false intuition: the number of possible microstates in the box is constant and shaking the box just moves the balls from one microstate to another. As mentioned, in a vast majority of cases, shaking the box will change the system into a less ordered microstate, because there are many more disordered microstates than ordered ones.

When all the balls are on one side, the system is not in equilibrium, whereas when the balls are scattered throughout the box the system is closer to equilibrium. This too is an erroneous intuition. In fact, non-equilibrium would exist only if specific microstates have lower probabilities than the others.

It was the intuitive yet erroneous idea that an ordered microstate has lower entropy and a disordered microstate has higher entropy (an intuition based, as noted, on the fact that there is a far greater number of disordered microstates than ordered ones), that gave entropy its bad name, because it gave rise to some other misconceptions. For example:

Order and entropy are opposites. Since the higher the entropy, the higher the disorder, it stands to reason that there is always a tendency for disorder to increase. Lord Kelvin claimed that the second law of thermodynamics would consume the universe by bringing upon it thermal death – a state in which everything would be in chaotic thermal equilibrium (the same conjecture is attributed to Helmholtz too). In practice, though, *entropy is a measure of uncertainty, not disorder.* The entropy of a system defines the number of possible ways (that is, the number of microstates) in which it may be found *if every possible microstate has an equal probability!* The only meaning of this definition is that entropy is the uncertainty one has when asked the question, what microstate is a system in? As we shall see in Chapter 4, von Neumann and Shannon understood this point well. Yet Boltzmann's error, namely interpreting the meaning of entropy as disorder (a mistake stemming from the fact that there are many more disordered than ordered microstates) has continues to haunt us to this day. All the more so since, as we shall see later, there are situations where an increase in uncertainty actually means an *increase* in information.

A spontaneous creation of life contradicts the second law, since living systems seem to be highly ordered and consequently their entropy is low. But in fact, increasing the complexity of a system (as in a living system), increases its uncertainty, and therefore its entropy. Thus, the spontaneous creation of life not only does not contradict the second law, but, as we shall see later, is driven by it.

The second law is not necessary. Since entropy is the disorder generated by random processes such as rolling dice, we have no need for any law in order to understand that the world is statistical. However, a law of nature is the point, in a process of analysis, where one stops asking questions and says instead, "That's the way it is." Take for example gravity, the attraction between masses. Were we to ask an expert on general relativity why masses are attracted to each other, we may get a lengthy and learned answer, but the bottom line will be, "because that's the way it is." And indeed, there is something that seems almost trivial in the second law. If the second law of thermodynamics would be exclusively based on probabilities, then events with low probabilities can also occur occasionally, meaning that there is a chance – albeit a low one – to witness some event that seems to be in violation of the second law. In fact, some scientists occasionally do "show us" some violation of the second law in some system or another. But the passage of a system from a microstate of disorder into one that is more ordered *does* *not* violate the second law of thermodynamics. A violation would mean that the system spontaneously lowered the number of its possible microstates. If that could happen, we shall be able to build air conditioners that require zero energy to run.

In conclusion, the number of microstates – both ordered and disordered – in a closed system is constant, and the logarithm of that number is the system's entropy (which means that the entropy of a closed [isolated] system remains constant). The reason entropy increases in a non-isolated system is because there tends to be a spontaneous increase in the number of microstates that the particles can be in. If the number of possible microstates does not increase, then there is no spontaneous change in the system! To decrease the number of possible microstates for a system, there must be an input of energy (work). For example, work is required to compress gas, because the number of possible microstates has been lowered.[10]

Boltzmann's and Clausius's Expressions of Entropy

The expressions given by Clausius and Boltzmann for entropy were as different as can be. While the Clausius entropy is the ratio between two physical quantities – heat and temperature – Boltzmann's entropy (as defined above) makes no direct mention

---

[10] In 1895, Jules Henri Poincaré published a theorem that showed that any closed mechanical system must at some point return to its initial state. That is, it will pass from one microstate to another, until it returns at one time or another to its initial microstate. This theorem seems to prove that Boltzmann's intuitive idea, on which he based his *H*-theorem, and according to which the random scattering of particles increases the number of microstates (and thus increasing entropy), was incorrect. However, it is important to realize that Boltzmann's entropy deals with a closed system and is solely dependent on the *number* of possible microstates, which is constant, and not at all dependent on the *dynamics* of the changes from one microstate to another, which was what Poincaré was studying. Simply put, collisions between atoms do not increase the number of microstates.

of either heat or temperature. So how is it that these two expressions describe the same quantity? The reason is that the number of possible microstates is dependent on the amount of energy possessed by the particles, which is dependent on the overall amount of energy possessed by the gas, namely its temperature. The arrangement of particles illustrated in Fig. 2 above is actually an over-simplification of a microstate, because in addition to its physical location, every particle actually also has velocity – a speed-and-direction vector conventionally depicted by an arrow. If we distribute the energy between the particles in one particular way, the number of possible microstates will be different than when the energy is distributed in another way. But entropy must be defined in equilibrium, that is, when the number of microstates is at a maximum. Therefore, there must be some point at which the energy distribution gives the maximum number of microstates. This distribution satisfies Clausius's inequality. The distribution at which there is a maximum number of microstates is generally a function of temperature: for each temperature, there is a different distribution.

Appendix A-4, which deals with the derivation of the bell-shaped distribution, shows how the distribution of energy between atoms is calculated to yield the maximum number of microstates. Planck used this same principle to calculate the energy distribution in the thermal electromagnetic radiation of matter, and thus made one of the most important discoveries in the history of physics: energy can only be absorbed or emitted in discrete quantities – a discovery that laid the foundations of quantum theory.

It can said that just as Carnot's theorem led to the more general formulation of entropy by Clausius, so Clausius's inequality led to Boltzmann's even more general formulation. Boltzmann's definition now connects a physical concrete value (the Clausius entropy) with the uncertainty that exists in a system. The disadvantage of Boltzmann's definition of entropy is that in many cases its value depends on how the problem is outlined (as we saw in the lots and houses example), and one macroscopic system may be assigned different values of entropy depending on the specific statement of the problem. In addition, Boltzmann's entropy requires complex calculations to determine the number of microstates. On the other hand, as we shall see in the second part of this book, the generality of Boltzmann's expression does allow us to extend it beyond the physical sciences to other fields, such as logic, networking and sociology.

The Gibbs Entropy

"The whole is simpler than the sum of its parts".[30]

\- Josiah Gibbs

At approximately the same time that Boltzmann was working out his statistical explanation for the second law of thermodynamics, in 1877, an American scientist named Josiah Willard Gibbs, working at what was in those days a backwoods scientific center – Yale University in Connecticut – published the results of his research on the same topic. Today, his contribution is regarded as one of the greatest breakthroughs of 19th century science, a cornerstone of physical chemistry.

As mentioned before, Boltzmann expressed entropy as a function of the number of microstates, a value that derives from the extensivity of the entropies of multiple systems. The Gibbs entropy was derived by mixing these systems. In fact, Gibbs's expression is not a function of the *number* of microstates, but rather a function of their *probabilities*. Of course, the final result yielded by both expressions will give the same value for entropy, but Gibbs's expression for entropy is more useful for many cases, especially in calculating the entropy of information, which will be discussed in the second part of this book.

Josiah Willard Gibbs

Josiah Willard Gibbs, 1839-1903

Josiah Gibbs was born in New Haven, Connecticut, on February 11, 1839, the only son of a professor at Yale University (like five previous generations before him). As a boy, he was somewhat withdrawn socially in school life and of rather delicate health, but he proved very diligent student.

When he was fifteen he began studying at Yale College, where he won prizes for excellence in Latin and mathematics. He graduated in 1858, and remained at the college where he undertook research in engineering. Most of his engineering knowledge was self-taught: in college he was taught mathematics, the classics, and just a bit of science. As was common at the time in many universities, the entire science curriculum was a one-year course called "natural philosophy," which included chemistry, astronomy, mineralogy and the like, alongside with physics. But as a graduate engineering student, Gibbs also did some experimental work in the laboratory – quite unusual in those days, since it was not part of the usual science curriculum.

His dissertation, *On the Form of the Teeth of Wheels in Spur Gearing*, in which he used geometric techniques to investigate gear design, won him the first Ph. D. degree awarded by Yale in engineering. He received his degree in 1863 and remained to teach in Yale for three years: two teaching Latin, and then teaching "natural philosophy." In 1866 he patented a design for an improved type of railroad brake.

Gibbs was never short of means, as his father's death in 1861 (his mother had died some time before) had left him and his sisters a fair amount of money that allowed them to travel to Europe, and Gibbs took advantage of this opportunity to meet with distinguished scientific colleagues and learn from them. Among other places, he spent a year in Berlin and another one in Heidelberg.

In those days, the German academic institutions were world leaders in chemistry, thermodynamics and theoretical natural sciences. As a rule, in the 19th century, the European scientific standards were far higher than in the United States, in all sciences. (In engineering, though, the U.S.A. did not fall this far behind.) Gibbs used well this unique opportunity (after returning to the U.S.A., he never left New Haven again) and put all his efforts into acquiring knowledge that was not available at the time in his homeland. Looking at the lecture notes he took there, it is impossible to tell which subjects he found particularly interesting, but there is no doubt that during his stay in Germany he was influenced by Kirchhoff and Helmholtz.

In June 1869 Gibbs returned to New Haven and resumed his work. Just two years later, when Yale University decided to upgrade its science program, Gibbs was appointed professor of mathematical physics – before he had published even one paper. He received no remuneration for his lectures, which was not unusual in those days even in important scientific centers. His students found him an efficient, industrious lecturer, as well as a patient, encouraging and considerate one, and often amusing.

It was not until 1873, when Gibbs was 34 years old, when he published his theory of thermodynamic equilibrium, that the scientific community began to recognize his genius. It was an extremely original and innovative work, published as two papers. The first one, *Graphical Methods in the Thermodynamics of Fluids*,[31] included his formula for free energy. The second one had the title *A Method of Geometrical Representation of the Thermodynamic Properties of Substances by Means of Surfaces*.[32]

In these papers Gibbs used a wide range of novel graphs and illustrations of the kind now called phase diagrams. These make it possible to present various combinations of quantities, such as pressure, volume, temperature, energy, entropy and the like, in extremely useful ways.[11] For instance, a graph of entropy vs. volume showed when gas changed to liquid, or liquid to solid. In his second paper he presented three-dimensional graphs whose axes represent three thermodynamic qualities, i.e. entropy, energy and volume, at the same time. For each substance, the three-dimensional space was divided into areas suitable for gas, liquid or solid, and the interfaces between them provided more information (for example, the temperature and pressure of a phase transition). In such a seemingly simple representation there was a wealth of information that used to be provided separately in the past, but could now be presented as a whole.

Maxwell was impressed by Gibbs's work, and in a 1875 lecture spoke about it to the Chemical Society in London, in an attempt to draw British scientists' attention to this enormous contribution to thermodynamics. He even went so far as to build a three-dimensional model of Gibbs's thermodynamic surface for water. Shortly before his death, Maxwell sent this model to Gibbs.[33]

---

[11] The cost of printing Gibbs's papers was exceptionally high because of their length and the abundance of mathematical formulas and graphics, and in order to have them printed, it was necessary to raise donations from the journal's subscribers as well as New Haven businessmen, many of whom could not make head or tail of these papers, but nevertheless subsidized them.

In 1876 Gibbs published the first part of his *On the Equilibrium of Heterogeneous Substances;* the second part appeared in 1878.[34] This work added another important layer to the study of thermodynamics, and finally earned him the fame he deserved. In these papers Gibbs used thermodynamics to explain some of the physical phenomena associated with chemical reactions – until then, there was little overlapping between these disciplines, and their effects on each other were presented merely as a series of isolated facts – and triggered a revolution in classic thermodynamics. In fact, Gibbs applied thermodynamics to chemistry, and since then, every chemistry student solves problems about the concentrations of chemicals in chemical equilibrium using to Gibbs's methodology. In the third and longest part of his work, Gibbs dealt with the problem of thermodynamic stability (namely, equilibrium).

Gibbs's papers are now regarded as highly important, but a number of years were to pass before their significance was widely acknowledged. It was claimed that the reason for the delay in recognizing the importance of Gibbs's work was due to his style of writing, which was difficult to follow, and also to the fact that he chose to publish his papers in an obscure journal, *Transactions of the Connecticut Academy of Science.* His brother-in-law, a librarian, was the editor of this journal, and if it had few readers in America, they were even fewer in Europe. Gibbs therefore took pains to send reprints of his papers to the one hundred scientists, more or less, who in his opinion could understand and appreciate his work. Maxwell, Helmholtz and Clausius were on the list; Boltzmann's name was added only by the time the third part was published.

In 1880, the newly established Johns Hopkins University in Baltimore, Maryland, offered Gibbs a professorship with a salary of $3,000 a year. Yale responded by offering him $2,000, but Gibbs accepted Yale's offer and remained in New Haven.

Between 1880 and 1884 Gibbs developed vector analysis by combining the ideas of William Hamilton and Hermann Grassmann. This work is still of immense importance in both pure and applied mathematics. Among other things, he applied his vector methods to chart the path of a comet by observations from three observatories. The method, which needed far fewer calculations than the previously used Gauss method, described the path of the Swift Comet in 1880. Between 1882 and 1889 Gibbs published a series of five papers on the electromagnetic theory of light.

From 1890 and on, Gibbs devoted most of his time to teaching, and his research during those years was of less importance than his initial contributions to thermodynamics. Only in 1902 was he was persuaded to compile his views and ideas on numerous subjects in an important volume, *Elementary Principles in Statistical Mechanics*,[35] that was to provide a general mathematical framework for both Maxwell's electromagnetic theory and subsequently quantum theory. With this work, Gibbs has laid the principles of statistical mechanics on a firm foundation.

Initially, as noted above, not many physicists and chemists recognized the importance of Gibbs's contributions. Only after Wilhelm Ostwald translated his papers into German (then the leading language in science) in 1892, and Henri Louis Le Châtelier into French in 1899, did his ideas begin to have an impact on European science. Gibbs's papers, noted Ostwald in his autobiography, had far-reaching impact on his own development as a scientist.[36]

At long last, then, Gibbs's work was becoming known, appreciated and acknowledged by his contemporaries, but Gibbs himself never made an effort to explain his ideas beyond what he wrote in his scientific papers, and these – even to his admirers – were abrupt to a point that defied full understanding. Preferring to present his ideas mainly as calculations and diagrams, he was a man of few words.

To his critics he would respond that on the contrary, his papers were too long and unnecessarily wasted his readers' time. He was also known to keep his ideas to himself until he had fully developed them, and never explained how he got his inspiration for doing the research about which he wrote.

Apart from those few years in Europe, Gibbs lived all his life in the home his father had built, a short distance from the school in which he studied and from the college and university in which he worked all his life. He died at the age of sixty-four. J. G. Crowther, author of a book about famous American scientists, summed up Gibbs's life as follows:

> [Gibbs] remained a bachelor, living in his surviving sister's household. In his later years he was a tall, dignified gentleman, with a healthy stride and ruddy complexion, performing his share of household chores, approachable and kind (if unintelligible) to students. Gibbs was highly esteemed by his friends, but U.S. science was too preoccupied with practical questions to make much use of his profound theoretical work during his lifetime. He lived out his quiet life at Yale, deeply admired by a few able students but making no immediate impress on U.S. science commensurate with his genius.[37]

American physicist H. A. Bumstead, Gibbs's colleague in Yale, eulogized him thus:

> Unassuming in manner, genial and kindly in his intercourse with his fellow-men, never showing impatience or irritation, devoid of personal ambition of the baser sort or of the slightest desire to exalt himself, he went far toward realizing the ideal of the unselfish, Christian gentleman. In the minds of those who knew him, the greatness of his intellectual achievements will never overshadow the beauty and dignity of his life.[38]

Gibbs's contribution was only fully recognized in 1923, when Lewis and Randall published their book *Thermodynamics and the Free Energies of Chemical Substances*,[39] which presented Gibbs's methods to chemists worldwide. Since then, chemical engineering is based on it.

Whereas Boltzmann's entropy, for a system with Ω microstates, is the product of the logarithm of that number by a constant now called the Boltzmann constant, Gibbs defined the same entropy as the sum of the entropies of the individual microstates. Since the entropy of each microstate is dependent on its probability, Gibbs showed that entropy can be written as the sum of the probabilities (see Appendix A-3). Gibbs's expression for entropy is

$$S = -k\sum_{i=1}^{\Omega} p_i \ln p_i,$$

that is, the sum of all the microstates of $p_i \ln p_i$, where p_i is the probability of microstate i. Sometimes it is more convenient to calculate this expression, rather than Boltzmann's. Also, using Gibbs's equation for entropy we can divide a system into its components according to our needs. In fact, the Gibbs entropy has become the most common means for calculating entropy, now used in thermodynamics, quantum physics (where it is called the von Neumann entropy) and information theory (where it is called Shannon's entropy).

Gibbs's expression for entropy is the one that appears in most textbooks on statistical mechanics or information theory, and it can be interpreted as a generalization of Boltzmann's entropy. Indeed, the Gibbs entropy allows us to assign a different probability to each particular microstate (or to a number of specific microstates). Returning to the example of the six lots, three of which have houses, the result obtained using Boltzmann's expression was $S_B = \ln 20$. Using Gibbs's method and the assumption that all microstates have the same probability, 1/20, the entropy will be the sum of twenty identical units

$$S_G = -(\frac{1}{20} + ... + \frac{1}{20}) \ln(\frac{1}{20}) = \ln 20 \approx 3$$

.

This result is indeed the same as the one was obtained using Boltzmann's expression (recall that $\ln \frac{1}{x} = -\ln x$).

However, what will happen to the entropy if the owner, who lives in one of the houses, prefers that the lots adjacent to his property on both sides will remain empty? Previously, there were twenty microstates, represented as follows (1 represents a lot with a house, 0 represents an empty lot):

111000	110100	110010	110001	101100

101001	100110	100101	110001	101010

000111	001011	001101	001110	010011

010101	010110	011001	011010	011100

By adding the constraint that one house at least will not have any neighbors, the number of microstates is reduced to ten:

110100	110010	101001	100101	101010

001011	010011	010101	010110	011010

Let us complicate the problem even further and assume that the owner will be willing, with reservation, to live in a house that has one neighbor, the reservation being that the house should have a view to the west. We assume that only 50% of the lots have a view to the west. Thus the probability for ten of the microstates is 2/3, whereas ten microstates have only one half of this probability, that is, 1/3. Therefore, every lot among those ten without any neighbors has a probability of $p = \dfrac{2}{30} = \dfrac{1}{15}$, and the ten microstates with one neighbor each has a probability of $p = \dfrac{1}{30}$. Thus, the entropy according to Gibbs is

$$S_G = -(\frac{1}{3}\ln\frac{1}{30} + \frac{2}{3}\ln\frac{1}{15}) = (\frac{1}{3}\ln 30 + \frac{2}{3}\ln 15) \approx 2.94.$$

This result is smaller than Boltzmann's entropy. In general, adding constraints always decreases entropy, and thus the Gibbs entropy will usually be lower than Boltzmann's. So the Gibbs entropy is useful when dealing with situations that are not in equilibrium, meaning that often it should not properly be called *entropy*, since entropy is defined only in equilibrium. Nevertheless, its importance is enormous, as we shall see below.

The example used above, the entropy of lots and houses, seems utterly useless. It is inconceivable that any member of any zoning committee would care about the logical entropy of lots and houses in a particular area. However, the implication of such calculations for other areas cannot be overstated. Recall that according to Clausius, $S = Q/T$, and thus $Q = TS$, meaning that the entropy produced by some process multiplied by its temperature gives heat. This is the heat that *cannot* be used for work, since it goes into increasing entropy – as is necessary to prevent a decrease in total universal entropy (recall that this is the heat that reduces the efficiency of the Carnot machine). Therefore, when energy is released in some process and we want to know how much of it can be used for other purposes; we must subtract the value of TS from the amount of released energy. The released energy minus TS (the energy which is consumed to increase entropy) is called *free energy*. Every chemist knows how important this value is in calculating the efficiency of chemical and nuclear reactions, from power stations to batteries. In fact, free energy is Carnot's efficiency of a chemical reaction, and it was Gibbs who gave science the necessary tool for calculating it, by defining the entropy of constraints.

Putting lots and houses aside, let us review a more practical example. Two gases, A and B, are put in a container at a ratio of one to one, namely, there is an identical number of molecules of each gas. Now, assume that we divide this container into two equal sections, and that some demon has contrived to put all the A molecules on one predetermined side of the partition, and all the B molecules on the other side. This is a system with a constraint, since there are no microstates that have molecules of A among the molecules of B, or *vice versa*. Before the demon's interference, one section of the container had a 50% probability of having molecule A and a 50% probability of having molecule B. The entropy per molecule is:

$$S = -(\frac{1}{2} \ln \frac{1}{2} + \frac{1}{2} \ln \frac{1}{2}) = \ln 2$$

due to the fact we have two microstates, AB and BA.

After the demon's interference we have full knowledge about the A's and B's molecules location in the sections, namely, we have one microstate, and zero entropy. In other words, the entropy of the mixed system is greater by ln 2 per molecule. Now, multiplying this by the Boltzmann constant and the number of molecules, we get that the entropy of mixing is: $S = N k \ln 2$.

This means that there is a loss of free energy by an amount of $Q = T N k \ln 2$ in favor of the entropy of mixing. (Generally, if the amounts of A and B are not equal, we would use Gibbs's general equation.)

Applying thermodynamics to chemistry and Gibbs's phase diagrams allows chemists to predict how the boiling or freezing points of solutions will change, calculate the concentrations of reactants and products in chemical reactions in equilibrium, design distillation processes, calculate the rate of chemical reactions as a function of the temperature, and so forth. Gibbs's calculations constitute a very important contribution to the thermodynamics of chemical reactions. But most astonishing is the fact that his expression ended up being the basis for information theory, which will be discussed in Chapter 3.

The Maxwell-Boltzmann Distribution

The true logic of this world is the calculus of probabilities.
-James *Clerk Maxwell*[40]

Up to this point, it has been shown that entropy has two faces, a physical one, described by Clausius, and a statistical one, described by Boltzmann and Gibbs. Connecting between these two expressions is the distribution function of the energy called the Maxwell-Boltzmann distribution (which was independently derived by both scientists). This distribution is not unique to gases; if fact, it turns up in many other areas, and therefore merits a special discussion.

James Clerk Maxwell

James Clerk Maxwell, 1831-1879

Maxwell's biography appears here not only because of his calculation of the speed distribution of molecules in gas (the so-called Maxwell-Boltzmann distribution), but also, even mainly, in acknowledgment of his contribution to our understanding the nature of electromagnetic radiation. As we shall see later, understanding the thermal distribution of radiation is what brought Max Planck to the conclusion that energy comes in discrete, indivisible quantities called quanta (singular, quantum). The amount of energy in a quantum is proportional to its frequency. This conclusion ushered in a new era in the history of physics, and Maxwell is generally regarded as one of its founding fathers.

Indeed, James Clerk Maxwell was one of the greatest scientists ever. To his electromagnetic theory we owe some of the most significant discoveries of modern science and almost all the technology that serves us today. Maxwell also made significant contributions to mathematics, astronomy and engineering, but first and foremost, he will always be remembered– and justifiably so – as the founder of modern physics. Albert Einstein, for example, arrived at his special theory of relativity due to his interest in a curious consequence of Maxwell's equations: that the speed of electromagnetic radiation propagation is independent of the speed at which its source moves. On this Einstein said: "The special theory of relativity owes its origins to Maxwell's equations of the electromagnetic field."[41]

Much of today's technology draws from Maxwell's understanding of the fundamental principles of the universe. Many developments in the fields of electricity and electronics, including radar, radio, television and other communication devices, have been based on his discoveries. Rather than synthesize what was known before him, Maxwell completely changed our understanding of the interaction between material substances that until then was based on Newton's views. This change deeply influenced modern science and informed the later stages of the industrial revolution.

James Clerk Maxwell was born to John and Frances Clerk on June 13, 1831, in a house Edinburgh, Scotland, that his father had built in a new, elegant area of the city. John Clerk (who later changed his surname to Clerk Maxwell) was a lawyer, and both he and his wife were quite involved in their city's cultural life. A short time after the birth of their only son, James, the family moved to

Glenlair, to a grand house on Middlebee Estate which they had inherited. The estate was in a rather isolated area (at least a day's ride by horse and carriage from the nearest city, Glasgow), and there Maxwell spent the first ten years of his life. His mother was responsible for his early education until her death when he was just eight years old, and then a local 16-year-old boy was hired to tutor him privately. However, this tutor was unable to get young Maxwell to apply himself to his studies or to discipline him, and this unsuccessful experiment came to its end after two years when Maxwell's aunt came visiting, saw what was happening and put an end to it. In 1841 Maxwell was sent to a public (namely, in Britain, private) school, the Edinburgh Academy, and stayed with his widowed aunt.

Maxwell's father and uncle, both members of the Royal Society of Edinburgh, encouraged his interest in science. At the age of 10, his uncle took him for a visit at the laboratory of William Nicol, the inventor of the Nicol polarizing prism, who gave Maxwell two of his prisms. This meeting made a huge impression on the young boy, and later Maxwell described this visit as the turning point of his life, when he realized with certainty that his vocation in life should be scientific research.

Despite this, his first years at school were quite difficult. His peculiar accent, strange shoes and the unusual clothes his father's designed for him singled him out among his peers, who used to call him "Dafty." However, after two mediocre years, Maxwell began to show his talents. He made some friends, including Lewis Campbell, later professor of classics at St. Andrew University and his biographer, and Peter Guthrie Tait, future Professor of Natural Philosophy at Edinburgh University, who became his lifelong friend and partner in solving mathematical problems.

At fourteen, Maxwell met an artist by the name of D. R. Hay, who was looking for a way to draw oval shapes. The young boy generalized the definition of an ellipse, successfully producing actual ovals identical to those studied by René Descartes in the 17th century. He then published his first paper, *On the Description of Oval Curves, and Those Having a Plurality of Foci*.[42] Maxwell's father showed the method to James David Forbes, an experimental physicist at the University of Edinburgh. Forbes was impressed, and presented the paper in Maxwell's name at a meeting of the Royal Society of Edinburgh in April 1846 – without a doubt, an outstanding accomplishment for such a young boy. Of course, his ideas were not new, but it was remarkable that a young boy of 14 could conceive them.

When Maxwell, at the age of sixteen, completed his studies in 1847, he was ranked second in his class. Another exemplary student at the Academy was Peter Tait, one year younger than Maxwell, who at the age of twenty would become a senior wrangler in Mathematical Tripos – the youngest in the history of Cambridge University. Maxwell continued his studies at the University of Edinburgh. He chose to study the sciences even though his father encouraged him to pursue law, and remained there for three years. He also studied philosophy with great intensity. At the age of seventeen, Maxwell presented a paper to the Royal Society of Edinburgh on *The Theory of Rolling Curves*, and then, at eighteen years of age, another paper – *On the Equilibrium of Elastic Solids*.

In 1850, Maxwell moved to Cambridge University. Despite the great importance accorded to the study of the classics in those days, the uppermost target for ambitious students was to win first place in the Tripos, a series of mathematics exams: quite remarkably, mathematics dominated the teaching methods in Cambridge at the time. Here Maxwell received excellent training in applied mathematics. He read a book on analytical statistics by Belgian mathematician, Adolphe Jacques Quetelet, which made him realize that physics could benefit from statistics. In one of his letters, he wrote: "The true logic of this world is in the calculus of probabilities"; and in another: "This branch of Math., which is generally thought to favor gambling, dicing, and wagering, and therefore highly immoral, is the only Mathematics for Practical Men."[43] (And indeed, in 1859, he applied this insight to the explanation that he gave for the stability of Saturn's rings.)

In 1855 Maxwell was made a fellow of Trinity College in Cambridge, and then published his first study in electromagnetics, which dealt with Faraday's lines of force.[12] This paper linked Faraday's field theory with the electrical force, and showed how magnetic induction can be expressed by a differential equation. It later became clear that this was the key to the analysis of electromagnetic waves, and also to field theory in general. Thus Maxwell showed that a few rather simple mathematical equations can express the electrical and the magnetic fields and the interactions between them.

Maxwell's stay at Trinity was short-lived. Early in 1856 his father fell ill, and Maxwell wanted to return to Scotland. He therefore applied to Marischal College in Aberdeen for the fellowship in Natural Philosophy. His application was accompanied by a letter of introduction from William Hopkins, a Cambridge scientist and mentor of its most promising mathematical students of the time (besides Maxwell, they included also William Thompson, the future Lord Kelvin, George Stokes, one of the founders of fluid theory, Tait, and others), which said:

> During the last 30 years I have been intimately acquainted with every man of mathematical distinction who has proceeded from the University, and I do not hesitate to assert that I have known no one who, at Mr. Maxwell age, has possessed the same amount of accurate knowledge in the higher departments of physical science as himself... His mind is devoted to the prosecution of scientific studies, and it is impossible that he should not become (if his life is spared) one of the most

---

[12] Michael Faraday, 1791–1867, was one of the pioneers in this area.

distinguished men of science in this or any other country.[44]

Nevertheless, Hopkins believed that Maxwell, despite his fine aptitude in physics, was somewhat lacking in mathematical ability, as his solutions were generally presented in graphic-geometric methods, rather than mathematical analysis.

In April of that year, at the age of 25 years, James Forbes informed Maxwell that a position at Aberdeen University had become available. During the Easter vacation, Maxwell went to Edinburgh, and a short time later, his father died. He returned as planned to Cambridge, but upon his arrival, he was offered the Chair of Natural Philosophy at Aberdeen, which he accepted.

In Aberdeen he met the daughter of the Principal of Marischal College, Katherine Mary Dewar, and married her. Not much is known about her other than that she was of great help to her husband in his experiments, but was not well-liked by his friends. She was, apparently, a hypochondriac, and Maxwell attended to her devoutly.

When St. John's College in Cambridge announced that the topic of their Adams Prize for 1857 was "The Motion of Saturn's Rings," Maxwell immediately became interested. When still a student at the Edinburgh Academy in 1847, he and Tait had considered this problem. He now decided to compete for the prize, and his first two years at Aberdeen were devoted to the studying of this subject. Maxwell showed that solid rings could not be stable and thus they must be composed of small, solid particles. He won the prize, and his explanation was later proved correct by observations.

In 1860, Marischal College and King's College merged to form the University of Aberdeen, and Maxwell, still junior in his department, found himself – despite his accomplishments – out of work and with a pension of only 40 pounds. This was a paltry amount even for those days. However, with a private income of 2,000 pounds a year from his estate, he was far from destitute.

In 1859, after Forbes moved to St. Andrews College, the Chair of Natural Philosophy became available at the University of Edinburgh. Maxwell applied for the position, but again, his scientific accomplishments did not help much, and the post went to Tait. Writing about the announcement, the daily *Courant* commented: "Professor Maxwell is already acknowledged to be one of the most remarkable men known to the scientific world," and yet: "... there is another quality which is desirable in a Professor in a University like ours and that is the power of oral exposition proceeding on the supposition of imperfect knowledge or even total ignorance on the part of pupils."[45] In fact, even though Maxwell's writing was the epitome of clarity, his lectures and discussions were incomprehensible and abrupt. It seemed that his thoughts outpaced his tongue.

However, this was for the best, since he almost immediately joined King's College at London University, where he remained until 1865. These were the most productive years of his career, for then he began his research in electromagnetism. In 1864, in a lecture on The Dynamical Theory of the Electromagnetic Field, given at the Royal Society of London, he stated: "We can scarcely avoid the conclusion that light consists in the transverse undulations of the same medium which is the cause of electric and magnetic phenomena."[46]

In 1865 Maxwell left King's College to oversee the completion of his house in Glenlair. Thanks to his private fortune, he could retire from the burden of teaching and use his time to run his estate, traveling through Europe, handling an extensive correspondence, and writing his book, *Electricity and Magnetism*.[47] The set of a few partial differential equations, known today as Maxwell's equations, appeared there for the first time in their full form; undoubtedly, this was one of the greatest scientific accomplishments of all time. Apparently, one of the reasons he wrote his book (which was published in 1873) was frustration, since no one could be bothered to compare his and Faraday's theories, which dealt with electromagnetic fields, with the prevailing German theories that dealt with electric and magnetic forces. In the introduction to his book he wrote:

> Great progress has been made in electrical science, chiefly in Germany, by cultivators of theory of action at a distance... the electromagnetic speculation carried out by Weber, Riemann, Neumann, Lorenz etc. is founded on the theory of action at distance... These physical hypotheses however, are entirely alien to the way of looking at things which I adopt... it is exceedingly important that the two methods should be compared... I have therefore taken the part of an advocate rather than a judge.[48]

His retirement ended in 1871 when he was persuaded to accept, without much enthusiasm, the Cavendish Chair of Experimental Physics at Cambridge – though not before both Joseph John Thomson, who was to discover the electron 25 years later, and Hermann von Helmholtz had declined the appointment. He devoted most of his energy to designing and building the Cavendish laboratory. Officially opened in 1874, it was destined to give the world many important discoveries in physics.

Apart from his talents as a theoretician, Maxwell also had a very practical side. He showed great facility in the design of mechanical instruments to demonstrate various phenomena in physics. Among others, he built a colored spinning top that showed in an astoundingly simple way how a fourth color is obtained from the correct mixture of the three primary colors, and how colors are perceived by the human eye. He also built, as mentioned earlier, a model of Gibbs's thermodynamic surface for water (a phase diagram). A short while before he died, Maxwell sent it to Gibbs, and to this day it is on display at Yale University.

On May 17, 1861, at the Royal Society of London, Maxwell presented the world's first color photograph. The photograph was made using three filters – red, green and

blue – and the image was remarkably true to the original.
During his sixth year at Cambridge, the first symptoms
of stomach cancer began to show, and he began a long,
arduous battle against the disease. On November 5, 1879,
at only 48, Maxwell passed away. He was buried on his
estate.

In 1859, after reading Clausius's paper on the collision of gas
molecules, Maxwell began to investigate the statistical mechanics
of gases. In 1866, concurrently with Boltzmann yet independently
of him, he derived what is today called the Maxwell-Boltzmann
distribution. (A diagram of the distribution of the speeds of the
particles appears in Fig. 3; the calculations upon which this is
based can be found in Appendix 4-A.) The Maxwell-Boltzmann
distribution describes how energy is distributed among molecules
of gas. Since (in the case of a monatomic gas) the energy of a gas
is directly related to the speed of its atoms, the distribution of
energy between the atoms can be defined by Newton's laws of
motion to give the distribution of speeds of the atoms in the gas.

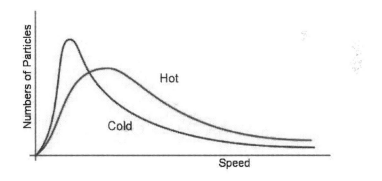

Figure 3: This graph depicts the relative number of particles in a
system as a function of their speed. In an ideal gas, the average speed
rises with temperature. The number of particles with the hightest
speeds is small, due to exponential decay.

This distribution of energy in equilibrium has great importance in nature, and its far-reaching consequences are the main issue of this book.

According to the second law of thermodynamics, the function of the energy distribution in equilibrium will result in a maximum value for entropy, that is, both the number of microstates, Ω, and the entropy as defined by Clausius, will be at a maximum. From the derivation of this distribution (see Appendix A-4), a bell-like speed distribution, the so-called Maxwell-Boltzmann curve, is obtained (see Fig. 3). In statistics, a bell curve is often referred to as a "normal distribution."[13] In a normal distribution, the probability that an atom will have a given energy decreases exponentially as the energy rises.

The bell-like Maxwell-Boltzmann distribution is derived from the *exponential* decay of the number of particles with a given energy. That is, the relative number of particles carrying a particular energy decreases exponentially as energy rises according to $e^{-\frac{E}{kT}}$, where k is the Boltzmann constant, E is the energy and T is the temperature. It follows that most of the particles possess low energy. Multiplication of the increased energy, E, by the exponentially decreasing number of particles yields an energy distribution which is a rising function at low energies and a falling function at high energies. The result is a bell-like distribution.

The exponential decay is drastic: the number of deviations from the average decreases rapidly; most of the particles in the distribution have energy close to the average. For many phenomena in nature the average has the highest probability; however, there are also some natural distributions which include substantial probability to the extremes. These distributions, the "long tail distributions," will be discussed in detail further on.

One of the astounding things in thermodynamics is the ubiquity of its consequences. Amazingly, one can glimpse them not only in

---

[13] It is worth noting that the normal distribution, without the long tail to the right, is the distribution that is described in most textbook and is an approximation of the Maxwell-Boltzmann distribution that is shown in the figure.

the exact sciences such as physics, chemistry or biology, but also in pure mathematics, computer science, sociological studies, and more. The bell curve appears in thermodynamics because it was developed using the gas laws as a starting point, but – as we shall see below, and as we saw earlier in the examples of lots and houses – the notion of logical entropy is much more general, and thus can be applied to many other areas. These days, science is making its first steps towards the understanding of complex systems; even though we still do not understand the parameters that determine their statistical distributions, the fact is that such distributions are similar to the Maxwell-Boltzmann one. For example, if we observe the distribution of the height of a sufficiently large group of people of the same race and sex, we obtain a bell curve. The factors that determine a person's height are many and complex: genetic, nutrition, hormonal, etc. Yet the distribution obtained is identical to the one obtained from inert gases in thermodynamic equilibrium.

An even more surprising example is the distribution of the length of the cars in any given country. The factors that influence the length of a car are both engineering-related and psychological. Sometimes, the significance of a larger car is prestige: a dimensionless quantity that cannot interact in any measurable way with other quantities. Such quantities are called "logical quantities." As you have probably guessed, the distribution of car lengths is also bell shaped: there are a few short ones, most are of average length, and there are a few long ones. Therefore, a graph of the number of cars as a function of length is a bell-like curve. This distribution characterizes many other quantities, too, including intelligence as measured by IQ tests. Similarly, if we were to ask a group of people to estimate the weight of, let us say, a sack of flour, we could predict that the distribution of their answers will also produce a bell-shaped curve around the correct value. In fact, this is the thermodynamic basis for the concept of "the wisdom of the crowd": our tendency to assume that the average answer is the correct one. Perhaps we naturally sense that a system in equilibrium, in which every microstate has an equal chance, is a "just" system.

The exponentially determined, bell-like curves, appears in nature in many different ways, and what characterizes them is, as stated, the preference for the average. For example, when we examine mortality tables, according to which insurance companies determine the chances that a person of a certain age will die within the next year, we see that the chance of dying increases exponentially with age. That is, the older a person is, the greater are the chances that he will die within the next year. Correspondingly, most people will die at or near the average age of death (in Israel, approximately 80 years), and fewer will die at an age far removed from the average, that is, much older or much younger.

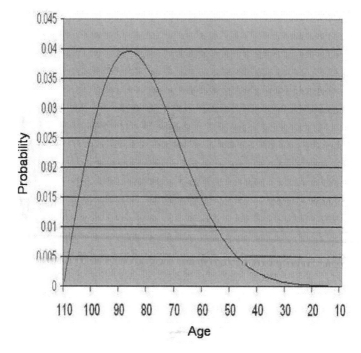

Figure 4: The distribution of death rate/age resembles, astonishingly, the speed distribution in gas. In the figure: theoretical death rate/age in Israel. Source: CIA, World Factbook , (est.) 2010

Nevertheless, it must be kept in mind that thermodynamic equilibrium does not *always* provide an exponentially determined, bell-like curve. There is in nature another distribution, no less common, that yields finite distribution to values far from the average. The decay in these cases is not exponential but a power law decay; for example, the distribution of wealth in a given population. In economics, this distribution is known as the Pareto Law, or the 20:80 rule (sometimes called also Zipf's Law, or Benford's Law). Later on, we shall see that these distributions are also consequences of the second law and its tendency to increase entropy.

Chapter 3

The Entropy of Electromagnetic Radiation

Electromagnetic Radiation

This chapter discusses the entropy of electromagnetic radiation: beginning with the nature of the radiation itself, as explained by Maxwell, going through to Max Planck's discovery that radiation energy is discrete (quantized), and leading up to the calculation of the energy distribution of radiation in thermodynamic equilibrium.

As mentioned above, in 1873 – in the golden age of science – Maxwell published his monumental work which describes, using a set of equations subsequently named after him, both electric and magnetic forces and the interactions between them. The unification of these two important forces in a single formalism was a historical achievement, but furthermore, Maxwell's equations explained what electromagnetic radiation actually *is*.

Electromagnetic radiation, it turns out, is the periodic motion of an electric field and a magnetic field perpendicular to it. An electric field is a property of a particle or object with an electric charge: in the space surrounding it there operates a force that attracts to it particles with an opposite charge, and repels particles with a like charge. A magnetic field is generated when there is a change in the electric field – for example, when an electrically charged object moves within it – and influences objects that have magnetic properties. The electric and magnetic fields are properties of the space. Unlike sound waves, which are vibrations of medium (such as air), the electromagnetic radiation does not require any medium in order to exist.

One counterintuitive result of Maxwell's equations is that the speed of propagation of electromagnetic radiation is independent of the speed of the source that emits it. If a person travelling in a car throws an object backward, the object's speed (as measured by an observer by the roadside), will be the sum of the object's speed, determined by the force with which it was thrown, and the car's speed relative to the observer. Yet the speed of the light emitted from the car's headlights (as measured by any observer, inside the car or outside) will always be the same, whether the car is moving or not. From this peculiar result Einstein concluded in 1905, in his paper on the special theory of relativity, that the speed of light (it being a form of electromagnetic radiation) is a universal constant. Among the implications of this astounding result were his statements that time is relative, that mass is a form of energy, and that the ratio between energy and mass is the speed of light squared.

The periodic motion of electromagnetic radiation can be described as an oscillator characterized by its frequency. Perhaps the simplest oscillator imaginable is a mechanical pendulum, that is, a weight (bob) suspended from a string of a certain length that swings back and forth in a periodic motion. Galileo Galilei discovered in 1602 that the period time (the time required for the bob to complete one back-and-forth cycle) is independent of both the energy of the pendulum and its mass, and depends only on the string's length. This property, called isochronicity, is used to measure time in grandfather clocks.[49] It is worth noting that all oscillators are isochronous. In old style mechanical watches, a spring pendulum with a frequency of several hundred vibrations per minutes is used. Due to isochronicity, the watch does not speed up or slow down when the spring is tighter or looser; rather, it keeps at a constant pace.

Most watches today use electronic oscillators, and only a few still use mechanical ones. An electronic oscillator includes a resonant circuit in which an electric charge moves in periodic motion and a piezoelectric crystal. The oscillating charge causes a change in pressure on the piezoelectric crystal – a crystal that applies mechanical pressure as a result of an electric field, similar to a spring that applies pressure when a mechanical force operates on it. In electronic clocks, the piezoelectric crystal is usually quartz, hence they are called quartz clocks. The frequency of a quartz circuit is a few million oscillations per minute, and thus quartz clocks are much more accurate than mechanical ones.

In fact, pendulums are used not only to measure time, but also to measure length. The first standard definition of the unit of length, the meter, was proposed in 1668 by English philosopher John Wilkins, who suggested that the meter is the length of a pendulum string with a period cycle of two seconds (that is, the time required for the bob to move from one side to the other is one second). However, because the frequency of a mechanical pendulum is not only dependent on the string's length, but also on the gravitational force, which differs with the distance from the center of the earth, the measurement must be performed at sea level.

The definition of the standard meter changes from time to time. One of the most famous definitions was the one accepted by the French Academy of Sciences in 1791: one meter is one ten-millionths the length of a quarter of the meridian passing through Paris – from the equator to the North Pole. Based on this definition, the mythological platinum-iridium meter bar was cast, which is stored in the Republic Archives in Paris. In 1960, the definition of the standard meter was once again made dependent on an oscillator, this time the electromagnetic radiation emitted by the isotope 86 of the element krypton. The International Bureau of Weights and Measures determined that one meter is exactly

1,650,763.73 wavelengths of the orange-red light emitted by krypton-86 in vacuum. (A wavelength is the distance that light passes in one cycle; frequency is defined as the number of vibrations of the oscillator in a unit of time, and thus frequency multiplied by wavelength yields the speed of light; in other words, frequency corresponds to the inverse of wavelength.) In 1983 the meter was redefined once more, as the distance travelled by light in 1 / 299,792,458 of a second, again in vacuum. This definition is derived from the fact that the speed of light, as measured in the most precise experiments, is 299,792,458 meters per second. At the time of writing, this is the accepted definition.

Some sources of electromagnetic radiation emit it in one frequency or in a very narrow range of frequencies (laser, maser). Others emit it in broader ranges: some stars emit radiation all across the board, and our sun covers most of the whole range. Even a simple light bulb emits radiation in a range broader than the human eye can see.

The various frequencies of electromagnetic radiation are useful to us in many different ways. At relatively low frequencies, it is used for radio broadcasts; at higher frequencies, called microwaves, it is used for short-wave broadcasts and for cooking; at even higher frequencies, in the range called infrared radiation (that is, it is below the frequency of the color red that is visible to the human eye), and its energy is felt as heat. When the frequency increases even more, radiation passes into the visible spectrum – the colors of rainbow visible to the human eye, beginning with red and going on to with blue and violet (when all these frequencies are combined, we perceive "white" light). At still higher frequency, the radiation is called ultraviolet; it is damaging to living cells, and for this reason we are warned to use sunscreens when at the beach. Next are x-rays, used in medicine and other applications, and at even higher frequencies are gamma rays, which are emitted in radioactive decay. The highest frequencies belong to some of the cosmic radiation that comes from outer space, most of which is scattered by the atmosphere.

The types of interaction between electromagnetic radiation and matter are numerous, and we use them for a vast variety of applications; however, such details are beyond the scope of this book. Here we shall limit ourselves to the absorption and emission of a light ray of a given frequency. A ray can either pass through matter without any change, or be scattered in it, or be absorbed by it, or be perfectly reflected from it (as in the case of a perfect mirror). The electromagnetic wave can be described as an oscillator because, as mentioned before, the vibrations of its electric and magnetic fields are synchronized. Oscillators absorb and emit energy only if its frequency is similar to their own. This is familiar to anyone who tried to push a child in a swing at the playground: we must apply a periodic force which corresponds with the frequency of the swing. If the swing is pushed forward at a constant force, it will not move periodically; but if the force applied is synchronized with the swing's motion, the swing will absorb energy from the person pushing it and continue its back-and-forth motion.

Similarly, in order for a ray to be absorbed by matter, its wavelength must be much shorter than the thickness of the material slab through which the light is passing, so that the electric field will be able to oscillate within that slab a number of times – at least once (in order to transfer the energy to the electrons in the slab). Waves whose wavelength is very long for the width of the absorbing slab will not be able to oscillate within it, and therefore will not be absorbed. This phenomenon is called diffraction. The higher the frequency (a shorter wavelength), the higher the interaction of the radiation with the matter. Generally, radiation energy is absorbed by the matter's particles (its atoms and molecules) and a short time later is reemitted. If, between the moment of absorption and the moment of reemission, the particle moves, the ray will randomly change its direction according to the particle's motion. This is called scattering.

The higher the radiation's frequency, the higher is its tendency to scatter. The reason is that the electrons surrounding the atom's nucleus responds to changes in the electric field; a higher frequency means a faster change in the field. For this reason, very long wavelengths (that is, with very low frequency) are used for radio broadcasts. They can travel long distances, up to thousands of kilometers, without being absorbed or deflected from their path. The scattering of visible light is the reason for the sky's blue color. Blue light in the sun's radiation has a higher frequency than red, and thus it scatters much more in the atmosphere, coloring the sky blue. (The blue reflection from the sky colors the sea blue.) The sun's light, after the blue has been scattered, turns red, and thus toward evening, the sky appears reddish. This was first explained by British physicist Lord Rayleigh, and therefore the scattering of light due to wavelength is called Rayleigh's scattering.[14] Rayleigh also gave, along with Sir James Jeans, a partial explanation for black body radiation, which will be discussed later on.

Electromagnetic radiation is absorbed and emitted by matter in interesting ways. Maxwell's equations show that an electric charge vibrating at a given frequency will emit electromagnetic radiation at the same frequency. In fact, radio transmitters are based on this principle. Similarly, a static oscillator with no energy (analogous to a mechanical pendulum at rest) will absorb an electromagnetic wave moving toward it and begin to oscillate, provided the frequency of the wave is the same as the inherent frequency of that oscillator. Radio receivers are based on this principle. Most of the electromagnetic radiation that surrounds us is a result of the absorption and emission of energy by atoms and molecules, and therefore it is possible to describe their electrons around the atomic nucleus as microscopic transmitters and receivers.

Black body Radiation

If both transmitters and receivers are electrical oscillators, what causes one to emit radiation and the other to absorb radiation, not the other way around? This is a thermodynamic problem, because heat is one of the forms of radiation (i.e. the infrared radiation). We know that heat is transmitted from hot bodies to cold ones. Since the statements of thermodynamics are universal, energy must flow from hotter oscillators to colder ones. But what is the temperature of an oscillator? In order to find out, we must first calculate its entropy.

---

[14] Recall that this was the topic of Clausius's dissertation, but his explanation, which was based on the absorption and emission of light, was erroneous.

Already in Boltzmann's days it was known that an oscillator's energy is proportional to its temperature, that is, the energy is equal to the Boltzmann constant times the absolute temperature: $E = kT$. This conclusion was derived in the study of the properties of ideal gases, as explained in Appendix A-5.

Since entropy according to Clausius is energy divided by temperature, and since energy is proportional to temperature, we obtain $S = \dfrac{E}{T} = k$. That is, *every oscillator has the constant amount of entropy of one Boltzmann constant![15]* This is surprising, because it means that the entropy of every single oscillator is a constant, independent of its energy or frequency. (Recall that an oscillator's frequency is also independent of its energy). This remarkable result implies that the amount of entropy of any oscillator is the same, even if it is as massive as an entire star, or as small as one molecule of an ideal gas. On the other hand, the oscillator's temperature is proportional to its energy. To demonstrate this, we may calculate the temperature of a swinging bob with energy of one joule. Since Boltzmann's constant is approximately 1.38×10^{-23} J/K, the temperature of such an oscillator should be an extremely high 7.25×10^{22} K – greater by fifteen orders of magnitude than the temperature at the core of the sun, where nuclear fusion takes place.

Can such a temperature be "real"? As a matter of fact, it can. First of all, experience shows that a pendulum tends to stop its movement (due to friction among other reasons), just as a hot object tends to cool down. Secondly, it is well known that mechanical motion can be used to obtain high temperatures. Prehistoric man would light a fire, among other methods, by rapidly spinning a hardwood stick in an indentation in a block of softwood. Nevertheless, it is impossible to measure the pendulum

---

[15] In principle, a single oscillator is a single microstate, and therefore we would expect it to have zero entropy. Yet the uncertainty associated with it as a result of its vibration gives it finite entropy of one Boltzmann constant. This result, which is empirically consistent with the gas laws and the study of blackbody radiation (as we shall see below), is a law of nature.

with a home thermometer, because the bob's motion would break the glass...

What about the oscillator's energy? A vibrating mechanical oscillator is extremely hot in comparison to its surroundings and is very "anxious" to get rid of its energy. The reason is obvious – a lot of entropy will be generated by the transfer of the hot oscillator's energy to the numerous colder oscillators around it. For example, if we take a swinging bob and transfer its energy to an environment that includes N oscillators, we increase entropy from k to Nk. In the air, for instance, N is the number of gas molecules absorbing this energy.

We can treat electrical oscillators the same way, thanks to the universality of thermodynamics. Like mechanical oscillators, an electrical oscillator will also lose its energy (as an emission of electromagnetic radiation), and since an electric oscillator has both energy and entropy, it also has temperature.

The source of electromagnetic radiation is the vibration of an electrical charge, and so too is its demise. The molecules around us have electrons (which for the purpose of this discussion can be viewed as minuscule oscillators) that vibrate at various frequencies, and their energy can be emitted or absorbed depending on their temperature relative to the environment. A temperature that is higher relative to the environment will make them emit radiation, and a lower one, to absorb it. When radiation encounters an electric charge that can oscillate at all, it will induce the charge to vibrate and lose some if its energy to that charge.

What happens if both oscillator and the environment have the same temperature? The answer is called a "black body." In a black body, all oscillators are at the same temperature, and therefore the probabilities for an oscillator to either absorb or emit radiation are equal. By definition, this is a state of thermodynamic equilibrium.

The abundance of sensational discoveries made during science's golden age, at the end of the nineteenth and at the beginning of the twentieth centuries, also included the solution to what was then one of the most important problems in science: the question of black body radiation.

Black body radiation, despite its name, refers to the electromagnetic radiation that is emitted by any material body (not necessarily black). The characteristic of a black body is that the frequencies of the radiation it emits are a function of its temperature only. The energy emitted is completely independent of its composition, structure, or any property other than temperature. Since every object in the universe (including the universe itself) apparently has some temperature, every object in the universe emits black body radiation, even if it also emits some other type of radiation.[16]

Black body radiation is similar to the Maxwell-Boltzmann distribution, in that both are functions of temperature. But there is a great difference in the way they were derived. The atomic hypothesis, which was the basis for calculating the distribution of gas particles' speeds, was not accepted at the time by the majority of the scientific community because "it was impossible to observe atoms," and the distribution itself was not measured experimentally; rather, it was derived through a theoretical calculation. So in this case, calculation preceded experimentation. In contrast, the black body radiation emitted by any body can be observed and easily measured. These measurements were the basis for the calculation of the black body radiation frequencies distribution, which was to lead to the monumental conclusion that energy is quantized.

As can be seen in Fig. 5, black body radiation has a characteristic distribution at various frequencies (and thus various wavelengths).

---

[16] In 1893, Wilhelm Wien discovered that as the temperature of an emitting body increases, the maximum frequency of the radiation (the frequency with the most energy), v_{Max}, increases according to the equation $v_{Max}(2T) = 2v_{Max}(T)$. That is, if the temperature is doubled, the maximum frequency also doubles. Josef Stefan (who was Boltzmann's dissertation advisor) discovered that the intensity of the radiation of a blackbody is proportional to the fourth power of its temperature. That is, $I = \sigma T^4$, where I is the intensity of the radiation (intensity is energy per unit time per unit area). The constant σ is called the Stefan-Boltzmann constant. This means that the hotter the body, the higher the intensity and the frequencies of the radiation it emits.

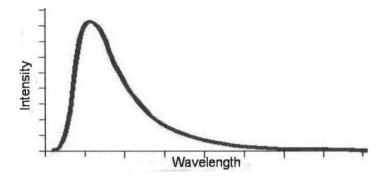

Figure 5: The relative intensity of radiation energy emitted from a black body as a function of the radiation's wavelength.

Black body Radiation and Black Holes

An interesting example that shows how thermodynamic thinking can be useful even without the rigorous calculations common in science comes from a subject that has recently become very popular – black holes. A black hole is a mass that has been compressed to such a density that even electromagnetic radiation cannot "escape" its gravitational field. According to Einstein's general theory of relativity, electromagnetic radiation would be unable to escape from a gravitational field whose intensity exceeds a specific value. Yet the second law of thermodynamics, as we shall see immediately, forbids the existence of a body that does not emit any radiation.

Einstein's special theory of relativity deals with effects that are based on the assumption that electrical and magnetic fields are properties of our space. In his general theory of relativity, Einstein added gravitation as a property of the space. More precisely, mass bends space around it. It is hard to imagine a three-dimensional bent space. A helpful two-dimensional analogy would describe a tight rubber sheet on which we place iron balls of various weights. Each ball creates a depression of a different depth, depending on its weight, that is, it distorts the rubber sheet in a way that is consistent with its mass. If we roll a marble along this sheet, its path will not be a straight line: wherever it approaches one of the depressions, its path will deviate from the straight line, in a way that depends on the depression's depth. Now try to imagine this in three dimensions rather than two...

If Einstein was right and his description of a curved space was correct, then light – even though it has no mass – should also deviate from its path when it passes near a mass. The bending of space by a mass is quite miniscule, but it is still measurable. In order to verify the validity of Einstein's assertion, it was suggested to observe a star whose celestial position is precisely known, at such a time when the line of sight from us to it runs very close to the sun. According to the general theory of relativity, the line of sight – the path on which the light from that star travels toward us – should curve. As a result, the star will appear to us as if its location is different from its known position. The problem is, of course, that it is impossible to observe stars when the line of sight runs close to the sun, since sunlight would make the star's light invisible to our eyes (and to our instruments). However, this can be done during a full eclipse of the sun, because then, for a few moments, this problem vanishes.

Einstein published his general theory of relativity in 1915. The next eclipse of the sun happened in 1919, and the renowned English astronomer, Arthur Eddington, headed a scientific mission to Africa, where the eclipse would be full, to test the theory. Legend has it that the measurements were not entirely conclusive, but in any case, Eddington announced that the stars observed did, indeed, seem to deviate from their actual, known positions. In his photographic plates, they showed up at the locations predicted by the general theory of relativity – in other words, Einstein was right. The next day all the major world papers, led by *The Times* of London, ran sensational headlines: NEWTON'S LAWS HAVE COLLAPSED!

Einstein seemed to have been the only one who was unperturbed. He was invited to the conference in which Eddington was to announce the results of his observations, but Einstein said that he was busy. When the announcement was telegraphed to the University of Berlin, where Einstein worked at the time, a spontaneous celebration erupted, and one lady said to Einstein, "You probably didn't sleep last night." Einstein answered that actually he had slept very well. "But what would have happened," she insisted, "if Eddington would have proclaimed that you were wrong? "If that happened," responded Einstein, "I would have had to pity our dear Lord. The theory *is* correct all the same."[50] Despite his nonchalance, Einstein became overnight a celebrity of a stature equaled today only by rock stars. No other scientist ever, even in the golden age of science, has received anywhere near the publicity and honor that Einstein did.[17] No scientist in human memory has gained the acclaim and respect accorded Einstein. The name Einstein is now a synonym for a wise person, and his face, with the emblematic hair and moustache, has practically turned him into a brand-name.

Modern cosmology is based entirely on the general theory of relativity, and one of its most fascinating topics is the study of black holes. A black hole is a massive celestial body with a gravitational field so powerful, that not only does it force light to deviate from its path, it does not even allow light to escape its grasp. A black hole can be visualized as a pit with smooth walls that devours everything and emits nothing, not even electromagnetic radiation. Although black holes research began more as logical speculation rather than as solid science based on observation, it ignited the popular imagination, and the scientists' response was not long in coming. In the scientific search engine, Google Scholars, there are over half a million links to scientific papers on black holes (although only about fifty actually claim to relate them to actual observations). The high priest of black holes study is Stephen Hawking, a fascinating and inspiring scientist, who, in spite of being completely paralyzed in all four limbs, can be said to be alive and kicking. We may be assumed that anyone reading this book is familiar with his image. His fame as a scientist today, among the general public, is second only to Einstein himself.

---

[17] In 1952, Israel's prime minister David Ben Gurion, offered Einstein the presidency of the State of Israel (that had become vacant after Chaim Weizmann's death), explaining that he had to make the offer first of all to the greatest Jew alive then. Einstein politely declined.

One of the most peculiar things about black holes is the minute amount of information they provide: a regular physical system has plenty of properties, but a black hole has only four at most: mass, electrical charge (if it has one), angular momentum (*ditto*), and the diameter of its "event horizon." (An event horizon is a sphere surrounding a black hole, such that anything that passes through it is swallowed by the black hole and cannot escape.) That is all. And if we omit the event horizon, because it is a function of the mass, we are left with a mere three properties. Even a single atom has more properties.

With respect to thermodynamics, the black hole presents a paradox: if a black hole is a "point," it must have no entropy at all. Hence, a black hole that swallows up some material object decreases the universe's entropy, but then, it is well known that the entropy of a closed system can only remain unchanged or increase – and obviously, the universe is a closed system.

The answer to this paradox was provided by a young post-doctoral fellow at Austin University, Texas, by the name of Jacob Bekenstein (now a professor at the Hebrew University, Jerusalem). Bekenstein knew that theoretical calculations showed that when two black holes merge, the area of the event horizon of the resulting black hole is the sum of the horizon areas of the two original ones. This is exactly the extensivity property we used in order to derive Boltzmann's entropy. On the other hand, no physical mechanism was known which was capable of making the area of the event horizon smaller. This analogy between the area of the event horizon and entropy intrigued Bekenstein, and he contemplated this problem until he finally determined that black holes do indeed have entropy, which is proportional to their event horizons.

But if a black hole has entropy, then according to Clausius, it must have temperature. Hence a black hole must emit black body radiation – yet by definition, a black hole is not supposed to emit any radiation whatsoever. Bekenstein's claim irritated Hawking, who lashed out at Bekenstein quite nastily. Yet later on Hawking accepted the notion (though not without a final snipe at Bekenstein: "[I]t turned out in the end that he was basically correct, though in a manner he had certainly not expected"[51]), and even characterized the radiation that a black hole must emit in view of its finite entropy. The explanation for this radiation is complicated and requires rather a long digression into quantum mechanics, which is beyond the scope of this book. However, the bottom line is that the event horizon of a black hole must emit radiation in the form of energy-bearing elementary particles, and thus black holes do not exist forever. Every black hole will eventually (over tens of billions of years) evaporate through this emission and disappear. Today, this radiation is called Hawking radiation, although many call it Bekenstein-Hawking radiation.

This is how the second law of thermodynamics led to the conclusion that a black hole, even though (according to its initial definition) it was incapable of emitting radiation, must emit some radiation after all, just like any other object. The story illustrates the phenomenal change that has occurred in science during the last few decades. In the golden age of science, in the 19th century, there were only about one thousand physicists in the whole world – people who believed (sometimes too firmly) in experimentation and observation according to the principles of logical positivism. It seems that today, with about half a million links in Google Scholar pertaining only to black holes (and of those, about fifty thousand on their entropy), and despite the fact that no one has actually managed to "see" even one of them, the pendulum has swung the other way.

The Distribution of Energy in Oscillators – Planck's Equation

> *"A new scientific truth does not triumph by convincing its opponents and making them see the light, but rather because its opponents eventually die, and a new generation grows up that is familiar with it."*
> - Max Planck[52]

The man who explained the frequency distribution of black body radiation was a German scientist, a cultured man and a broad-minded intellectual named Max Planck. Planck, who at the end of his career saw (rather passively, some say) the collapse of German science with Hitler's rise to power, is mainly known for the explanation he gave for black body radiation, based on his revolutionary determination that the energy of electromagnetic radiation is quantized, that is to say, comes in discrete, indivisible "packets". This hypothesis eventually led to the development of quantum theory, an area of utmost importance in physics today.

Max Karl Ernst Ludwig Planck

Max Karl Ernst Ludwig Planck, 1858-1947

Max Planck was born in Kiel, Germany, on April 23, 1858. He was the sixth child in the family. His family was highly educated, and his father was a law professor. When Max was nine years old, his father was appointed to a chair at the University of Munich. His son attended the Maximillians Gymnasium there, where he emerged as a gifted and diligent student. He excelled in all disciplines, but stood out in music and philosophy particularly. He was a gifted pianist with a perfect pitch, played the organ and cello as well, and even composed *lieder* and operas. He completed his studies in the Gymnasium at the age of 17 with distinction, and began to consider which subject he should pursue at the university. As is often the case, an acquaintance with a charismatic math teacher, Hermann Müller, who discussed with him a variety of subjects – including the principles of conservation of energy – led

---

him to decide finally on physics. He was not dissuaded by the words of Philip von Jolly, a physics professor in Munich, who advised him against this subject since "in physics they have discovered just about everything, and all that is left is to fill a couple of holes."[53] To his lecturer at the university he said that his goal was not to discover new things but to understand the known fundamentals of the field.

Planck began his studies at the University of Munich in 1874. His teachers there were good, but none were scientists of note, and he found refuge in self-study. In 1877 he transferred to Berlin for a year, where he was fortunate enough to study under leading physicists Hermann Von Helmholtz and Gustav Kirchhoff, whose names are celebrated to this day. Young Planck was not very enthusiastic about their lectures (he said that Helmholtz was never quite prepared for his lectures, spoke slowly, made numerous miscalculations, and bored his listeners; whereas Kirchhoff gave carefully prepared lectures that were dry and monotonous). Nevertheless, studying in Berlin, then a major scientific center, broadened his horizons immensely. In particular, Clausius's papers on thermodynamics kindled his interest and imagination, and this remained a topic that would play a major role in his scientific career. In 1879, having returned to the University of Munich, he presented his dissertation, *Über den zweiten Hauptsatz der mechanischen Wärmetheorie* (*On the second fundamental theorem of the mechanical theory of heat*).

One year later, at 22 years of age and after completing his academic requirements at Munich, he was accepted as a *Privatdozent* – lecturer without pay. As can be expected, this position did not improve his financial situation, and he continued to live with his parents – much to his chagrin, since he felt that he was a burden to their household. He continued to work on the theory of heat, and independently discovered the thermodynamic formalism that Gibbs had developed. Clausius's ideas about entropy greatly influenced his thinking, and he believed that the second law of thermodynamics and entropy play a major role in physics.

He remained in Munich for five years, and then, in 1885, his father's connections helped secure him an appointment as an associate professor of theoretical physics at the University of Kiel. He remained there for four years, continuing to work on entropy. Now that his annual income was 2,000 marks, he finally felt, at the age of 27, that he could afford a home of his own. In 1887 he married his childhood friend, Marie Merck.

Planck was a family man – warm and gregarious – and his home became an active social center frequented by well-known musicians and scientists. In the evenings they would often play music – with Planck at the piano and famous violinist and composer Joseph Joachim on the violin. On choral evenings, his students would join in. In later years, his guests included Albert Einstein (with his violin), as well as Otto Hahn and Lise Meitner, who subsequently became pioneers in the study of nuclear fission. In addition to music, Planck loved hiking and mountain climbing, an activity he was to pursue well into his senior years (at the age of 80 he was still fit enough to climb 3,000-meter peaks in the Alps).

In 1889, following the death of Gustav Kirchhoff, the first and only chair of Theoretical Physics at the University of Berlin became available, and Planck received it. He remained there as an associate professor, but was also appointed director of the Institute for Theoretical Physics (where he was the only professor). The University of Berlin was then the most important center of physical and scientific research in Germany, and a world leader in theoretical physics. This appointment indicated that his outstanding talents were recognized even before he had done his monumental work. In 1892 he was appointed full professor. He lectured on all branches of theoretical physics and was the advisor to a total of nine doctoral fellows. He was considered a good lecturer; Lise Meitner noted that he was "dry, somewhat impersonal, using no notes, never making mistakes, never faltering; the best lecturer I ever heard."[54]

Planck decided to be a theoretical physicist at a time when theoretical physics was not yet a field in its own right. About this period he later wrote:

> In those days I was essentially the only theoretical physicist there, whence things were not so easy for me, because I started mentioning entropy, but this was not quite fashionable, since it was regarded as a mathematical spook.[55]

In 1894 Planck became interested in black body radiation, and in 1901 he presented his revolutionary solution to a problem that had been occupying the world of physics for years (one of those "holes" that still needed filling, according to von Jolly), as described below. In 1905 Albert Einstein used Planck's ideas to explain the photoelectric effect (and for this, not for the theory of relativity, Einstein received the 1921 Nobel prize). Plank was one of the first major physicists to adopt Einstein's theory of relativity immediately upon its publication in 1905, and supported it against its numerous opponents. In 1918 Planck received the Nobel prize for his achievements.

In 1909 after twenty-two years of happy marriage, Marie Planck died, apparently of tuberculosis, and left him with two sons and twin daughters. Following his second marriage in 1910, he had another son, but tragedy kept stalking him. His eldest son was killed in the Battle of Verdun in the First World War (1916), his daughter Grete died in childbirth one year later, and in 1919, his second daughter, Emma, also met the same fate.

In 1914 Planck succeeded (in collaboration with physical chemist Walter Herman Nernst) to bring Einstein to the Kaiser-Wilhelm Institute for Physics in Berlin. After the World War I he also brought to Berlin his favorite student, Max von Laue, a pioneer in the research of x-ray diffraction. Planck continued his activities at the University of Berlin for over half a century, until 1928. Upon Planck's retirement, Erwin Schrödinger, one of the fathers of quantum mechanics (which originated, as mentioned above, from Planck's research on black body radiation) was appointed to fill his place. For a time, Berlin continued to play a role as a major center of theoretical physics – until January 1933, when Adolf Hitler rose to power.

In addition to his great academic achievements, Planck was involved in the science community as a leader and educator. He nurtured promising young students, found creative solutions for problems in the organization of scientific work, and filled a number of administrative posts from 1930 to 1937 in the German Physical Society, the Kaiser Wilhelm Society[18] (known today as the Max Planck Society), and the respected scientific journal, *Annalen Der Physik*. These were very influential positions.

Even though Planck's activities remained within the boundaries of science, he was a prominent public figure due to his scientific reputation and his exceptional achievements. His political views were typical of German Empire – conservative and patriotic. He found it hard to stomach the liberalism of the Weimar Republic, yet accepted the National Socialist Party's policies without any public protest. Nevertheless, he spared no effort to aid his colleagues who lost their jobs because of Nazi persecution, and attempted to work behind the scenes for the freedom of science. There is no doubt that the Third Reich took advantage of his compromising attitude for its political purpose. When Jewish scientists were being expelled from Germany and some of their non-Jewish colleagues were seeking to emigrate, Planck urged them to stay put in order to preserve and promote German science.

---

[18] The Kaiser-Wilhelm Society, founded in 1911, was an umbrella organization for a large number of scientific research facilities in Germany. In 1959 the Society and all its institutes were renamed after Max Planck.

Otto Hahn, later a Nobel laureate, asked Planck to gather well-known professors for a public demonstration against the regime's treatment of Jewish professors. Planck's answer was:

> If you are able to gather today 30 such gentlemen, then tomorrow 150 others will come and speak against it, because they are eager to take over the positions of the others.[56]

During those years, Planck and others struggled to preserve science in Germany. At Planck's direction, the Kaiser-Wilhelm Society avoided outright dissension with the Nazi regime, yet he had no qualms about praising Einstein, at a time when the Nazis' fiercely condemned him and his work. He even met with Hitler in an attempt to stop the persecution of Jewish scientists and to discuss the fate of Fritz Haber, but to no avail.[19]

About Planck's behavior during this period Einstein said in 1934:

> He tried to moderate where he could and never compromised anything by his deeds or words ... And yet ... even as a *goy*, I would not have remained president of the Academy and the Kaiser-Wilhelm Society under such conditions.[57]

Einstein had good reasons for saying this. Planck believed that Einstein should have supported the regime no

---

[19] Haber, a Jew and a wholehearted German patriot, was one of Germany's greatest chemists, the first to synthesize ammonia from its components. The importance of this work to the chemical fertilizers industry and agriculture on the one hand, and to explosives and other materials of war on the other hand, was immense. He was also the father of Germany's chemical warfare in Wolrd War I. Before the Hitler's rise to power, Haber was at the forefront of science in Germany, but the Nazi regime stripped him of his position and rights and he was forced to leave Germany. One year later, in 1934, Haber died in exile, before he could see how his invention, Zyklon B, was used to slaughter his people, including members of his own family.

matter the circumstances, and since he failed to do so, Planck recommended his expulsion from the Academy. Ironically, Haber supported Planck on this issue; von Laue was the only one who opposed him. When Einstein was later asked if he wanted to send his regards to anyone in Germany, he answered: "Only to Laue, and to no one else."[58]

At the end of 1938, The Prussian Academy of Science lost its independence and was taken over completely by the Nazis. Planck resigned its presidency in protest (some say that the Nazi regime put pressure on him not to seek another term in office). The political climate was becoming more and more hostile, and the Nazi Johannes Stark, a member of the German Academy of Physics and a 1919 Nobel prize laureate, attacked Plank, Arnold Sommerfeld and Werner Heisenberg, whom he labeled "white Jews," because they continued to teach Einstein's theory of relativity. The Nazi government office for science investigated Planck's ancestry, but all they could find was that he was only $1/16^{th}$ Jewish.

World War II deeply affected Planck's final years, a time of deep personal suffering and severe blows. He lost almost all his property and all his notebooks and scientific diaries in an Allied bombing raid on Berlin in 1944. His son Erwin, with whom he had a unique relationship, was cruelly executed by the Gestapo following the unsuccessful attempt on Hitler's life in the same year. During those war years, Planck lived near Magdeburg, in the country estate of an industrialist friend. At the war's end he was 87 years old.

In his last few years, Planck concentrated on philosophical and ideological issues in modern science, and worked tirelessly to bring his findings to the public's attention and to instill his deep faith in the contribution of science to humanity. He was often interviewed by the press and on radio, wrote articles for daily newspapers and popular science magazines, and lectured all over Germany and the world. He himself explained the motivation behind this work as follows:

> At my age of 89 I cannot be productive in science anymore: what remains for me is the possibility of reaching out to people in their search for truth and insight, above all young people.[59]

His final years were spent modestly in a relative's house in Göttingen. He was sick and weak, but active nonetheless. He even traveled to England to take part in the Royal Society celebration of Newton's tricentennial in 1946 (which had been postponed for obvious reasons; actually, Newton was born in 1642). In 1947, at almost ninety years old, Plank died in Göttingen.

In 1894, Max Planck became interested in black body radiation. Electric equipment manufacturers commissioned him to find a way to produce light bulbs (invented in 1878) that emit the maximum amount of light for a minimum amount of energy. The problem of black body radiation had already been introduced in 1859 by Kirchhoff: How does the intensity of the electromagnetic radiation emitted by a black body (a perfect absorber, also known as a cavity radiator) depend on the radiation's frequency? The problem was explored experimentally, because there was no consensus at the theoretical level. A law discovered in 1896 by Planck's colleague Wilhelm Wien, linking the maximum frequency to temperature, intrigued him greatly, and he decided to derive Wien's law from the second law of thermodynamics. The result was a work whose scientific importance cannot be overstressed, and here are its main principles:

Given a material object that contains within it all possible oscillators (also called "radiation modes") – a dense object, either solid or liquid, is preferable for this purpose, since unlike gas, which is mostly vacuum, electrons can move in solids and liquids in many more orbits – the number of possible radiation modes is represented by $N(\nu)$ (the Greek letter ν, nu, denotes frequency).

How would the expected energy emission look like as a function of frequency at any given temperature?

If you have carefully read the text to this point, your answer should be $N(v)kT$. Since the energy of each oscillator is kT, the energy of each oscillator times the number of possible frequencies $N(v)$, will produce the spectrum illustrated in Fig. 5. This idea was introduced by Lord Rayleigh and Sir James Jeans in 1897.

This elegant solution has one considerable disadvantage – it is not consistent with experimental results. The number of radiation modes $N(v)$ in a given volume increases as the frequency increases (since the wavelength becomes shorter, and therefore more of them can exist within this given volume), and becomes astronomical at very high frequencies. According to Rayleigh and Jeans, if every radiation mode emits kT of energy at high frequencies, the energy emission will become infinite – which both contradicts the first law of thermodynamics (conservation of energy) and is inconsistent with experimental results.

Planck first guessed the correct solution already in 1900, but proved it using the second law only a year later, and then published his paper *"On the Theory of the Energy Distribution Law of the Normal Spectrum"* in *Annalen der Physik*.[60] To this day, there are those who claim that Planck's result was merely a conjecture, but the truth is that like other lions of science, he guessed first and proved later. Planck's solution included a significant, far-reaching assumption: the idea that energy is quantized, that is, rather than existing in any arbitrary amount, it only comes in quantized amounts which he named "quanta" (plural of "quantum", Latin for "how much"). The idea is that an oscillator vibrating at frequency v can emit or absorb energy only in multiples of hv. The constant h, nowadays called "Planck's constant," was calculated empirically from black body radiation (as described in Appendix A-6). Remember that at that time, prominent scientists were still arguing whether matter was discrete or continuous, and all of a sudden there appeared the idea that even energy was discrete. The quantum of electromagnetic radiation is called a *photon*.

Mysterious are the ways of science. Newton had claimed, more than two hundred years before Planck, that light was composed of particles, but this was perhaps his only idea rejected already by his contemporaries, because it was wave theory, rather than the theory of the mechanical motion of particles (which he had formulated), that gave a better explanation for optical phenomena such as interference and diffraction. On the other hand, light also showed particle-like properties, and for many years scientists have struggled with the problem, whether matter was particulate or a wavelike. Putting the question this way is misleading, since it implies that matter must be either this or that – particulate or wavelike – where in fact, matter shows properties of both particles and waves. The wavelike properties of matter were demonstrated in experiments involving interference of massive particles, such as electrons or protons. And now Planck demonstrated, in his studies of black body radiation, that electromagnetic radiation too, which has no mass, nevertheless has both particulate and wavelike properties.

Planck used Boltzmann's entropy to calculate the distribution of P particles in N states (radiation modes), such that entropy would be maximized. He was the first scientist to use Boltzmann's equation for a calculation of thermodynamic distribution.[20] In his derivation, he made two assumptions: first, that radiation is quantized; and second, that the amount of energy embodied in a quantum of electromagnetic radiation depends on its frequency. That is, the higher the energy of a photon, the higher its frequency. No less important, he proved that an oscillator's energy is proportional to its temperature (that is, $E = kT$) *only* when the number of photons in each radiation mode is very high, that is, at very low frequencies. When the frequencies are very high, the number of photons in one radiation mode decreases exponentially and thus the energy emitted is lowered dramatically. Thus Planck solved the problem of infinite radiation at high frequencies that arose from the Rayleigh and Jeans model. The calculation of Planck's equation is shown in Appendix A-6.

---

[20] In Appendix A-6 we derived the Maxwell-Boltzmann distribution using Planck's method. Both Maxwell's and Boltzmann's methods were different. In this book, we unified all the derivations and used the Lagrange multipliers technique.

Planck's monumental work has many ramifications, not the least of which is quantum mechanics, but another one of its major consequences was in explaining the entropy of electromagnetic radiation and its quantization. Four years later, Einstein used the quantization idea as an explanation for the photoelectric effect, and spared Planck the Via Dolorosa traveled by Boltzmann with the atomic hypothesis. The term that Planck coined, "quantum," became part of physics with the development of quantum mechanics, which unites the wavelike and material properties of particles in one formal theory. Yet Planck himself cannot be properly regarded as one of the pioneers of quantum mechanics. On the contrary, he disapproved of it from the start. Quantum mechanics was developed, beginning twenty years after Planck's great discovery, by scientists such as Niels Bohr, Werner Heisenberg, Paul Dirac, Erwin Schrödinger, and others whose fascinating stories exceeds the scope of this book.

Physical Entropy – A Summary

To sum up our discussion up to this point, entropy can be defined in two complementary ways:

The first is **Clausius's macroscopic entropy** which is involved in the transfer of energy from a hotter object to a colder one. When energy flows from hot to cold, entropy spontaneously increases. This flow of energy is perfectly analogous to the flow of water from a higher place to a lower one. This is the second law of thermodynamics.

Clausius's entropy, which is based on our understanding of the concept temperature, uses a system's temperature of as a measurable physical quantity, in the same way as its mass or length, and is defined only in equilibrium. In a nutshell, the change in the system's entropy, according to Clausius, is its heat divided by its temperature – in equilibrium.

The second definition of entropy is **Boltzmann's statistical entropy**, or **Gibbs's entropy of mixing**. Boltzmann's entropy is the logarithm of the number of a system's microstates times a constant today called the Boltzmann constant. Neither temperature nor energy appear explicitly in Boltzmann's expression for entropy, although the number of microstates is usually dependent on them.

To calculate Boltzmann's entropy, the number of microstates must be counted. In equilibrium, every microstate has an equal probability, so that a system in any particular microstate has no statistical incentive to shift to another microstate.

Furthermore, the second law requires that entropy be calculated in equilibrium, since in this state, the number of microstates is at a maximum. When the number of microstates is not dependent on energy and temperature (as with the example of inert particles in a box), the number of microstates is constant and calculating the system's entropy is straightforward.

In contrast to Clausius's macroscopic entropy, which requires the use of a calorimeter and a thermometer for its direct measurement, Boltzmann's statistical entropy – which cannot be measured directly – is related to the distribution of energy among particles, or the radiation modes. The energy distribution can be measured, as we saw in the case of a black body, and entropy can be calculated from it either by calculating the number of possible configurations (according to Boltzmann), or by calculating their probabilities (according to Gibbs). Both Clausius's and Boltzmann/Gibbs's methods must yield the same value for the entropy.

Let us now review the assumptions which led to each of the two different energy distributions, Maxwell-Boltzmann's and Planck's.

Maxwell-Boltzmann: The Maxwell-Boltzmann energy distribution is calculated by maximizing the number of microstates and is based on the assumption that the number of particles is constant and much smaller than the number of possible states. This distribution is exponential, and is called the canonic distribution. The distribution of velocities derived from the canonic distribution produces the normal (bell-like) curve.

Planck: The energy distribution of a black body, as calculated by Planck, assumes that the number of particles can be greater than the number of states (radiation modes).

Since it was not known at the time that light has particulate properties, Planck had to make another assumption, namely, that energy can be absorbed by or reemitted from an oscillator only in multiples of a quantum, which is an indivisible unit of energy. The value of the energy in a quantum is directly proportional to the oscillator's frequency. This assumption was applied to the number of the microstates, and the temperature was calculated from Clausius's inequality. In the approximation where the quantum's energy was low compared to kT and energy could be removed from an oscillator (almost) continuously, Planck's equation yielded the energy of the radiation mode as $E = kT$, which is the case of the vibration of a diatomic molecule in an ideal gas, or a mechanical oscillator. When the amount of energy that could be removed was greater than the oscillator's energy kT, Planck's distribution gave the Maxwell-Boltzmann distribution.

The quantum approximation, which yielded the canonic distribution, was a surprising result. In a classical system, it is impossible to obtain from an oscillator (or from any other object, for that matter) more energy than it contained, in accordance to the law of conservation of energy. Yet in the quantum approximation, it is possible for a photon emitted from an oscillator to have more energy than the oscillator itself!

What is the meaning of this strange result? The explanation is that a number of oscillators collect their energy and emit it via one oscillator chosen at random, the same way that a lottery winner gains much more money than he or she invested; of course, this is the money contributed by many other ticket-buying participants. Most of the energy in black body radiation – and as we shall soon see, in other systems in equilibrium as well – is found in classical quanta, whose energy is lower than the average energy. On the other hand, there are very few quanta with higher energy, much greater than the average. The electromagnetic quantum energy distribution greatly resembles the distribution of wealth: many quanta are energy poor, and a few are quite energy rich. We shall discuss this similarity between the numbers of "poor" photons and poor people thoroughly later on, when we'll discuss the economic aspects of entropy.

Part II

Logical Entropy

Chapter 4

The Entropy of Information

Shannon's entropy

"My greatest concern was what to call it. I thought of calling it 'information,' but the word was overly used, so I decided to call it 'uncertainty.' When I discussed it with John von Neumann, he had a better idea. Von Neumann told me, 'You should call it entropy, for two reasons. In the first place your uncertainty function has been used in statistical mechanics under that name, so it already has a name. In the second place, and more important, no one really knows what entropy really is, so in a debate you will always have the advantage."

- Claude Shannon[61]

So far we have discussed entropy in the context of physical and chemical processes. However, it does appear in other areas as well. American engineer Claude Shannon was the first to point out the important role entropy has in communications. Before discussing the thermodynamics of communications, it is very important to define the concepts we used – *communication, information* and *content.* In technical contexts, these terms have quite specific meaning, different than their everyday use. For example, when we say something like, "the communication between Bob and Alice is terrible because they tend to yell at each other," the word *communication* refers to the quality of their personal relationship. However, in the context of our discussion, *communication* means the process of *transferring content*; therefore, communication by yelling is not always a "bad thing": it may actually prove quite efficient. Similarly, the concept of *content* has nothing to do with the amount of "wisdom" being transferred in communication, but simply refers to a sequence of transmitted signals, such as letters and digits (commonly referred to as character strings).

The word *information* as we use it daily is not well defined. However, Shannon defined information as the number of signals, e.g. in the sequence of the binary characters zero (0) and one (1), that can be transferred over a given communication channel. That is to say, information is a series of choices between "yes" and "no" (represented by "one" and "zero"); or more concretely, Shannon defined information as the logarithm of the number of possible different contents that can be transmitted along a channel.

In the technological sense, then, communication is the transfer of information from a transmitter to a receiver (or multiple receivers). Content transfer happens only when the sender and the receiver of information can interpret the information signals exactly the same way. For example, if your newly purchased electrical appliance is accompanied by a user's manual in Chinese, and assuming that you cannot read Chinese, you have received quite a large amount of information, but no content whatsoever.

People communicate among themselves through a wide variety of means. The most common are speaking, reading, writing, and even body language. In a face-to-face conversation, each person takes alternately (or occasionally simultaneously...) the roles of both "transmitter" and "receiver." The transmitter can be our vocal chords, bodily gestures, or even released chemical substances, and the receiver will then be our ears, eyes or noses. Many technological developments, including the telegraph, radio, television, landline and mobile phones, fax, and computer, have steadily enriched our means of communication and have allowed us to communicate over practically any distance. While listening to the radio, the communication comes from the broadcasting station, which transmits to a large number of receivers at different locations. Two users (ignoring, for the moment, conference calls) can communicate using messaging, telephone or fax, no matter where they are and how distant from each other they may be.

Until recently, information was transmitted through telephone, fax, radio, and television using analog methods. Even today, many public radio broadcasts are analog. To understand analog transmission, let us look at the radio. Here, a transmitter emits electromagnetic waves at a given frequency in which the sounds of speech or music have been incorporated in a process called modulation, and a receiver receives the modulated waves, extracts the voice information and transform it into vibrations of sound. There are two main modulation methods: One of them, known as AM (amplitude modulation), changes the amount of energy carried by the wave at any point in time, according to the intensity of the voice. In other words, the wave's amplitude is modulated. When the sound wave reaches the receiver, the amount of energy absorbed rises and falls according to the wave's amplitude, continuously changing the characteristics of the sound emitted from the receiver. The second method, FM (frequency modulation), changes the wave's frequency according to the characteristics of the sound it carries. The amplitude of the wave stays the same over time, but its frequency fluctuates. The higher the deviation of the carrier's resonance frequency from that of the receiver, the lower the intensity of the sound emitting from the receiver.

Analog broadcasts have great advantages because they are less sensitive to *noise* (extraneous signals) during transmission, and this is the reason that they have dominated the field until recent years, when the quality of transmission improved to a level that allows efficient digital data transfer. The reason that analog transmission is less sensitive to noise is the data redundancy. For example, when a color picture is transmitted by analog modulation, the transmitted image is similar to the original picture that is formed in our eye's retina. If during transmission, noise is added to the picture, such as optic distortion or a blur, the quality of the image formed in our retina will be reduced, but not totally destroyed. An analog picture of a blue sky presents a blue pixel for every point in the sky's area, and corrupted data for this pixel would create only a blank or differently colored spot in the sky. With a digital transmission, however, the blue area of the picture is encoded by a few *bits* (explained below) defining the entire area of the sky's picture and its color: one incorrect bit would change the color of the whole sky, and "noisy" bits will, in many cases, completely corrupt the whole picture. All the same, there are great advantages to digital transmission as well: If we fax a document (a fax is an analog device), the receiver never obtains a document as sharp as the original, either because of the finite resolution of the electro-optic scanner of the fax machine, or as a result of noise on the telephone line, or both. If we forward this received fax further on, the quality deteriorates with each sending. In fact, repeating this process many times will eventually corrupt the document entirely, due to the accumulated noise. In contrast, digital information sent by e-mail retains the same quality, no matter how many times it was forwarded.

There is in information theory a "sampling theorem" that states that it is possible to express any analog information by a digital file, and *vice versa*. Therefore, the relevance of the thermodynamic analysis that will be done hereafter for digital files is applicable for analog files as well. However, a discussion of the sampling theorem would be beyond the scope of this book.

Computers enable simultaneous digital communication between many users. That is, they transfer information files – sequences of "ones" and "zeros" – as short, electrical or electromagnetic pulses. The pulses travel from one computer to another via a device called a "modem" (**mo**dulator-**dem**odulator). When a received pulse reaches a computer's modem, the modem orders the computer's central processing unit to write a "one" in its memory; when there is an interval between pulses, the computer is programmed to write a "zero" in its memory. When the computer sends a sequence of pulses (a file) via the modem, they are processed successively: When the processor reads "one," it instructs the modem to send a pulse, when it reads "zero," the modem does nothing. The content of the file itself is thus expressed as a series of "ones" and "zeroes," and is independent of the intensity of the pulse: the value of any pulse is "one." This is in contrast, for example, to AM transmission, where intensity is the content.

A file made up of "ones" and "zeroes" is called a binary file. A file that consists of logical characters (not just "one" and "zero," but also other characters) is called a digital file. All binary files are therefore digital. By the same token, a file that consists of decimal digits – the multiplication table, for instance – is digital and decimal.

During the last few decades, the analog transmissions that had once dominated electronic communication media (telephone, radio, television, fax, and so on) have been largely replaced by digital transmissions; hence the impression that the analog method of communication is the "simpler" one. In fact, the opposite is true: technologically, it is much simpler to transfer information in digital form than in analog. Digital communication, so common today, is naturally associated in our mind with modern computer technology, but in fact it predates the computer era. The first to use this technology was the American painter and inventor Samuel Morse, with his invention of the telegraph in 1836 – forty years exactly before Alexander Graham Bell invented the telephone (an analog device).

Morse (1791-1872) was a professor of art and painting at New York University and an important artist in his own right. His interest in communication was kindled in 1832 when, on the deck of a ship on its way from Europe to America, he met and had a casual conversation on that subject with an expert on electromagnetism. The meeting inspired him with the idea of a telegraph, and he was so carried away that he abandoned his art, which had provided him with a handsome income, and devoted all his time and energy, with a great personal and economic sacrifice, to the development of the telegraph. The result was a method of transferring text based on strong and weak "taps." (Today, after subsequent modifications, they are called "dashes" and "dots," respectively.) These taps were produced using a key, today named after Morse, to close an electric circuit which includes this key as well as the receiver, a source of electric power (such as a battery) and an electric wire of suitable length connecting the key to the receiver. The main principle behind the receiver is the existence of a small electromagnet that produces a weak or strong tap, depending on the strength of the signal received over the wire. Most importantly, Morse developed a code, also named after him, which converted the entire alphabet – that is, letters, numbers and punctuation marks – to combinations of the binary characters – that is, "dots" and "dashes." With such a system, it is possible to transmit text in any language, each language having its own Morse code. Expert operators can listen to the tapping and understand the sequences as if it were human language.

In 1836, the year in which he demonstrated his telegraph to colleagues at New York University, Morse also ran in (and lost) in the elections for mayor of New York. His repeated requests to the governments of the United States, France and Britain to allow him to establish telegraph lines were rejected. Only in 1843 did he finally succeed and, after much effort, received a budget of $30,000 to establish the first telegraph line between Capitol Hill in Washington, D.C., and Baltimore, Maryland; the rest, as they say, is history.

During the nearly one hundred years that passed between the invention of the telegraph and the arrival of Claude Shannon, the first person to quantify the entropy associated with the transfer of content, telegraph went through significant developments – mainly due to its enormous military, economic and social value. Over the years, the wired telegraph was joined by a wireless telegraph (just as today phones can be either landline or mobile) and a device was added to register the received signals (as dots and dashes) – a forerunner of today's fax. It is worth noting that Lord Kelvin – a scientist of great achievements and no little arrogance, after whom, we may recall, the absolute temperature scale is now named, and who enthusiastically claimed that no object heavier than air will ever fly (said about ten years before the Americans Wright brothers flew, but quite a few millions of years after the first uneducated, heavier-than-air, creatures were gently gliding through the skies) – was made Peer of the Realm not for his achievements in pure science, but for his contribution to the laying of a submarine telegraph cable between England and France in 1857. To this day, the telegraph is thought to be one of the most useful and successful inventions ever, and even though the computer has replaced it in general use, radio buffs still enjoy communicating among themselves using the Morse code.

Two significant technological developments allowed the present tremendous progress in the world of communication. First, with the invention of computers, enabled to process data quickly; second, but no less important, was the ability to transmit and receive short pulses with extreme accuracy of duration. Between them, they rendered the Morse code outdated and led to the replacement of its dots and dashes with the "zeroes" and "ones" of binary code. It is no wonder that at Bell Labs (the highly acclaimed research laboratories of the great telephony company, AT&T in New Jersey), engineers began investigating more efficient ways to transfer information over communication channels.

To understand the essence of communication, let us examine the following example:

Bob promises Alice that if he will be free to meet her for dinner, he will call her by seven o'clock p.m. If he does not call, it is a sign that he won't be free. As it turns out, Bob could not come, so he did not call. The message had been "delivered," and Alice, who knew now that she should not expect Bob to meet her, went for a cards game with her friends.

It appears that Bob, by not taking any action, nevertheless conveyed information to Alice. However, this is not so simple, as it is obvious that every time Bob does *not* call Alice does not mean that he *is* busy in the evening. A better explanation is that information is adaptive. In other words, it depends on the circumstances. The reason that the absence of a call before seven o'clock *could* be considered information was that Bob previously gave Alice specific instructions: she should expect *another* message from him before seven. If he sends another message, it is a sign that he is free to come, if he does not, he is not. In other words, Bob laid the groundwork and both he and Alice agreed that a call is a positive message and the absence of a call is a negative message.

In a way, this is the essence of communication and information. In terms of computer communication, Bob sent Alice a message of one bit: "1" = Bob is coming, "0" = Bob is not.

It was Claude Shannon who coined the term "bit" (a portmanteau of "**bi**nary" and "di**git**") and defined communication in terms of calculable probabilistic quantities. In order to calculate the amount of information, he had to define its elusive meaning.

He defined information as the number of bits, "0" or "1," that can be transferred over a channel, that is, as a series of choices between "yes" and "no" ("1" and "0"), expressed in binary code. Each such possible choice is called a bit. He defined the amount of information that can be transferred over a communication channel as the *uncertainty* within it, or, as the sum total of the *different possible choices*. The logic behind his definition is this: the higher the uncertainty in a communication channel, the higher the content that can be transferred.

To illustrate Shannon's definition, let us look at another example: Let us say that Bob wants to send Alice his telephone number, which consists of a three-digit area code followed by seven digits. Altogether, Bob wants to send Alice a number made of ten decimal digits. It is clear that at the end of his transmission, Alice will have received one specific number out of 9,999,999,999 (approximately 10^{10}) possible numbers, assuming that each one of these numbers has an equal probability. Any one of those 10^{10} numbers can be viewed as a microstate. Thus, as we saw in the discussion of Boltzmann's entropy, the entropy of Bob's message to Alice will be the logarithm of the number of microstates. Therefore, the entropy (or as Shannon called it at first, the uncertainty) that is associated with Bob's telephone number (which Alice does not know) is $N = \ln 10^{10} = 10 \ln 10$.

What will be the number of microstates if Bob transfers that ten digit number using binary code (that is, sends it in bits)? Since each bit can only be "1" or "0," we shall need to solve the equation $2^N = 10^{10}$ (since each additional bit doubles the number of microstates). Therefore, $N = 10 \dfrac{\ln 10}{\ln 2}$. The value N, which was obtained from the log of the number of possibilities, is the number of bits required to transfer the phone number, and thus it gives Shannon's entropy for a ten-digit decimal number. (Actually, engineers use the logarithm of base 2, since in this particular case the number of bits is exactly equal to Shannon's entropy, as we shall see later on.) In general, Shannon showed that the number of bits required to transfer a file with a given content is equal to its entropy. Shannon's definition for the number of possible choices on a communication channel, which is called either "Shannon entropy" or "Shannon information," differs from the concept of "information" which is used in everyday language and which in this book, as mentioned earlier, is called "content.

Claude Elwood Shannon

Claude Elwood Shannon, 1916-2001

Claude Shannon was born in 1916 in Petoskey, Michigan. His father was a businessman and his mother a teacher. The first sixteen years of his life were spent in the town of Gaylord, Michigan. While still a child, he already showed a talent for mathematics and mechanics, and built model airplanes, some of them radio-controlled. He once built a model telegraph that connected him to a friend's house more than half a mile away. His hero was Thomas A. Edison, who, as he found out later in life, was actually a distant relative. Like other American culture heroes, in his youth Shannon worked as a paper delivery boy and repaired radios at the local department store. (Perhaps being a delivery boy is a necessary condition for becoming great in America!)

In 1932 he began studying electrical engineering and mathematics at the University of Michigan. He received his BSc in 1936, and then began working as a research assistant in the Department of Electrical Engineering at the Massachusetts Institute of Technology (MIT), at the same time pursuing graduate studies. His master's thesis demonstrated how Boolean algebra could be used to analyze and synthesize relay switching circuits and computers. His first published paper on this subject (1938) aroused great interest. One should bear in mind that the first digital computers appeared only in the mid-1940s. In 1940 he received the Alfred Noble American Institute of American Engineers Award – an annual prize granted to a person under thirty for a paper published in one of the member companies' journals. (This is not the well-known Nobel prize, which he was never to win). A quarter of a century later, computer historian H. H. Goldstine described this work as follows:

This surely must be one of the most important master's theses ever written... The paper was a landmark in that it helped to change digital circuit design from an art to a science.[62]

In 1938 Shannon moved to the Department of Mathematics at MIT, and while working as a teaching assistant there, he began writing a doctoral thesis entitled *An Algebra for Theoretical Genetics*, in which he used algebra to organize genetic knowledge, similar to his previous work with switches.

At that time, Shannon began to contemplate various ideas concerning computers and communication systems. By the spring of 1940, he had fulfilled all the formal requirements for his master's degree, other than foreign language – his Achilles' heel. Desperate, he hired private tutors in French and German. Finally (after failing German once), he passed his exams and in April 1940 was awarded his MSc in electrical engineering for his paper on Boolean algebra. Immediately after that he received his PhD for his dissertation on the use of algebra in genetics.

In 1940 and 1941 he worked as a research fellow at the Institute for Advanced Study at Princeton, New Jersey, under the direction of Hermann Weyl, a German mathematician and a renowned expert on symmetry, logic and numbers theory. There Shannon began seriously to develop his ideas about information theory and efficient communication systems.

In 1941 Shannon joined AT&T's Bell Labs in New Jersey, and worked there for 15 years in diverse areas, most famously in "information theory," a field which he founded by publishing his famous paper, *A Mathematical Theory of Communication*, in 1948.[63] This study is widely regarded as Shannon's greatest contribution to science, since it fundamentally changed all aspects of communications, in theory as well as in practice. Shannon the mathematician was well-versed in statistical mechanics, and in his paper he demonstrated that all sources of information – telegraph keys, personal conversations, television cameras, and so on – have a "source rate" measured in bits per second, and that all the various communication channels have a capacity that again can be measured in the same units. It is possible to transfer information over a channel only if the source rate does not exceed the channel's capacity, said Shannon. He calculated the maximum information that can be transferred over a channel if it can transfer N pulses per second. Shannon believed that his theory could also be applied to biological systems, since the principles that operate mechanical and living systems are similar.

Shannon's work laid the theoretical foundation for a highly important field, file compression, which will be described below. However, it should be noted that when Shannon published his ideas, the vacuum-tube circuits which were then used in computers could not run the complicated codes needed for efficient file compression. The theoretical limit that a file can be compressed to is called the Shannon limit. As we shall show below, the Shannon limit corresponds to the thermodynamic equilibrium of the files undergoing ideal transmission over a channel without noise.

It was only in the early 1970s, with the development of faster integrated circuits, that engineers could reap the benefits of his contributions. Today, Shannon's insight is part of the design of virtually all storage systems that digitally process and transfer information, from flash memories on through computer and telephone communication, to space vehicles.

In 1949 Shannon married Marie Elizabeth Moore, a computer expert who was a pioneer in the development of a computerized loom in the 1960s. The couple had three children. Shannon and his wife enjoyed spending the occasional weekend in Las Vegas with Ed Thorp, an MIT mathematician, and John Kelly, Jr., a physicist who worked at Bell Labs. These three developed a gambling method combining information theory with game theory and won vast sums at roulette and blackjack tables. Shannon and Thorp also applied their theory, later called the Kelly criterion, to the stock market, with even more beneficial results.

Besides his interest in gadgets, Shannon loved music and poetry and played the clarinet. He occasionally wrote ditties, jogged regularly and enjoyed juggling. One Christmas, his wife, aware of his peculiar interests, gave him a unicycle. Within a few days, Shannon was riding it around the house; a few weeks later he was juggling three balls astride it. A few months later he had already invented a special unicycle where the rider bobs up and down while pedaling forward. He also designed a gadget for solving Rubik's Cube.

In 1956 Shannon was invited as a visiting professor to MIT, and from 1957 to 1958 he held a fellowship at the Center for the Study of Behavioral Sciences in Palo Alto, California. One year later he became a Donner Professor of Science at MIT, continuing his research there in various areas of communication theory. He retained his affiliation with Bell Labs until 1972.

Shannon's papers were translated into many languages, but most thorough in this endeavor were his Russian translators, who had displayed great interest in his work from early on. In 1963 he was presented with three 830-page copies of a collection of his scientific writings in Russian. Years later, while on a visit to the Soviet Union, he learned that he had earned some thousands of rubles in royalties from the sale of his books, but much to his regret, he could not take the money out of the country. With no choice but to spend the money there, he bought a collection of eight musical instruments.

At some point, Shannon began to sense that the communication revolution has gone too far. He wrote: "It has perhaps been ballooned to an importance beyond its actual accomplishments."[64] His personal feelings notwithstanding, the digital communication revolution *was* as important as the industrial revolution two hundred years earlier. Obviously, the labors of many people are involved in any revolution. But if the landmarks of the industrial revolution were the improvement of the steam engine by James Watt and the development of thermodynamics by Carnot, Clausius and others, then the information revolution can be attributed to the development of the thermodynamic theory of information by Shannon, as well as the inventions of microprocessors and integrated circuits by others. If the flow of information in copper wires or optical fibers can be compared to the flow of liquids in a pipe, then Shannon demonstrated how the flow of information can be quantified in a manner similar to measuring the flow of a liquid. What is amazing is that such a basic quantity in nature took so long to be defined. And perhaps no less amazing is the fact that the Nobel Prize Committee failed to appreciate the importance of Shannon's discovery. The quantified definition of information is an important cornerstone in information technology and computer science, and has changed not only the technical aspects of IT (Information Technology), but also, for better or for worse, the way in which we think about information – or, more specifically, the way we think about everything.

Claude Shannon died in 2001 at the age of 84 after a long struggle with Alzheimer's disease. In his final days, he was not even aware of the wonders of the digital revolution to which he had contributed so much.

In order to understand Shannon's entropy, let us return to Bob and Alice and assume that they have a communication channel that is capable of transferring one pulse by seven p. m. What Shannon did was to attempt to quantify the amount of information that Bob transfers to Alice. At first blush, it seems that the amount of information is the sum of probabilities. In other words, if the probability that "Bob is busy" (0) is p, then the probability that "Bob is free" (1), is $1 - p$, meaning that the total probability is one unit (one bit), no matter what the value of p actually is.

But Shannon gave a different solution, namely:

$$I = -[p \ln p + (1 - p) \ln (1 - p)],$$

That is to say, the amount of information, I, is a function of the probability of the bit being "0" times the log of this probability, plus the probability of the bit being "1", times the log of *this* probability. For this solution, Shannon deserved a place in the pantheon of great scientists.

First we have to understand why $I = p + (1 - p)$, that is, one bit, is not a good answer. It is possible that on the day Bob made his arrangement with Alice, he had already planned another meeting and that the one with Alice (who was aware of this) was a secondary option. If we suppose that the chance for this original meeting to be cancelled, so that Bob would meet with Alice, is ten percent, then the bit with a value of "0" carries less information to Alice (0.1 bits), while the "1" bit carries more information (0.9 bits). If we add these probabilities, the answer is always "1" regardless of the relative probabilities (as known to Alice) of the bit being "0" or "1." If Alice had not been aware that the probability was 90:10, she might have assumed that the probability was still 50:50, and the bit with the "0" value would carry the same value of information as the "1". Therefore adding probabilities overlooks the *a priori* knowledge that is so important in communications.

In the expression that Shannon gave, on the other hand – *and he was aware of the fact that this expression was the same as that of the Gibbs entropy* – summing up the probabilities does not disregard the 90% chance of the bit being "0" and the 10% chance of it being "1" (or any other value that Alice would assign to her chances of meeting with Bob).

If Alice evaluates the probability that Bob will be free that evening as 50%, the amount of information that Bob sends her is at a maximum, because Alice will be equally surprised by either value of the bit. Formally, in this case both possibilities have the same uncertainty, and the information that the bit carries is:

$$I = -\frac{1}{2}\ln\frac{1}{2} - \frac{1}{2}\ln\frac{1}{2} = \ln 2.$$

That is, the maximum amount of information that a bit can carry is equal to one half the natural log of 2 (50% chance that Bob will come), plus one half of the natural log of 2 (50% chance Bob will not).[21] Since engineers prefer to calculate base 2 logarithms rather than use the "natural" base, e, the maximum amount of information that a bit carries is 1.

If the probabilities that Bob will or will not show up are not equal, the bit that he sends to Alice carries less information than one unit; if they are equal, the information carried in the bit is equal to one unit. If Alice knows that the chance of seeing Bob is just 10%, the amount of entropy according to Shannon will be:

$$I = -\frac{1}{10}\ln\frac{1}{10} - \frac{9}{10}\ln\frac{9}{10} \cong 0.32.$$

That is, the bit carries information that is just 0.32/ln2 = 0.46 of the

---

[21] In communication theory, the numerical value $\ln 2 \cong 0.693$ is called a "nat".

maximum value.

Shannon's definition is superior to the one that is independent of the probability. If we send N bits, the maximum information is N bits. The reason for this is that Shannon's expression acquires its maximum value of one for each and every bit when "0" and "1" have equal probabilities; but when their probabilities are not equal, Shannon's information is less than one. And this was Shannon's great insight: for an N-bit file, there is a chance that its content could be transferred via digital communication using less than N bits. In principle, then, it is possible to compress files without losing content, and of course, this is very important for the speed, cost, and ease of transferring information.

Can Shannon's Information Be Regarded as Entropy?

Before Shannon published his seminal work in 1949, he pondered the question of an appropriate name for the quantity he was defining. In an interview he gave to Scientific American, Shannon related that John von Neumann had advised him to call the quantity "entropy," since the concept of entropy was vague enough to give him an advantage in debates. As we shall see immediately, von Neumann – one of the most brilliant mathematicians who ever lived – gave Shannon some very sound advice.

This advice notwithstanding, Shannon's theory is today called "information theory," although Shannon himself actually called his paper *A Mathematical Theory of **Communication*** [emphasis added]. There is nothing wrong with calling Shannon's theory "information theory," since it does concern the transfer of information, but it should be borne in mind that Shannon's "information" is actually entropy.

In previous chapters we saw that entropy is a calculated value based on the number of microstates. At any given moment, every statistical system, even a dynamic one, is in one and only one microstate. This is especially true for a data file, whose entire epistemological meaning is a single microstate, which is its content!

The confusion between Shannon's entropy and information – in the sense of content – is derived from our tendency to consider a stored computer file and a transmitted file as one and the same. In other words, for us, "information" usually refers to the content that we have received, while Shannon treated information as the uncertainty that accompanies the transmission of the content.

If a file is not transmitted from the computer's memory, the issue is just academic. Suppose we have in our computer memory a file with N bits and H Shannon information. The file has content, exactly in the same way as gas molecules in a vessel are at every instant in a single microstate (although, in contrast to gas, the microstate of the file in our computer is static, this is immaterial for our present discussion, which focuses on there being just a single microstate at any given time.)

What is the content of the file? There are three possibilities: (a) the content is unknown to us, and we want to know it; (b) we already know it; and (c), we do not know but we do not care either. If no one reads the file, we can leave the question of the content and its significance to the epistemologists. On the other hand, if someone does read the file, the problem becomes a thermodynamic one. In fact, in order to read a text, our eyes must scan the letters, whose forms are reflected by light onto our retinas and then interpreted by our brain. The transmission of content from the page to the eye involves energy expenditure, and is therefore subject to the laws of thermodynamics. All the more so with regard to a file in a computer's memory, when it is transmitted to some device that will change it to characters (or sounds, or pictures) through any number of processes.

It starts with the computer's magnetic head reading the bits of the file. If the value is "1", it sends out a pulse (of electric current or electromagnetic radiation) that is physically an oscillator. Normally, the electromagnetic or electrical vibration undergoes amplification. This amplification of a classical oscillator is comparable to the Carnot heat engine as we saw in Chapter Three, and the temperature of a classical oscillator is its energy divided by the Boltzmann constant. Thus, according to the second law of thermodynamics, the transmission of a file is essentially a flow of energy from the hot transmitter to the cold receiver. Since the transfer of energy involved in the transmission of the file is subject to the second law, and since Shannon's entropy, as will be shown, is thermodynamic entropy, it becomes evident that the transmission of the file increases entropy. Since entropy is proportional to the number of contents (microstates), it means that the number of contents tend to increases.

Now is the time to demonstrate how physical entropy, as described above, is connected to information, as Shannon defined it. Physical entropy, it will be recalled, has certain properties and characteristics: the flow of energy from hot to cold, uncertainty, extensivity, and a tendency to increase (as expressed by Clausius's inequality). And since Shannon's information possesses these very properties, this is enough to justify calling it "entropy."

Energy flow: In Shannon information, energetic bits are transferred from a "hot" transmitter to a "cold" receiver, similar to the way Clausius entropy is generated by transfer of energy from a hotter object to a colder one.

Uncertainty: When Alice is waiting for Bob to send his bit of information, she has no idea of its value. If she knew the value ("0" or "1"), Bob would not have to bother sending it. Therefore, the essence of the bit is the uncertainty inherent in it. Information that passes through a channel is the log of the number of possible contents similar to the number of possible microstates. (As mentioned above, Shannon was aware that his expression was the same as the Gibbs entropy.)

Extensivity: Given two files, A and B, the amount of information transferred if both files are transmitted will be the sum of the information in files A and B added together. This is analogous to the additive property of both the Boltzmann and the Gibbs entropies.

Clausius's inequality: As mentioned already, Shannon's expression for information was identical to the Gibbs entropy since he assumes that the probabilities of all possible contents are not necessarily uniform. Yet in a file where all probabilities for the contents are the same, the amount of entropy, I, is maximum. If we denote as H the value obtained from Shannon's expression when the probabilities are not uniform, we can write that $H \leq I$. This is identical with Clausius's inequality.

Thus, entropy as defined by Shannon is equivalent to entropy as defined by Clausius, Boltzmann and Gibbs.

If we have a file (a series of "1's" and "0's") N bits in length, and assume that each bit carries maximum entropy, that is ln2 nat, the file will carry $I = N$ ln2 nat. The number of possible ways that N bits can be arranged, where each bit has an equal probability of being either "1" or "0", is $\Omega = 2^N$. This shows that Shannon's expression is none other than the logarithm for the number of different possibilities for arranging a file, Ω, or in other words, the number of possible files (contents), that is, $I = \ln\Omega$. This expression is identical to the Boltzmann entropy, except that it lacks the Boltzmann constant.

The Boltzmann constant does not appear in the Shannon information because Shannon referred to bits as logical conceptual quantities. From a historical thermodynamic perspective, this is a pity. Had he considered the "1" bit to be a classical energetic oscillator (that is, a classical electrical oscillator) whose entropy, as we recall, is k, then information as he defined it, and entropy as Gibbs defined it, would have been identical. As we saw in the previous chapter, the entropy of a classical oscillator is one Boltzmann constant and is independent of its energy, in the same way that Shannon's entropy is independent of the energy of a "1" bit.

Accordingly, there are three analogues and one identity between Shannon entropy and the statistical entropy of thermodynamics:

An analogue between the number of different contents and the number of microstates;

an analogue between a state in which there are unequal probabilities for the "0" and "1" bits, and between the Gibbs entropy and Clausius's inequality;

an analogue between equal probabilities of the bits being "0" and "1," and between the equal probabilities of microstates in Boltzmann's entropy;

and an identity regarding extensivity for both the Boltzmann and Gibbs entropies and the Shannon's entropy.

To review: "Shannon's information," as it is defined, is the Gibbs entropy without the Boltzmann constant. The Boltzmann constant must be added when the information-carrying bits are oscillators, such as classical electromagnetic pulses, say, where each has an entropy of one Boltzmann constant. That is, the Shannon information is the logarithm of the number of possible contents of a file, which expresses the uncertainty of its content. The greater the uncertainty of a file, the greater the amount of content. Thus, one may extrapolate and say that *the second law of thermodynamics tends to increase the amount of content*. This point will be explored in more detail in chapter five.

Equilibrium and File Compression

The concept of equilibrium is integral to the definition of entropy, but we have yet to deal with it with respect to Shannon's entropy. Now we shall demonstrate that a state of thermodynamic equilibrium also exists in communications.

One way to formulate of the second law of thermodynamics is to state that every system tends towards equilibrium. The reason for this is that in equilibrium, the value for entropy is at a maximum. Therefore, with respect to information, one can express equilibrium as a state in which every one of the possible different contents has equal probability. It also means that each bit has an equal probability of being either "0 or 1" – as if each one of the bits is taking part in some sort of unbiased coin tossing for its value. (Of course, there is a chance, albeit miniscule, that an N-bit file in equilibrium – even though created using a fair, 50:50 coin tossing – may be, for instance, comprised only of "0"s.)

In a file in which the probabilities for a bit to be "0" or "1" are not equal, the uncertainty value is smaller. Therefore, even though the length of such a file may be equal to that of another one with equal probabilities, it may have less content. This leads to the conclusion that a file in equilibrium is the shortest possible file that can be sent for any given content. For economic and engineering reasons, engineers are obviously interested in sending the shortest file necessary to carry a given content. For this purpose they run some compression software, which compress the file before its transmission or storage. For example, if a file contains one million "1" bits, a compressed file will contain some short formula whose meaning is "a million 1's" rather than a string of one million "1's". Such a compression changes the probability of any bit to be either "1" or "0" to about 50%. Thus, an ideal compression maximizes the uncertainty of a file, making it reach thermodynamic equilibrium – that is, the shortest possible file that can carry the given amount of content. A file that was compressed to its maximum is said to have reached the *Shannon Limit*, that is to say, thermodynamic equilibrium.

Usually, communication channels transfer not only content, but also "noise." For example, in electromagnetic broadcasting, the transmission channels are exposed to electromagnetic radiation from many sources, e.g. black body radiation emitted from objects in their environment, radiation at various frequencies from all sorts of devices in use in the surroundings, cosmic radiation, and radioactive radiation. Since electromagnetic channels are affected by this random radiation, the content that Bob sends to Alice might get corrupted: the radiation may alter the values of some of the bits in the file, and Alice may receive a file different from the one that Bob sent. In fact, sometimes the file that Alice receives may lose virtually all its meaning because of this extraneous noise. Thermodynamically speaking, over a noisy channel, Alice will receive a microstate different from the one that Bob sent. Nevertheless, this noise actually *increases* the amount of information in the file (according to Shannon's definition). This paradox can be understood if we remember that even though the subjective content has been reduced, the uncertainty, i.e. the entropy – the Shannon information – actually increased. This process occurs spontaneously and reflects the tendency of systems to increase a file's entropy according to the second law of thermodynamics. In Appendix B-1, we shall discuss this more extensively.

Indeed, increasing entropy is often done purposefully in an attempt to correct errors due to random noise. To protect the integrity of the content that Alice is to receive, specific content –

called *control* – is usually added to the transmitted files explicitly for checking whether any errors were introduced during transmission and, if there were any, to correct them.

The Distribution of Digits – Benford's Law

The effects of the second law of thermodynamics occur in each and every spontaneous process in nature; however, sometimes these effects are overlooked. When we consider why water flows from a high place to a lower one, or why a pendulum gradually slows its motion until it stops, we think of the force of gravitation for the former case and friction for the latter one. Few will explain these phenomena in terms of the second law of thermodynamics, since our natural tendency is to give explanations based on deterministic forces, overlooking the inherent irreversibility and uncertainty of nature. But when we discuss distributions, the forces-based explanations become extremely complicated, if not impossible. We saw how the second law of thermodynamics explains the distribution of the velocities of gas particles – a cornerstone of gas theory, which contributed to the acceptance of atomic hypothesis. Similarly, we saw how the second law explains the frequency distribution of a black body's electromagnetic radiation of a given temperature – an explanation that led to the discovery of the quantum nature of radiation. Does Shannon's entropy yield similar logical distributions?

Indeed, what is a logical distribution, and how is it expressed? As we are going to see, logical thermodynamic distributions affect our lives no less than physical distributions.

We start with the equilibrium distributions of signals in files. A binary file in equilibrium is compressed. That is, if we sample a large number of files, we shall see that the number of "1" bits is equal to the number of "0" bits in them. There is no need to be familiar with thermodynamics to understand this. However, the distribution of decimal digits in random numbers, contrary to intuition, is not uniform. Experience has shown that high-value digits will appear fewer times than low-value digits. This phenomenon, which has been observed in numerous random files, is called Benford's Law. It had raised many problems for the mathematicians, until it became clear that this is a direct consequence of maximizing Shannon's entropy. In order to understand Benford's law, let us calculate the ratios among of the frequencies of digits in a decimal file in Shannon limit.

Digits (and the numbers composed of them) are different from letters (and the words made of them). The logical meaning of a number is clear and well defined. Whereas combinations of words may excite or annoy or bore, or, in most cases, lack any meaning, combinations of digits are always a number with some significance. The relationship between digits and numbers is defined by the laws of arithmetic, as opposed, of course, to letters and words.

It is possible to simulate a digit, *n,* as a box containing *n* balls. Thus, the ten decimal digits are analogous to ten boxes, in which the number of balls they contain is equal to their value, as shown in the following table:

0 =	0000000000	5=	1111100000
1=	1000000000	6=	1111110000
2=	1100000000	7=	1111111000
3=	1110000000	8=	1111111100
4=	1111000000	9=	1111111110

A possible way of coding the boxes-and-balls model for the transmission of a decimal digit is to form a sequence of 10 bits for each digit (as shown above), such that the number of "1" bits in each sequence is equal to n. The distribution of the n "1" bits in the sequence has no significance. For example, a number with 20 digits will be coded by twenty consecutive sequences of ten bits each, and the number of "1" bits in each sequence will be equal to the value of corresponding digit in the number.

To restore the number that Bob transmitted, Alice has to split the binary file she received into ten-bit sequences. Now she should count the number of "1" bits in each sequence and write down the appropriate decimal digit; finally, she has a sequence of digits that matches the number that Bob sent her. What will the distribution of the digits in the sequences be? If we imagine each "1" bit as a ball, and each sequence of ten bits as a box, the calculation of the distribution of "1" bits in the sequences will be identical with calculating the distribution of balls in each box such that Shannon's entropy is maximized. Calculating the distribution of P balls in N boxes is somewhat similar to the calculations that Planck did when he figured the distribution of photons in the radiation modes of a black body. Obviously there are differences: for example, with a decimal file, there cannot be more than nine balls in a box. Using a different method of counting, for example the hexadecimal system (based on 16), the number of balls cannot exceed fifteen. However, the number of photons which can be found in a radiation mode can be as large as P. In Appendix B-2, the standard method of Lagrange multipliers is used to calculate the distribution of digits that will yield the maximum number of microstates, and the obtained relative frequency of the digit n, $\rho(n)$, is given by the function:

$$\rho(n) = \log_{10}(\frac{n+1}{n})$$

This expression deserves some attention. Its significance is that it shows that in a random decimal file, the relative normalized frequency of the digits is given by a function that is the logarithm of the ratio between a digit plus one and the digit itself. Now it is possible to calculate the frequency distribution of the various digits in a file of random data, as shown in Fig 6.

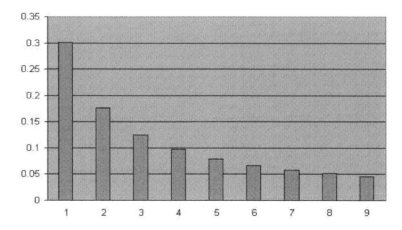

Figure 6: Benford's law – the relative frequency of a digit in a file of random numbers in not uniform. The frequency of the digit "1" is 6.5 times greater than that of the digit "9".

These results are counterintuitive, since we naturally expect a uniform distribution of digits. Yet the "1" digit appears 6.5 times more frequently than the "9" digit! The reason is that in equilibrium, each microstate has an equal probability, and thus every ball will have an equal probability of "drawing" any box. That is, in order to divide fairly P balls into N boxes, P drawings for N boxes must be performed. At each drawing, one box will "win" one ball. Obviously, the probability that in the end of our game one particular box will have won many balls is lower than the probability that it will have won only a few balls. Put simply, it is easier to win one ball than to win nine balls. Life is tough!

Does this imply that the second law of thermodynamics is also applicable to mathematics? Surprisingly, this very distribution – with the very same mathematical expression – was discovered empirically in 1881 by Canadian-American astronomer Simon Newcomb while he was looking at a booklet of logarithmic tables. (Before the era of the calculator, these tables were used for multiplication, division, finding the exponents of numbers, etc.) Newcomb noticed that the pages beginning with the digit "1" were much more tattered than the others. He concluded that if one randomly chose a digit from any string of numbers, the chance of finding the "1" digit is greater than finding any other digit. He examined the charts beginning with the digit "2" and so on, and came up with – as a conjecture – the very same formula that is derived in Appendix B-2.

In 1931, an employee of the General Electric Company, physicist and electrical engineer Frank Benford, demonstrated that Newcomb's Law applied not only to logarithmic tables, but also to the atomic weights of thousands of chemical compounds, as well as to house numbers, lengths of rivers, and even the heat capacity of materials. Because Benford showed that this distribution is of a general nature, it is called "Benford's Law." Since then, researchers have shown that this law also applies to prime numbers, company balance books, stock indices, and numerous other instances.

It should be noted, however, that if we were to allocate P balls among N boxes *not* by "drawing the lucky box" one ball at a time, but rather by using, for example, a top with ten faces bearing the digits "0" to "9", and allowing each spin of the top to determine one digit in a non-biased way, the distribution of the digits among the boxes will be uniform. Why? It is clear that the digit symbol marked on any face of the top does not affect the probability of it falling on that particular side. This is why the various lottery games use such techniques for drawing numbers as to give a uniform distribution, so that gamblers familiar with Benford's law will not have an advantage.

At first glance, Benford's distribution seems counterintuitive, because we tend to regard digits as symbols rather than physical entities. The fact that most people are not aware of Benford's distribution is used by tax authorities in some countries to detect tax fraud by companies or individuals. If the distribution of digits in a balance sheet does not match Benford's law, the tax authorities suspect that the numbers have been fixed, and may launch a more thorough inspection.

To illustrate briefly the ideas presented more fully in Appendix B-2, let us examine a model of three balls and three boxes. The number of possible microstates (or configurations), according to Planck, is ten, as follows:

$$\boxed{0\,|\,0\,|\,3}\;\boxed{3\,|\,0\,|\,0}\;\boxed{2\,|\,1\,|\,0}\;\boxed{2\,|\,0\,|\,1}\;\boxed{1\,|\,2\,|\,0}\;\boxed{1\,|\,1\,|\,1}\;\boxed{1\,|\,0\,|\,2}\;\boxed{0\,|\,3\,|\,0}\;\boxed{0\,|\,2\,|\,1}\;\boxed{0\,|\,1\,|\,2}$$

In equilibrium, each configuration has an equal probability. Thus we count the number of occurrences for each digit in all configurations. "1" occurs nine times, "2" occurs six times, and "3" only three. This is the distribution expected from the calculations in Appendix B-3 for the more general case (Planck-Benford), as applied to our case.

We therefore conclude that:

The distribution of digits in a decimal file that is compressed to Shannon's limit obeys Benford's law;

Benford's law is the result of the second law of thermodynamics.

Mathematical operations have a physical significance.

In the next chapter we shall see that this distribution, when expanded from decimal coding to any other numerical coding (as we have just seen in the case of three balls and three boxes), can explain many phenomena commonly present in human existence and culture, such as social networks, distribution of wealth (Pareto's principle), or the results of surveys and polls.

Chapter 5

Entropy in Social Systems

The Distribution of Links in Social Networks –

Zipf's Law

So far, we have reviewed the effects of entropy on the flow and distribution of energy, the transmission of information, and the distribution of digits in data files. During this journey, we came to realize that there is a significant difference between entropy and most the other physical quantities in nature.

Looking at quantities such as mass, time, length, electrical current, electrical charge, temperature, energy, speed, light intensity, and so forth, we notice that they all describe "something" measurable: each one (and many others) can be measured by some instrument or another. For instance, the instruments that measure the quantities listed above are, respectively, scales, clock, ruler, amperemeter, electrometer, thermometer, calorimeter, speedometer and photometer. But there is no "entropymeter." The fact that entropy cannot be measured directly is of great help for scientists in the field: they can write about entropy almost anything that comes to mind. At the same time, it demonstrates the fact that entropy is different from all these other physical quantities.

As we saw, entropy is *calculated for equilibrium*. When we observe gas in a vessel or read a transmitted file, we do not learn from the amount of entropy any of the system's details. On the contrary, entropy is a measure of our lack of knowledge about it. The uncertainty (lack of knowledge) about the system's configuration is the total number of its possible microstates, when we do not know in which particular microstate it is at a given moment — even though, at any given moment, the system must be in one and only one of these possible microstates. When we say that the system is in equilibrium, it means that all the possible microstates of the system have equal probability. Therefore, it is arguable that entropy is a property of a system, and not a physical quantity like the ones mentioned above.

The second law of thermodynamics states that every system tends to change in order to increase its entropy (specifically, the logarithm of the number of microstates), that is to say, it will tend to reach equilibrium, in which the number of microstates is at a maximum. The number of microstates in logical entropy is the amount of content possible, and therefore, as the number of microstates increases, so will the amount of content. Hence, the operation of second law of thermodynamics tends to increase content.

However, we should not confuse content and entropy: entropy is the uncertainty that accompanies content. If we transmit a file with N bits M times, we shall increase the entropy M times – exactly the same as it if we had sent M different files of N bits each. Nature does not care about the content, but about the uncertainty accompanying it. There is an old story about a man who crossed the U.S.-Mexican border every day with a bale of hay on his bicycle. The suspicious customs officers rummaged through those bales to no avail, and it took a long time before it dawned on them that he made his living by smuggling bicycles. The content that we consume is, in a matter of speaking, the straw through which we rummage with passionate curiosity, and the bicycles are the entropy in which nature is interested.

Is life itself a result of entropy's tendency to increase? Is the human "will" an expression of entropy's "will" to increase? It seems that the answers to both questions are "Yes". Changes in which entropy is increased are spontaneous and irreversible, just like biological activity and its accompanying human activity. Imagine a hypothetical observer stationed in space who has been looking down on earth for many millions of years. At the start he would have seen creatures appearing, plants and animals multiplying, and, in due course, also roads being paved, skyscrapers rising and electrical lights flashing; and flying through the air are not only birds, but also airplanes. Will this observer give credit to human ingenuity for some of these developments? It is more likely for it to think that it has all appeared spontaneously, according to the laws of nature. Humans are part of nature, therefore the human "will" is also part of nature, and hence, human actions and desires should also obey the second law of thermodynamics.

It seems that the basic characteristic of life is the replication of information. British biologist Richard Dawkins[65] claims that the purpose of natural selection is not necessarily the improvement of a species, but rather the replication of "selfish" genes. A living creature is a kind of smart coalition of cells, whose purpose is to replicate the genes within it. Obviously, biological reproduction is "desirable" according to the second law of thermodynamics, and thus it follows that our desire to reproduce is rooted in the second law. Dawkins even points out a connection between the replication of genes and the replication of information *à la* Shannon. In analogy to "gene", he coined the term "meme," which can be an idea, a song, or even a computer virus. Memes exist in the world of logical entropy of communication networks; they undergo spontaneous reproduction and instead of eating food, they are nourished by electricity.

Therefore, one may assume that our "will" drives us to increase entropy. Early in the nineteenth century, philosopher Arthur Schopenhauer claimed that the essence of all beings is its Will. In addition, he claimed that a man can do what he wills, but cannot will what he wills.[66] If we push further in this direction, we must conclude that it is not in our power to restrain our will to increase entropy. In other words, entropy, with its tendency to increase, determines what we want, and motivates us to do things that increase entropy. Any businessman will tell you that any step he makes is aimed to increase the number of options available to him. In other words, he will choose a course of action that will increase the number of alternatives he could choose from in the future. In thermodynamic terms, he is essentially saying: "I want to increase the entropy of the options at my disposal."

This tendency of entropy to increase is, if you will, the powerful driving force of all changes in nature. In general, these fall into four categories:

Physical changes, such as the tendency of water to flow down;

chemical changes, such as the tendency of iron to rust in damp air;

biological changes, such as the tendency for creatures to multiply; and

social changes, which are related to us, humans, and our culture.

Is it possible to characterize a social system using the same tools that serve us when we analyze a physical system? And if so, what is the social analog to a physical system? What is the analog to the flow of energy? And what is the analog to the distribution of energy in equilibrium? In other words, is it possible to analyze changes in a social system in terms of the second law of thermodynamics as formulated by Clausius, Boltzmann, Gibbs, Planck, and Shannon?

To answer these questions, we must first see what a social system is. Examination of the fabric of any social system, taking into account both human and environmental factors, immediately brings to mind a network. Looking at the definition of "network" in some dictionaries we find various kinds of relations: physical (railways, roads, etc.), human (family, support groups, work groups), or communication (the phone network, computer network, and of course, THE network, the internet). Any such network comprises nodes, that can be represented by dots or boxes, and links that connect the nodes, are usually represented by lines.

Is it possible to learn anything about the structure of a network from the second law of thermodynamics? Does entropy's tendency to increase influence the connections between the networks' nodes? To answer these questions, let us use the air transport network as an example.

In the air transport network, an airport is a node and the flights between one airport and another are the links. If one wants to fly from Tel Aviv to Recife, Brazil, one has to go through several airports (nodes), since there are no direct flights from Tel Aviv to Recife. The travel agent may suggest, for instance, flying from Tel Aviv to Paris, then from Paris to Rio de Janeiro, and finally from Rio to Recife.

Non-direct flights through several nodes are common because the airlines want to fill their planes. In our case, the number of travelers going from Tel Aviv to Recife on any given day is not enough to fill a plane. On the other hand, every day there are enough people to fill a plane to Paris. For travelers from Tel Aviv, Paris is a much more popular destination than Rio de Janeiro, let alone Recife. Had there been enough people to fill a plane from Tel Aviv to Rio, there would be direct flights, which save money, fuel and time. Since this is not the case, it is more efficient to create nodes with different numbers of links. For example, in a small country with a small volume of air traffic there is only one airport, from which one can reach a number of busier airports in other countries, and from any of them it is possible to reach many more international destinations. Nodes from which it is possible to go to numerous destinations are termed "busy nodes" – transfer points for those arriving from less busy nodes. At busy nodes, passengers change flights, so that they get to their desired destination, and the flights are filled, ideally to capacity.

What makes an airport a busy node? The answer is economic. In order for a node to be busy it must have certain characteristics, such as proximity to a large, dynamic economic center; a suitable geographical location; an appropriate distance from other busy nodes; the entrepreneurial aptitude of the landowners; and, of course, a heaping measure of luck.

Economically, a busy node is advantageous since it promotes the development of logistic-based services, such as shops and industry, which provide employment. The economic advantages must outweigh negative outcomes such as noise and pollution.

In a certain sense, social networks are similar to transportation networks (even though there is a significant difference, which will be explained later on). A person can be perceived as a node connected to a finite number of people (family, friends, neighbors, acquaintances, colleagues, and so forth). The number of links to other people varies from person to person. Some people have numerous links and other only a few. A person with many acquaintances is a busy node: the more links, the more likely that he or she is influential, that is, has the ability to exchange information with many people. Moreover, the more access a person has to other people who are themselves busy nodes, the more that person will benefit. The reason for this is that in times of need, he or she can reach – via a relatively small number of links – more people who are in a position to help, advise, or endorse them, cooperate with them in various areas, and so forth.

In 1976, social psychologist Stanley Milgram proposed the Small World Theory, according to which every person in the United States is connected to every other person in the United States through, at the most, six connections.[67] This theory, also known as "six degrees of separation" through six contacts, or "six acquaintances," has been examined in various ways, and there is no consensus among scientists on whether or not it is correct. Nevertheless, it is similar to our story about the traveler who wishes to go from Tel Aviv to Recife, Brazil. At first, it might seem that the number of connections that Milgram proposed is too small, yet one can argue that everybody knows at least one person who is a busier node than themselves. This busy node is similarly connected to an even busier node, and so on. Taking this line of thinking, the Milgram number does not seem surprising. In fact, by adding just one or two nodes, the American network can be extended worldwide.

As an illustration, consider the question: assuming that Mr. Levi from the Israeli town of Pardes Hanna and Mr. Smith from Oshkosh, Wisconsin, are complete strangers; how many people does Mr. Levi have to go through in order to reach Mr. Smith? As a resident of Pardes Hanna, Mr. Levi probably knows someone who is acquainted with the town's mayor. This worthy necessarily knows the Israeli Minister of the Interior, who probably knows his counterpart in the United States, who knows the senator from Wisconsin, who knows the mayor of Oshkosh, who knows one of his employees who knows Mr. Smith: eight degrees of separation, or fewer if, for instance, Mr. Levi knows his mayor personally.

Hereafter, we must make a distinction between two kinds of networks: symmetrical and asymmetrical.

Symmetrical networks are those that have bilateral equal connections between any two nodes, as for example, railroads and transportation networks in which it is equally possible to travel from node A to node B and from node B to node A along the same route. Telephone networks are also symmetrical: Bob speaks to Alice over the same channel that Alice speaks to Bob.

In *asymmetric* networks, the links between nodes are not bilateral, but rather hierarchic. Asymmetric networks are more common in general, and especially in social networks, as will be explained below. In an asymmetric network, Bob the TV newscaster is able to talk to Alice the viewer, but this does not necessarily imply that Alice has the ability to talk to Bob. The link resembles a one-way street. A simple example of an asymmetric network is the military. In this network, a number of soldiers are linked to their sergeant, a number of sergeants are linked to a junior officer, a number of junior officers are linked to a higher ranking officer, and so on up to the top. In such a network, a brigade's commanding officer, for example, can address a private soldier, but a private cannot immediately address a brigade CO. Generally, only those of the same rank can address each other directly. Yet if a sergeant from one brigade wants to communicate officially with a sergeant from another brigade, he or she will normally have to turn to their CO, who will call the CO in the other brigade, who will then make the connection with the other sergeant. Officers are "busier" nodes than sergeants, in the sense that the rules of hierarchy allow them to communicate with all privates and sergeants under their command and also with their counterparts in other units, with whom sergeants are not allowed to communicate officially. If the officer whom the sergeant approached is not authorized to contact his or her counterpart in the other brigade, one may expect that this officer will turn to one of higher rank, perhaps even as far as the brigade CO. In this case, the brigade CO will contact the other brigade CO, plowing a similar yet opposite route back down to the sergeant in question.

In general, if you consider Mr. Big to be your friend, it does not necessarily mean that Mr. Big considers *you* to be *his* friend. It may be that Mr. Big considers you merely an acquaintance – unless your name happens to be Mr. Bigger. It is obvious that the commanding officer of a brigade can freely address any of his subordinates (unless this is beneath his dignity), while the private usually has no access to the brigade CO. The basic idea behind a hierarchical network is the unequal distribution of links between nodes, which is derived from asymmetry in the connection between the nodes.

This links-and-nodes phenomenon is much more common than what may seem at first blush. As an example, most people in the world know the name of the President of the United States. On the other hand, it is conceivable that the President of the United States does not even remember the names of all the other nations' presidents, which are probably whispered on his ear when necessary. Most people cannot just phone the President of the United States, yet the American President has unlimited one-way access to almost anyone (in other words, he is a busy person of many links). Wealthy people enjoy a similar privilege. It can be assumed that you would not refuse to meet with Bill Gates, even if you are smart enough to know that Mr. Gates will not offer you, during that meeting, to share his wealth with you in one way or another. On the other hand, unless your name is Mr. Bigger, you will probably consider it an honor if your request to meet Mr. Gates will be politely rejected by none other than his personal assistant herself. It may be that the easiest way to estimate the wealth or status of someone is to count the people with whom he or she can make direct contact.

The human network is based upon an unequal distribution of links among nodes, because information transmission in a non-uniform network is more efficient. A non-uniform distribution of links to nodes is necessary, since a uniform distribution is problematic. To illustrate this, let us examine a group of people with a uniform distribution of links, where each member knows one tenth of the network's population. In this case, there is a high probability that closed secondary groups in which all the links begin and end within that group (a bubble) will be formed. This phenomenon was quite common in the past, when communication between various communities was not well developed. This is how such a wide variety of cultures and languages have evolved, whose existence has made communication between people from different countries problematic until very recently. Even now there are such bubbles in some remote corners of the world, as well as groups that choose to live in isolation, such as some closed religious sects. Surprisingly, the bubble phenomenon exists in academia too, where international groups of scientists conduct research that no one from outside the bubble is interested in. The existence of such groups limits the flow of information.

In Medieval Europe, a merchant who came to another country to establish business ties would find himself in difficulty – a strange language, a different culture, a natural suspicion of strangers, scant legal protection, etc. Yet, if he was Jewish, he could go into a synagogue and find people who, while denizens of the other country, still shared a language (Yiddish) and a culture with him, and were willing to trust him because he was, as they were, subject to rabbinical law and could therefore, if things came to that, be sued in a rabbinical court in his country of residence, under threat of excommunication. In other words, Jews had a unique ability to form "inter-bubble" connections, and thus fulfilled an important role in the development of trade and banking in Europe.

And so, the hierarchal system is analogous in its working mechanism to the connection between Mr. Levi from Pardes Hanna and Mr. Smith in Oshkosh. Since a hierarchal system, for instance a military one, prevents the formation of bubbles such as those that appears in an egalitarian system, it has been adopted by successful organizations no less important than the military – companies, corporations and institutions.

In a hierarchal system bubble formation is not possible, because the busier nodes are connected to many less busy nodes. The hierarchic distribution enables the connection of all nodes into one network with a minimum number of links. For this reason, there are many nodes with few links, and a few nodes with many. All this is the manifestation of entropy, which, in its tendency to grow, leads to the development of mechanisms which prevent bubble formation.

How can links be optimally distributed between nodes? Since we do not know with certainty how to define an ideal network, this is not a simple question. Moreover, systems – usually, and perhaps surprisingly – are not planned by some intelligent master planner but rather evolve spontaneously. For example, the internet uses the telephony network (landlines, cordless and satellite), and the cables infrastructure as well. These infrastructures were put in place by many individuals and firms, developed independently in separate locations before being linked together in one way or another. Obviously, whoever planned the telephone system in Pardes Hanna, Israel, never gave a thought to the cable network in Oshkosh, Wisconsin, and still there are direct telephone and internet services between Pardes Hanna and Oshkosh, using these combined infrastructures. As mentioned above, telephone communication is an example of a symmetrical network. When Mr. Levi talks with Mr. Smith, they each have the same ability to receive and transmit information. On the other hand, when we listen to the radio, we can only receive information. In internet and cable television, we usually receive much more information than we send. Social networks are a fairly novel exception in this sense, and they too are formed spontaneously. Even in an ideal world, where we could choose our acquaintances at will, we still would not be able, unfortunately, to choose our acquaintances' friends. In fact, no person ever controls an entire network.

If networks are indeed created spontaneously, this seems to warrant that they would tend to reach a state of equilibrium. But what is "equilibrium" in a network? If we try to relate it to Planck's formula, we can conclude that in equilibrium, the distribution of the links among the nodes will give the largest number of different ways to construct the network.

Paradoxically, the asymmetry of the links simplifies the mathematical calculations required to work out the entropy of networks. Let us say that we have a network of N persons, with P asymmetrical links. The essence of a one-way link is that one person's connection to another is independent of the number of links that these people have to him or her. In other words, one may say that a unilateral link is associated to a specific person in the same way that a particle belongs to a box. To calculate the distribution of links in equilibrium, we have to find the distribution of the links among the nodes that maximizes Shannon's entropy. The result thus obtained is in a way a generalization of Benford's Law, as discussed in the previous chapter.

The maximum entropy distribution of P links among N nodes (for the derivation, see Appendix B-3) is given by

$$\rho(n) = \frac{\ln(1 + \frac{1}{n})}{\ln(N+1)}$$

Here, n can be any integer, provided that it does not exceed the total number of links, P (i.e., $n \leq P$). It can be seen that the relative density of the links, $\rho(n)$, is a decreasing function of n. n expresses the ratio between the number of links (or particles) and the number of nodes (or boxes). We intuitively call this number a "rank." Nodes with a rank of 1 are the poorer nodes, because they have only one link. There are more nodes with a few links than with many, because as n increases, $\rho(n)$ decreases. This is not surprising, since we saw that Mr. Levi had to made contact with Mr. Smith through several busy nodes (including two ministers and one senator) and several less busy ones. A small number of busy nodes and a large number of poorly-linked nodes enable efficient communication. The intuitive explanation for this is that a remote node still offers at least one link to a busier node, from which connection to several busier destinations is possible, as in the airport example. Aircraft flying at capacity are analogous to well-exploited communication lines. The distribution of links in nodes is identical to the distribution of frequencies in the radiation mode of a black body at the classical limit.

It seems that this distribution is identical for many phenomena common in human society. For example, in a social network, a person is analogous to a node, and the number of people he or she has direct access to is analogous to the links. In an airline network, a node is an airport and the links are the direct-fight destinations. As we shall see below, a node may also be an internet site, or even a given book. In these cases, the surfers or readers are the links. Many other distributions follow this same equation.

This distribution, when plotted on a log-log scale, gives a straight line with a slope of -1 as can be seen on the left hand side of Figure 7. Therefore, this is called a power law distribution.[22] This distribution is also known as Zipf's Law, named after George Kingsley Zipf, an American linguist and philologist, who discovered this phenomenon in the frequency of words in texts. What he found was that in sufficiently large texts, the most common word appears twice as often as the second most common word, the second most common word appears twice as often as the fourth most common word, and so on. The Zipf distribution also gives a straight line of -1 slope on a logarithmic scale.

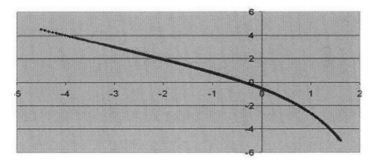

Figure 7: The logarithm of the relative frequency of nodes having n links (horizontal axis) plotted against the logarithm of the number of links, n, (vertical axis) produces a straight line with a slope of -1 for any integer n. This distribution is called a power law distribution. To the right of the vertical axis, the number of links is smaller than the number of nodes (n < 1), leading to exponential decay and a curved line.

In Appendix B-3, it is shown that Zipf's law is obtained for the maximum entropy distribution of P links (particles) in N nodes (boxes) when $P \gg N$ and $n = 1,2 \ldots \ldots, P$. In this case $n\varphi(n) = C$.

---

[22] The name derives from a polynomial distribution which, on a logarithmic scale, gives a straight line whose slope is the power of the polynom. A power law polynomial decays less steeply than an exponential decay. Therefore, the probability of a node to have many more "links" than the average is much higher than that in exponential distributions decay. For example, our chances of living much longer than the average is much smaller than our chances of being much richer than average, since life expectancy tends to decrease exponentially with age.

That is, the product of the relative frequency of a node with n links by n is constant – exactly what Zipf found empirically with regard to the relative frequency of words in texts. (Zipf's law is analogue to the classical limit of Planck's equation, namely, $E = nh\nu = kT = 1/\beta$, or $n\nu(n) = \frac{1}{h\beta} = C.$) The distribution of word frequencies in texts is an example of a poll in which the authors vote for words according to their popularity. Poll distributions in general are discussed later in this chapter.

To sum up, we assumed that a spontaneously-evolved network (without a master plan), like the networks that are formed in nature, is structured according to the second law of thermodynamics and therefore tends to reach equilibrium – the state in which the distribution of links among the nodes provides the maximum number of possible configurations.

We calculated the distribution of links between nodes in networks when the number of microstates is at a maximum, and demonstrated that there are more nodes with fewer links than nodes with many. This distribution is also called the "long-tailed distribution" (see Figure 8). The distribution of links among the nodes is identical with the distribution of frequencies in radiation mode in a black body at the classical limit, as suggested by Rayleigh and Jeans and calculated by Planck (figure 7 above).

If indeed an ideal thermodynamic network exists, a theoretical implication is that any link added may actually *reduce* the efficiency of the network! This apparent paradox can be expressed even more paradoxically: can the addition of a road to a transportation system *increase* traffic congestion? Is it possible that adding a road to the system would result in a reduction of the average road speed? Or the other way round, could shutting a road *improve* the flow of traffic? In fact, this is exactly what was observed in a number of cities, including Stuttgart, Germany, and Seoul, South Korea, where blocking a main road actually led to an improvement in the traffic flow.[68] Even more astonishingly, German mathematician Dietrich Braess predicted this effect in 1969.[69] The explanation given to this phenomenon – the so-called Braess's paradox – is that it represents a deviation from the Nash equilibrium in games theory,[70] which is based on optimal strategies that individuals choose basing on what they know at the time about the strategies of other players. In the case in point, many drivers who choose, in view of their experience on the road, an optimal route to bring them to their destination, would change their choice upon receiving the information that a certain road was blocked. As a result, the efficiency of the road system may improve. However, a full discussion of the Nash equilibrium exceeds the scope of this book.

This second law explanation has two advantages: it is quantitative, and it is purely statistical – that is, not influenced by non-measurable factors.

The Distribution of Wealth – The Pareto Law

Sultan Kösen soars to a height of 2.51 meters and is considered today (2013) to be the tallest man in the world. By comparison, Chandra Bahadur Dangi, only 0.55 meter tall, is regarded by the *Guinness Book of World Records* as the shortest adult in the world. (The ratio of their heights is about 1:4.5.) This means that the heights of the approximately 4.5 billion adults in the world range between 55 and 251 centimeters. The average of these two heights is 1.53 meters. No one knows precisely what the average height of an adult man is, but it can be assumed that the average of Kösen's and Dangi's heights is a pretty good estimate.

The statistical distributions and the laws that govern them were examined extensively because of the enormous importance of their fluctuation to our lives. Think, for example, about the distribution (congestion) of traffic on the roads, or the distribution of calls made to a telephone switch as a function of the time of day, or the distribution of electrical consumption as it relates to the weather, or any other similar example. All these issues have vast economic importance, since they allow one to evaluate the impact of various changes on the respective networks, which we all use on a daily basis. Should 30% of a bank's customers happen to withdraw instantaneously their savings, each for his or her individual reasons, the bank would collapse. Computer hackers topple internet sites by accessing the site numerous times simultaneously.

While every single act by every single person is taken for some specific, valid deterministic reason – perhaps known only to themselves – the behavior of a crowd is much more predictable. As Gibbs said, the whole is simpler than the sum of its parts. Let us assume that one clear morning; you wake up with a throbbing toothache. Your regular dentist, who lives on Main Street near your home, is on vacation (financed by you, needless to say). Therefore, you have to drive to another clinic, using the highway. Your decision-making ability is compromised because of that toothache, so you get on the highway at 8:30 a.m. on a weekday. For you, getting on the highway at this time of the day is an extremely uncommon thing to do, a result of both bad luck and bad judgment. Nevertheless, you find yourself caught in the usual eight-thirty-on-a-weekday-morning traffic jam. And although you see the other drivers in the traffic jam as criminal, and think that everyone would be better off if they all were behind bars, the fact is that you too are now taking just as much of a part as they are in creating this traffic jam, which normally has nothing to do with you. Traffic congestion is spontaneous and unplanned, yet common. It is formed by the nature's tendency to create non-uniform distributions. These phenomena are the driving force of economic activity.

Of all the distributions examined till now – energy in atoms, frequencies in electromagnetic radiation, digits in numerical data, and links in nodes   the most intriguing one is perhaps the equilibrium distribution of wealth.

Financial capital is not distributed among people the way body heights are distributed between Sultan Kösen and Chandra Bahadur Dangi. The majority of people know of someone who is many times richer than themselves. The richest person in the world is millions of times richer than most everybody. Our natural inclination is to think that being rich is neither fair nor just, although this belief is probably more common among poorer people than richer ones. Communism, the ideology that pretentiously aspired to create economic equality between all people, was never all that successful, and where it was enforced, it led to the poverty of nations and to extreme inequality within each one of them. The rich tend to think that their wealth is a result of their efforts, skill and vision. Economists sometimes tend to think that money attracts money – that is, it is easier to earn the second million than the first. This belief is also supported by the tendency of the rich to marry off their offspring to those similarly endowed. Yet this theory has many serious flaws, and it is not uncommon to see an enormous family fortune fade away within a few generations. As they say, the easiest way to make a small fortune is to start with a huge one.

Is the distribution of wealth influenced by the second law of thermodynamics? In order to examine this we shall look into a hypothetical country called Utopia, with a population of N residents. From time to time, money enters this country in the form of silver coins. Suppose that in Utopia, people do not have to work for a living because there is enough food, drink and accommodation for all. The Department of Justice and Welfare is entrusted with dividing up the coins between the residents. For this purpose it hires the services of the President's cousin (who gets a decent honorarium for his trouble), charging him with the distribution of these coins to all the people equally. In Utopia, it should be pointed out, everybody (except for the President's cousin) gets equal pay.

One day, however, this idyllic situation went awry. A group of residents, led by Mr. Envious, had noticed that the president's cousin has many more friends than any of them (probably because of the frequent parties he holds at his house). They gathered, all these bitter residents, for a very exhaustive discussion, and arrived at the logical conclusion that the reason for the cousin's many friends must be his having more silver coins. In order to rectify this inequality, they suggested buying a machine that will divide up the coins fairly. The reasoning behind their suggestion is that at the one-time cost of the machine, the smug smile will be wiped forever off the favorite's face – and this alone would be worth every penny! Envious, in person, guided the manufacturers in the construction of a machine that will draw, with equal probability, each coin that enters to Utopia among all the residents. The machine arrived, and the task of distributing the coins went from the favorite to the machine. However, when Envious the Idealist later saw the results of the draw, he was horrified: By introducing his so-called "unbiased" lottery machine, he himself has unintentionally introduced capitalism into Utopia.

Why should Envious be so horrified? How were the coins actually distributed between the residents? We have already seen in our discussion of Benford's law that if we draw P particles among N boxes, such that each particle has an equal probability of being in any box, the Plank-Benford expression is obtained. According to the second law of thermodynamics, the favorable distribution is the one that will yield a maximum number of microstates.

Theoretically, there is some chance that the coins will be equally distributed among the residents. However, as we saw when we were dealing with information, the probability of this particular microstate (which is the same as the probability of any other given microstate) is infinitesimally small. Conversely, the probability of an unequal distribution of some kind is almost a certainty. The most probable microstate is the equilibrium distribution. Obviously, an equal distribution has relatively lower entropy, because if we switch coins between residents A and B, the system does not change. Therefore, it is clear that in order for entropy to be at a maximum, every resident in Utopia must have a different number of coins.

The thermodynamic "justice" is the justice of configuration, and not that of the individual. It was for good reason that Gibbs claimed that the whole is simpler than the sum of its parts. The distribution of coins (that is, the distribution of wealth) is concerned with efficient system communication and has nothing to do with equality among individuals. Such an equality is foreign to nature. On the other hand, the idea of "equal opportunity" which is accepted throughout the civilized world (at least in theory) increases entropy by giving equal probability to every microstate *and* state. Equal opportunity removes the constraints inherent in a class-based society and provides an equal chance to each individual, even if, unfortunately, the chances for most people are to be poor.

The thermodynamic distribution of money has already been calculated in the section dealing with networks, which means that we already have a formula with which we can describe the distribution of coins in equilibrium. To illustrate the injustice that is created by an unbiased lottery machine, let us assume that there are 1,000,000 people in Utopia. What portion of the coins will the richest person get? From Zipf's law we may conclude that the richest person in Utopia will receive a million times more coins than the poorest person.

Looking at the table below, we can see that those at the lower decile by income, 289,000 men and woman, have one tenth of the wealth enjoyed by the upper income decile, 40,000 people!

As a result of the outrageous injustice perpetrated by presumably fair means, the citizens of Utopia changed the name of their country to Realia and started working in order to improve their luck. The richest person, for his or her part, will have to work even harder to maintain their fortune.

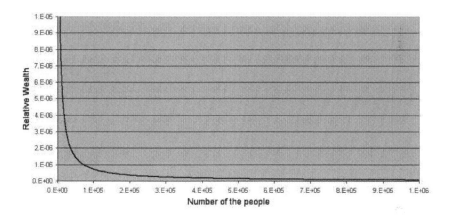

Figure 8: The thermodynamic distribution of wealth in a country with one million residents.

Entropy cannot predict who will get rich and who will be poor. The desire of each and every one of us to increase our links and our number of coins in order to increase entropy is the source of the dynamics and activity that characterizes Realia.

One of the interesting features of the Planck-Benford distribution is its self-similarity – that is, its insensitivity to the order of magnitude of the numbers (this is a property of any function that produces a straight line on a log-log scale.). The Planck-Benford distribution is insensitive to either the actual number of persons or the actual amount of wealth. That is to say, the distribution of wealth between the deciles in countries in equilibrium will be identical, regardless the size or relative wealth of the country.

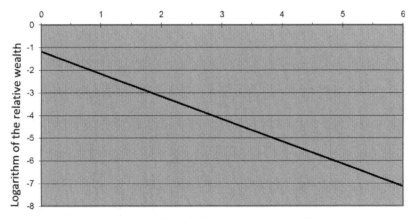

Figure 9: Full Logarithmic graph of the distribution of wealth gives the typical straight line of a power law function.

We can calculate the relative distribution of wealth from the Planck-Benford formula,

$$\rho(n) = \frac{\ln(1 + \frac{1}{n})}{\ln 11} \; .$$

When relative wealth ranges from 1 (lowest) to 10, we get the respective percentage of the population with the relative wealth as follows:

n Relative Wealth	10	9	8	7	6	5	4	3	2	1
$p(n)\%$ Percent of Population	4	4.4	4.8	5.6	6.5	7.6	9.3	12	16.9	28.9

That is, 4% of the population will have 10 times the wealth of the 28.9% poorest in the population (rank 1). We see that the strongest group, ranking 6 through 10, comprise 25% of the population and has 72% of the wealth.

This phenomenon is known as Pareto's law, named after Italian economist Vilfredo Pareto (1848-1923), a contemporary of Max Planck, who empirically suggested the approximate rule to be 80:20. Pareto's rule, as we could expect from any thermodynamic law, is also valid for other social phenomena. For example, it is common to think that 20% of the drivers are responsible for 80% of the traffic accidents; or that 20% of the customers are responsible for 80% of any business's revenues. Pareto himself suggested his empirical rule when he discovered that 80% of Italy's property was held by 20% of the population. Obviously, his 80:20 ratio was not quite precise. As we saw, the thermodynamic ratio is more like 75:25, and it might be more fitting to call Pareto's rule the "75:25 law.

Vilfredo Pareto

Vilfredo Pareto, 1848-1923

Vilfredo Pareto, an Italian industrialist, sociologist, economist and philosopher, was born in Paris in 1848. His mother was French; his father, an Italian marquis, was an engineer who, like other Italian nationalists during that period of foreign rule, had left Italy for France in 1835.

In 1858 the family returned to Italy. Young Vilfredo pursued his academic studies in the classics and engineering at the Polytechnic Institute of Turin. His doctoral thesis in engineering was entitled *The Fundamental Principles of Equilibrium In Solid Objects.* Upon completion of his studies in 1870, at the top of his class, he received his first position as manager of Rome's railway company. Four years later he was appointed manager of an iron and steel corporation in Florence. Exasperated with government bureaucrats, and having observed that economic legislation was motivated solely by protectionism and political advantage, he turned to political activity. At the time, he was a liberal-democrat who embraced the ideas of free trade, free competition and social welfare. He believed in meritocracy and detested the corrupt collusion between the nobility and the government. In 1882 he ran for the Italian parliament as a representative of the opposition party in the Pistoia region, but failed to get elected.

Upon the death of his parents, in 1889, Pareto inherited the title of marquis, but never used it. He married a penniless Russian woman whom he had met in Venice, and they moved to a villa in Piazolla. Here he began to lecture and write articles critical of the government. He quickly became the subject of police investigation, and as a result was unable to obtain any university post. Nonetheless, his papers attracted the attention of the leading neoclassical economist in Italy at that time, Maffeo Pantaleoni, who taught Pareto the basics of economic theory. Using the mathematics he had acquired in his engineering studies, Pareto began to publish sophisticated papers on economics. In 1893, on Pantaleoni's recommendation, he was appointed head of the Department of Political Economy at the University of Lausanne, Switzerland. Living in Switzerland did not stop his ongoing condemnations of the Italian government in the newspapers. He assisted escaping socialists and radicals threatened by the government, and even gave them shelter. During the Dreyfus affair in France, he denounced the anti-Semitic French authorities. At the same time, he published three volumes of his lectures (1896-1897).[71] He examined the distribution of income in populations and was the first to discover that in every country and during every era, incomes are distributed according to the law that today bears his name – the law that reflects the long-tailed distribution explained above. Some say that his doctorate thesis in engineering, which dealt with equilibrium, motivated him to find equilibrium in economy too. Later, Joseph Juran extended Pareto's distribution to include other areas of human activity besides income, and called it "Pareto's Law."

In 1900, in a famous paper called *Revista*,[72] Pareto made an about-face and spoke out against democracy. The political instability of the 1890s in Europe led him to the conclusion that radical movements do not truly seek equality and social justice, but rather take advantage of the masses in order to substitute one elite for another. Disillusioned, he realized that all ideologies, of whatever brand, were just smokescreens for the central motive – domination and power, as well as the desire to enjoy the benefits of power.

Pareto's social observations were the basis of his later ideas. One of them was that economic planning and economic forecasts, despite the logic inherent in them, could not pass the test of reality, because most human actions are governed by illogical, rather than logical considerations. Therefore, all forecasts based on rational economic reasoning were empirically doomed to failure.

In 1907 Pareto resigned the chair at Lausanne and moved to a place near Geneva. He suffered from heart problems, and nursed them surrounded by a dozen cats, an astounding library, a cellar full of excellent wines, and a cabinet stocked with fine liqueurs. His wife had left him in 1901, and since then he was living with a Frenchwoman whom he married only in 1923, after he was able to resolve the problem of divorcing his first wife (not a minor issue in Catholic Italy). During this period he wrote his book, *Trattato di sociologia generale* (*Treatise on General Sociology*),[73] published in 1916, in the midst of the First World War. In this book he claimed that ideologies are rationalizations that people make up for irrational actions. And indeed, today economists accept that irrationally-motivated actions are an important driving force in economics. In 2002, Daniel Kahneman received the Nobel Prize in economics on his research (in collaboration with Amos Tversky, who died before the Prize was awarded), on irrational decision making in economics.

Pareto's theory on irrational motives attracted many fascists. When Mussolini and the fascists grabbed power in Italy, Pareto, in his sickbed, muttered sadly, "I told you so." He was unhappy about this, but his disapproval did not prevent the fascists from bestowing honors upon him; they even appointing him as senator. He rejected most of the honors, but spoke favorably about some of the reforms that were made. Nonetheless, he warned against tyranny, censorship and economic incorporation. When the fascists decreed against freedom of speech at the universities, he wrote a letter of protest.

In Mussolini's reign Pareto saw a transition period at the end of which, he believed, "pure" market forces would be released, since at first, Mussolini indeed had replaced public management with private initiatives, eliminated various taxes, gave preference to private-sector industrial development, and so on. Pareto died less than a year after Mussolini had come to power, before the more dreadful aspects of his rule became apparent. The fascists continued to use his writings as scientific justifications for their methods. Pareto's theories did not make an impression in his time, but gained prominence years later – mainly for what is known today as Pareto's law, or the 80:20 law (rule).

Polls and Economics – The Planck-Benford Distribution

We have observed a remarkable phenomenon: not only does the physical world behave according to thermodynamical statistics, but sociology too does so. In fact, the Planck-Benford distribution worked out above yields Benford's Law, which pertains to the distribution of digits, and also Zipf's law, which governs the distribution of links in network, words in texts, and even wealth among people (Pareto's law). The Planck-Benford distribution is a generalization of the Maxwell-Boltzmann distribution (the normal distribution) for systems where the number of particles can be greater than the number of available boxes.

We can extend this thermodynamic line of thinking even further: We intend to argue that even our thoughts (or more specifically, our opinions) are the result of the second law of thermodynamics. Since "thinking" is not a well-defined action, we shall reduce the concept of "thinking" into "the expression of an opinion," which will be further reduced to choosing among various answers to a specific question.

For the sake of simplicity, let us distinguish between two kinds of questions. The first is the kind of question that has an absolute answer. For example, it is accepted that the correct answer to how much is one plus one is two. If you disagree, people will probably say that you are either very stupid or very smart.

The second kind of questions is where the answer is a matter of a personal opinion. For example, what was the best movie produced last year? Obviously, not everyone will pick the same movie. Questions with non-definitive answers are also called polls.

Contrary to lottery drawings, which are random by definition, our opinions are the results of logical operations. We do not understand the considerations that lead any individual to make one decision or another, and usually we cannot be certain whether the decision finally made was correct or not. Moreover, it is difficult to apply the Planck-Benford statistics to the decision making processes of a single person in a way that is empirically verifiable, since a single person usually decides only once on any particular matter.

Therefore, the way to test our theory is by using polls, in which many participants choose their favorite answer out of a range of options. There are two reasons for this: (a) in polls, the number of choices, N (the boxes or nodes or words) is an integer; and (b) the number of participants, P (the particles or links or authors) is also an integer and much larger that the number of choices.

Polls are highly important in our lives, not only because so many countries in the world choose their leaders by popular vote which is in effect a poll, but also, and perhaps mainly, because in a free economy, goods, assets, and services are priced basing on the opinion of buyers as to their value: if more buyers are interested in certain goods, services or assets, the price gets higher. Take, for example, a book. A copy of a specific book (after it has been written and prepared for publication) is a commodity that can be printed on demand. The more people that want to read this book, the more copies are sold. Bookshops can then charge a higher price, which would increase their revenues as well as the publisher's, and hopefully the author's, too.

On the face of it, we would expect that the number of copies of a specific title sold would directly reflect its quality. In other words, if title A is a thousand times better than title B, it should sell one thousand times more copies. Yet this is an unrealistic expectation, for a number of reasons: first, we do not know for certain that title A *is* regarded as better than title B in everyone's opinion; and second, even if we knew that it is better, there is yet no criterion for evaluating exactly *how much* better it is. Nevertheless, there is one quantitative measure for evaluating a title, which is simply the number of books sold – the bestsellers' list. Effectively, the number of copies sold is a kind of "vote" based on the considered opinion that each potential buyer uses in making a purchase. If nature worked this way, one would have expected the distribution of the number of books sold among the various titles to be random. We know, of course, that people do not buy books necessarily according to their quality, whatever "quality" means in this context. In fact, we buy a book before we read it! Thus, we can conclude that the number of copies of a book sold is a reflection not of *our* opinion, but rather the opinion of those who bought the book before us. However, those who bought the book before us also had not read it before buying, and so their opinion, too, is not reflected in their decision to buy.

How then do we decide which title to buy? Which politician to vote for? Where to go on vacation? Or what to watch on television?

It is not clear that this question has a clear-cut answer, and even though it is intriguing, it is not the focus of our discussion. However, polls, as we shall soon see, tend to obey the Planck-Benford statistics. Obviously, the Planck-Benford statistics do not tell us *which* title (or product, or political party) will be the hit that will enrich its copyright owners or sway the electorate. But it does tell us what the relative success of the second title will be compared with the first one – or more generally, it tells us what will be the distribution of books sold among of the various titles.

Predicting bestselling titles or predicting the next fashion trend, or as it is called in the industry, "the next big thing," is the holy grail of any entrepreneur. Is it possible? According to the second law of thermodynamics, it is *impossible*. The quantity that tends to grow is not the microstate itself, but rather the amount of uncertainty that accompanies it. The Planck-Benford distribution was derived under the assumption that the uncertainty of the system is at a maximum.

A dynamic financial system is characterized by inherent uncertainty. There is no economics without uncertainty. It is impossible to make money from the knowledge that the sun rises in the morning and sets in the evening; however, the stability of the earth under our feet, which is not certain, does provide an opportunity for making money: Insurance companies are doing exactly that. Think what would happen should NASA announce that in one year's time Earth will be struck by a massive, unstoppable meteorite: It is conceivable that in the course of the year between announcement and impact, civilization will exterminate itself without the help of that meteorite. The very existence of civilization is based on both the expectation of continuity and on uncertainty. It is reasonable to assume that we want to know the future only in terms of probability. Most people would not want to live out their life counting down toward a known date of death.

Economics means business, and business means risk management under uncertainty, or in other words, entropy. A best-selling title may have been a success because it was good, but it also had to tackle a number of hurdles put up by chance and luck. The first one is a review by an editor at the publishing house. Would the greatest Hebrew poets have made it? Not necessarily. "*O Bird*," Chaim Nachman Bialik's first published poem (1892), is considered a masterpiece of Hebrew poetry. Googling "O Bird" + Bialik (in Hebrew) brings up more than one hundred thousand links. In the Hebrew Wikipedia there is an entry dedicated just to this one poem. Every schoolchild knows by heart its first stanza – "Welcome back, O lovely bird, returning from warm climes to my windowsill..." (it was written when the poet still lived in Russia) – and possibly the next one. Problem is, there are 18 stanzas in all, which hardly anyone would recognize beyond the first and second ones. According to an apocryphal but funny story, in the 1990s an Israeli journalist sent out the last five (and virtually unknown, except to a few scholars) stanzas of this immortal masterpiece, under a pseudonym, to the literary supplements of all the daily newspapers in Israel. Each and every editor summarily rejected it, except for one, who happened to be familiar with the poem from beginning to end (even the unexpected does, sometimes, occur). This editor's answer was: "Welcome back, O Chaim Nachman Bialik, returning from the dead."

In 1988, British mountaineer Joe Simpson wrote a book called *Touching the Void*, about an incident in which he was almost killed while climbing the Andes in Peru. The book was not an impressive success. Ten years later, Random House published John Krakauer's book, *Into Thin Air*, which also tells of a climbing tragedy. This book became a sensational bestseller. And then, surprisingly, the sales of *Touching the Void* began to increase too. Random House, recognizing the trend, printed a new edition and promoted this book alongside Krakauer's. Sales grew even more. The new edition was on the *New York Times'* Bestsellers' list for fourteen weeks. At the same time, a docudrama of Simpson's book was released on television, and the sales of *Touching the Void* now doubled those of Krakauer's. In retrospect, it is possible to explain the dynamics that led to the sales of these two titles, but it is obvious that it could not have been foreseen.

In the city of big business, New York, millions of dollars are invested in Broadway productions. The night after a production's debut, the reviews come out – and in many cases, the cast is summarily dismissed. Is it possible that a tiny heartburn pill taken in advance by the reviewer of the *New York Times* would have saved the investment?

The most prestigious award in the world is the Nobel Prize. It is hard not to admire the Royal Swedish Academy of Sciences (RSAS) for doing a wonderful branding job over the years for their prize, and there is no doubt that most of its prestige is due to the outstanding achievements of those who have received it: the crème de la crème. And yet, Boltzmann never won the Nobel, even though Planck (who was a recipient) highly recommended him. Neither Gibbs nor Shannon were honored in this particular way. We shall not try to list the names of scientists who *did* win the prize, but whose work, as seen today, had been marginal at best, and sometimes even erroneous. It is not our aim to deride the work of the RSAS, just to point out that chance and luck are inevitable, even in the best-informed decisions made within systems operating at the uppermost professional level.

These were just a few examples of the first stages on the way to success, namely passing through the "filter of luck." Is it possible to estimate with certainty the value of a work of art? It can be presumed that the value of a painting by *avant garde* artist Jackson Pollock (1912-1956) climbed dramatically after someone in Hollywood decided to make a movie about him. Would that someone have made a movie about Pollock had he not been so eccentric? Was the movie successful only because the quality of Pollock's art? It is impossible to tell.

It is reasonable to assume that if you had written something good and then jumped off the top of the Eiffel Tower, this act will benefit the sales of the book (and enrich the beneficiaries of your will). Even if the book was not very good, but you went on to commit some cruel and unusual crime, you may be remembered sufficiently to increase its sales significantly. On July 21st, 356 BC (entirely by coincidence, the date of Alexander the Great's birth), a Greek called Erostratos set fire to the Temple of Diana in Ephesus, one of the seven wonders of the ancient world, and burned it to the ground. Erostratos never tried to hide his crime, on the contrary, he declared publicly that it was he who had burnt the temple – in order that his name be remembered by history. The Ephesians had him executed, and even proclaimed that anyone who uttered his name would be punished by death, but this did not help. Erostratos achieved his goal, and history does indeed remember his name. About 2,300 years later, Mark David Chapmann gave a similar reason for his assassination of John Lennon, and his name, too, is remembered by many. Brutus won a place in history for the murder of Julius Caesar, and John Wilkes Boothe for the murder of President Lincoln, and so forth. We do not need to check the Internet to know who assassinated JFK. His name is well-remembered, better than for instance the guy who invented Teflon, for example – what's his name? (Oh, yes, Roy J. Plunkett.) It is not surprising that it is in the United States, where fame can be cashed in at the best exchange rate, that the most outstanding crimes are committed.

It is thus clear that our decision-making on subjects which are not absolutely defined is a process in which chance plays a major part. Presumably, the probability that an Iraqi will think Mohammad a more important prophet than Jesus is very high, and equally, an Italian will think that the opposite is true. Being born in a country where almost everybody believes in Mohammad, as compared to being born in a country where almost everybody believes in Jesus is a purely probabilistic process. And if the second law of thermodynamics states that the number of microstates tends to increase to a maximum, we should therefore be able to calculate the most stable distribution between prophets, even though we shall not be able to tell which one will be the more popular. Let us now examine the Planck-Benford distribution using a concrete example. A recent poll in Israel asked respondents to complete the sentence "The greatest incentive for me is...", and got the following distribution:

cash, here and now – 59% of the respondents;

promotion, credit and responsibility – 23%;

personal development and creativity – 18%.

The results we would expect from a distribution based on the second law of thermodynamics would be:

$$\rho(1) = \frac{\ln 2}{\ln 4} = 0.5, \ \rho(2) = \frac{\ln 1.5}{\ln 4} = 0.29, \ \rho(3) = \frac{\ln(1.3333)}{\ln 4} = 0.21$$

In other words, in equilibrium we should expect that 50% of the respondents will choose answer (1), 29% will pick answer (2), and the remaining 21% will give answer (3) – a result which is fairly close to the actual poll cited above.

Obviously, the theoretical distribution has nothing to do with the meaning of the questions asked, or the answers given. As we can see, that the answers in this particular case deviate somewhat from the theoretical expectation, giving a greater emphasis to the preference for money; this can be explained as a reflection of our materialistic society. However, if we took numerous polls with different questions, we may expect the average to be in very close agreement with the Planck-Benford distribution, since the effects of culturally biased or any other deviation, in any individual poll, will tend to cancel each other out. The following table and illustration present the average of eight three-choices polls, each answered by 1,500 respondents each. And indeed, we can see that the agreement is much better.

	1	2	3	4	5	6	7	8	Average Distribution	Theoretical Distribution
Ques. 1	55%	39%	47%	64%	46%	56%	65%	47%	52%	50%
Ques. 2	32%	38%	31%	20%	37%	30%	19%	33%	30%	29%
Ques. 3	13%	23%	22%	17%	17%	15%	16%	19%	18%	21%

Figure 10. The combined results of eight polls on various subjects, answered by about 1,500 respondents each, show that the average distribution of answers is in good agreement with the theoretical distribution.

Figure 11. A graphic presentation of Figure 10's results. The solid line shows the actual distribution, and the dashed line, the theoretical distribution obtained by maximizing Shannon's entropy.

In conclusion, let us revisit bubbles. A common phenomenon, bubble formation actually reflects a tendency to disequilibrium, and this is also significant to the present discussion.

In equilibrium, the number of microstates is at a maximum and is therefore characterized by a non-uniform distribution. The thermodynamic distribution in equilibrium may sometimes resemble a bell-like curve, as we saw in the case of ideal gases, and sometimes it has a long tail. A poll distribution in which most respondents think alike is analogous to a network in which all nodes are connected to a single central node (a star-shaped network). This type of network is not in equilibrium, because the entropy is not at a maximum. Similarly, a network in which every node has an equal number of links is not in equilibrium. A network in disequilibrium is an unstable one, and hence strives to reach equilibrium. That is to say, the second law of thermodynamics "dislikes" uniformity, as in polls which show that everyone thinks alike. By the same token, it does not favor situations where each idea has an equal number of supporters. We can pursue this analogy one step further, and say that while the second law of thermodynamics dislikes dictatorship, it also dislikes anarchy.

Bubble formation is an essential stage in the development of large networks, since bubbles tend to combine eventually and become a larger network. Occasionally, however, a natural desire for communication may lead to the formation of suicidal bubbles. An astounding example of a suicidal bubble is a school of herrings attacked by a killer whale. Contrary to any logic, as an outside observer may see it, the school converges into a sort of virtual ball, in which each fish swims at amazing speed in a path wondrously synchronized with all other herrings. But then the whale opens its mouth and "poof!" – about thirty percent of the herrings are swallowed at once. Obviously, a herring that distanced itself from the school at such a time would greatly increase its chances of survival. After all, even a not too hungry person, armed with just a roll and a hard-boiled egg, would rather chase several herrings rather than a solitary one.

Are humans smarter than herrings? It seems that occasionally people do behave like a school of herrings. One of the more appalling examples history provides is the German Third Reich. Germany, a cradle of rational culture, the birthplace of many of the ideas discussed in this book, entered in the third decade of the twentieth century into a tailspin that ended up in a way not dissimilar to a school of herrings which forms a ball when a whale approaches it. Astonishingly (from the standpoint of the tendency for pluralism in nature according to the second law of thermodynamics) an entire nation united, democratically and almost unanimously, around the disastrous ideas of Adolf Hitler – just like those herrings. The usual range of ideas that existed when it was a plural society disappeared almost at once. This disappearance of pluralism – a result of equilibrium derived from the maximization of the number of microstates – dragged the human race into inconceivable horrors and slaughter. Germany's departure from internal equilibrium, as a result of developments which took place after the First World War (the harsh terms imposed by the peace agreement, the world-wide economic depression, and the rise of communism in Europe), which can be depicted as analogous to the whale that stirred the school of herring out if its equilibrium.

In economics, "bubbliness" is a motive force. Wherever a consensus develops among investors about the desirability one thing or the other – say, a new technology, or a wondrous invention – a bubble is likely to form. The most well-known bubble in economics is perhaps the gold rushes that took place in the US, Canada, Australia, South Africa and elsewhere in the 19th century. An enormous wave of immigration developed following the spread of rumors about rich gold deposits in remote areas. For many of these gold-diggers the result, so poignantly depicted in Charlie Chaplin's film *The Gold Rush*, was eating their scruffy shoes.

We all recall the Internet bubble. Without a doubt, the importance of the invention of the World Wide Web was second only to the invention of the printing press (which is considered by many to be the greatest invention of the second millennium). Around 1999, it became widely believed that most of the trade will soon move into the Internet, that Internet services will be free, and that the main source of income for Internet services providers will come from advertising. Therefore, the way television ratings determine profits, the number of hits on a site will determine the cost of advertisement, and consequently the site's profitability. The obvious conclusion drawn was that creating a "sexy" Internet site, to attract numerous hits, was the path to wealth. The excitement about the new network technology was justified in itself, and led to a consensus concerning its glorious future – but at the same time, many excited people tended to ignore the fact that a business model based on selling advertisement is inherently constrained (for instance, by the amount of money people are ready to spend for content, as well as by the low technological barrier in which competitors could enter). No less important was this simple logical truth: it is impossible for everybody to get rich from the same resource.

In spite of all this, anything that had something to do with the Internet was assessed at astronomical prices. High tech shares skyrocketed. In a sense it looked like a pyramid scheme, where no actual profits are necessary in order to get rich, as long as enough people are joining in, pouring ever more money into the pot; of course, there comes a moment when the number of people wanting to realize their profits is greater than the number of new participants (such a moment is inevitable in any finite-sized system). Then prices plummet, and existing investors rush in to realize whatever profits left to be had, and finally make every effort to cut their losses. And indeed, high-tech stock quotations started spiraling down during 2000, creating a sort of bubble within bubble – a bubble that came into being from the new aversion to high-tech stocks. Finally, in 2001, the share prices of technological companies and associated sectors collapsed in a way the market could not recover from for a whole decade. The collapse was not the result of disappointing technology. On the contrary, Internet technology continued to be overwhelmingly important. Even the aforementioned problematic business model was not the cause of the collapse. The bubble burst was a result of bubbliness itself, that is to say, of the pyramid mechanism that produced profits from the very rush on high tech shares, caused by a consensus that did not maximize the entropy.

Take another example: sometimes house prices go up, sometimes down. An increase in house prices reflects one and only one fact: demand is greater than supply. Accordingly, a drop in prices reflects the fact that more people want to sell than buy. Thus, fluctuations in the housing market indicate that the numbers of potential buyers and sellers vary in time: there are times when it is considered worthwhile to buy a house (and lo and behold, the prices go up) and there are times when buying a house is considered a bad idea (and sure enough, the prices drop). In fact, price increases and decreases are both bubbles. In equilibrium, the price of a house reflects the potential profit it may yield or the costs of building it, and price fluctuations should be negligible. In periods of equilibrium, house price dynamics will only reflect local changes in supply as certain areas become more or less desirable, rather than an overall rise or fall in demand, such as sometimes happens.

Sharp changes in prices based on consensus are bubbles, whereas in equilibrium, opinions are distributed so that the number of possibilities is at a maximum.

The problematic nature of economic prediction is rooted in bubbles. Anyone who can predict price fluctuations have his or her future assured, since all they have to do in order to get rich is to apply the age-old formula: buy low, sell high. And in fact, there are some who succeed in doing this. As we saw in the discussion of the distribution of wealth, the distribution of success is also determined by the second law of thermodynamics.

Conclusion

We have traveled a long way – from Carnot to Shannon – toward understanding of entropy and the second law of thermodynamics, which states that entropy can never decrease, and tends only to increase. Our journey began with Carnot, who derived the expression for the maximum efficiency of a theoretical machine that produces mechanical work from the spontaneous flow of energy from a hotter object to a colder one. Next, Clausius identified entropy in Carnot's efficiency equation, and gave it its definition: heat divided by temperature. Clausius also formulated the second law of thermodynamics, which says that all systems tend to reach equilibrium, a point where entropy is at a maximum.

A huge breakthrough in the understanding of entropy was independently made by Boltzmann and Gibbs, who showed that the entropy of a statistical system is proportional to the logarithm of the number of distinguishable arrangements in which it may be found. Each possible arrangement of a system is called a microstate, and since every system, at any given moment, can only be in one microstate, the entropy thus acquires the meaning of uncertainty. This is because if a system is in one particular but unknown to us microstate, the more microstates possible, the greater the uncertainty. Thus the second law of thermodynamics obtained a new meaning: Every system tends to maximize the number of its microstates and its uncertainty.

How does nature maximize the number of microstates? If we consider an ideal gas as an example, its energetic particles are distributed among the possible locations (states) within a system in a way that maximizes the number of microstates. The distribution in which the number of microstates is at a maximum is called the equilibrium distribution.

We examined two important distributions that are common in nature: one kind, an exponential one, occurs in systems where the number of particles is smaller than the number of states – for example, the distribution of the energy of particles of gases, or the distribution of heights among peoples. These distributions (graphically depicted by bell-like curves) favor the average. Another kind includes power-law distributions (graphically, these are long-tailed curves), which occur in systems where the number of particles is greater than the number of states. These distributions allow much greater divergence from the average and are observed, for example, in the classical limit to the energy distribution of black body radiation and in the distribution of wealth.

Up to that point, we have reviewed the contributions to the understanding of entropy made by Carnot, Clausius, Boltzmann, Gibbs, Maxwell and Planck. Their works were carried out between the early 19th century and the early 20th century, during the golden age of the physical sciences.

Later on it was also shown that the uncertainty associated with data transmission, such as receiving a computer file, is in fact the file's entropy. This entropy is named after Shannon, who was the first to calculate it. How is Shannon's entropy different from the entropy of, for example, a container full of gas? The difference is due to the fact that a digital file is transmitted by electric or electromagnetic harmonic oscillators. The oscillators used to transfer files are much hotter than their surroundings – that is, they have a lot of energy. As we saw, when an oscillator is very hot, its entropy is independent of its energy and has a value of one Boltzmann constant. In such cases, as in digital transmissions, where the entropy of a file is not a function of its energy, we call it logical entropy. By way of analogy, one plus one is always two, regardless of the amount of energy each digit one may have. This contrasts with oscillators (such as the molecular oscillators in a gas, for example) whose temperature is closer to the environment's, such that a change in the oscillator's energy leads to a change in its entropy. It thus follows that if oscillators whose temperature is closer to the environment were used to transfer files, any change in the energy of the file during transmission would affect its entropy. Since it is impossible to transfer files without losing energy during transmission, content transfer using oscillators with a temperature similar to their surroundings is inefficient.

If the laws of thermodynamics also apply to logic, they should be observed in logical distributions. And indeed, based on this assumption, we showed how the non-uniform distribution of digits in random numerical files, such as balance sheets, logarithmic tables and so forth (Benford Law), does, indeed, obey the second law of thermodynamics. This distribution we call the Planck-Benford distribution, after Planck who first calculated it and Benford who discovered this distribution in numerous databases.

We next examined the effects of the Planck-Benford distribution in social systems, and we found it in many networks, such as social, transportation and communication networks. All these networks are generated by a spontaneous linking of nodes. The invisible hand that distributes the links among nodes is entropy, namely, the tendency of spontaneous networks to increase the number of microstates. Calling the relative number of links a rank, we saw that texts obey Zipf's law, which states that the product of the rank and the frequency of any word in a long enough text is constant. In other words, nodes with many links appear less frequently, and nodes with few links appear more frequently.

We explored the distribution of wealth and saw a surprising result: When particles (coins) are distributed among states (people), such that every microstate has an equal probability, a highly non-uniform distribution is obtained (Perato's 80:20 rule), which is reflected in the distribution of wealth in free economies. In other words, there is a high probability that a small number of randomly chosen individuals will have huge amounts of money, whereas most individuals will have to make do with much less – a counterintuitive result in view of our equal probability starting point, yet all too familiar in real life. No less surprising, we saw that surveys and polls tend to obey the same Planck-Benford statistics.

Is our thinking also influenced by the second law of thermodynamics? Let us rephrase the question: do we humans aspire to increase the number of possibilities (microstates) at our disposal? Business people will certainly agree without hesitation, and even go so far as to add that anyone who does not act in this way is a sucker. To reinforce this point, let us tell an anecdote we heard on Israeli radio by author and journalist Amnon Dankner.

Dankner was good friend of another author, Dan Ben-Amotz. Ben-Amotz's personal philosophy was based on his firm belief that nobody should give anybody something for nothing. This philosophical school is also known as "penny-pinching." One day, while Ben-Amotz was on an extended stay in New York, Dankner paid him a visit, and the two went for breakfast in an inexpensive eatery. When Dankner saw the paltry bill, he offered to pick up the tab. To his surprise, Ben-Amotz frowned. Now, had Ben-Amotz been your typical cheapskate, his reluctance when offered a free meal would have been peculiar indeed. But, as mentioned, Ben-Amotz was something of a philosopher, and his explanation for rejecting the offer was this: the next time they would dine together, the place would probably be classier, hence the bill would be larger, and since it will be his turn to pick up the tab, this morning's "free meal" would eventually cost him more.

Unconvinced, Dankner did some back of envelope calculations and showed Ben-Amotz that even if he (Ben-Amotz) would always end up paying for the more expensive meals, it would not cost him more than fifty dollars over a whole year. So he asked him: "Why does this bother you so much?" (Ben-Amotz was a man of means.) Ben-Amotz answered: "I hate being a played for a sucker." And then Dankner asked him a really profound question: "Why is it so important to you not to be played for a sucker?"

The rest of the story has nothing to do with the topic at hand, that is, why do we so hate to feel that we are suckers? But we shall continue with it anyway, so as to not leave it unfinished.

Ben-Amotz's answer, which came after a long reflection, was: "Let me think about it." Dankner himself, so he said, totally forgot about it as soon as the meal was over. But four years later, Ben-Amotz, on his deathbed at home, called for Dankner. When Dankner arrived, Ben-Amotz, his remaining strength almost spent, whispered: "Do you remember that you asked me why I hate so much being a sucker?" Dankner nodded. And Ben-Amotz told him: "I don't know."

Any one of us sometimes does things which are plainly irrational because of this aversion to being a sucker. Kahneman and Tversky[74] discussed the illogical economic decisions that people make just because of loss aversion. But before turning to loss aversion, we must deal with a more fundamental question: Why do we want to get richer and richer? This is an interesting question, because we always seem to want more money than we have, no matter how much we actually have. It seems that no amount of money can satisfy our hunger for even more money – as opposed to food: everybody understands that there is no need to have infinite amounts of it.

If we interpret a microstate as an option, we can understand that money increases the number of options open to us. The greater the budget, the greater the selections of products we can choose from as best suits us. Therefore, our desire to increase the number of options open to us is an outcome of entropy's tendency to increase.

Let us return now to Ben-Amotz and to his grumpiness at Dankner's offer to pay for his meal. According to Ben-Amotz's reasoning, what Dankner did was reduce the number of options open to Ben-Amotz in the future: declining the offer, it would be up to him whether or not to invite Dankner for a meal later on; accepting it, only one of these options would be left. In general, receiving an expensive gift may make us feel distressed because we become indebted to the giver. Suppose you are celebrating your only son's Bar-Mitzvah. You invite your good friend, who happens to have two sons, ages eleven and twelve, and he gives the boy a present worth one thousand dollars. Chances are you may feel somewhat like Ben-Amotz because now your allegedly good friend has reduced the number of options open to you upon receiving successive invitations to his sons' Bar-Mitzvahs. His present actually cost *you* one thousand dollars! What a dreadful man.

Reducing the number of options available to us thus means a net loss. Every system in nature "wants" to increase its entropy, that is, the number of options available to it. But reducing the entropy of a system is possible only by applying work (power) from the outside.

Freedom, then, is the ability to choose at will from the greatest number of options available to us. In other words, entropy is freedom; and the equal opportunity (rather than equality *per se*) that maximizes the number of options available is the second law of thermodynamics. When the number of options available to us is infinite, choice becomes random and the microstate in which we exist is our fate that is determined by God's game of dice.

Appendices

Appendix A-1

Clausius's Derivation of Entropy from Carnot's Efficiency

Clausius realized that it is possible to rewrite Carnot's efficiency,

$$\frac{W}{Q} \leq \frac{T_H - T_L}{T_H},$$

in a slightly different way, namely,

$$\frac{Q}{T_H} \leq \frac{Q - W}{T_L},$$

where Q is the heat removed from the hotter object (let us designate it Q_H) and $Q - W$ is the heat transferred to the colder object (designated Q_L). Now Carnot's inequality can be written as

$$\frac{Q_L}{T_L} - \frac{Q_H}{T_H} \geq 0.$$

The meaning of this inequality is that the energy absorbed by the colder object, divided by the temperature of the colder object, is always higher than the energy removed from the hotter object divided by the temperature of the hotter object. In the case of reversible action, the two ratios are equal. Namely, the entropy that is generated in the colder object is always greater than the entropy that is reduced in the hotter object, except in the case of reversible action, where the system is in equilibrium and the two entropies are equal, namely:

$$\frac{Q_L}{T_L} = \frac{Q_H}{T_H}.$$

Clausius called the quantity $\frac{Q}{T}$ in equilibrium "entropy," and designated it S. Strictly speaking, since Q is energy in transit (like work, heat is energy that is added or removed), S designates the change of entropy. Thus, in general,

$$S \geq \frac{Q}{T}.$$

Appendix A-2

Planck's Derivation of Boltzmann's Entropy

Working under the assumption that the "atomic hypothesis" was correct, Boltzmann wanted to find out the statistical meaning of entropy. He built a model of an ideal gas consisting of "billiard ball" particles involved in elastic collisions, in which no kinetic energy is lost. To find such a system's entropy, we have first to calculate the number of different states in which the system can be found. In figure 12 we have a schematic vessel, with N states and P particles. Although in the figure below we show only the spatial location, the word "state" refers to a particle, its velocity (its speed and direction) as well as location. We assume that the number of particles is much smaller than the number of states, namely, $P \ll N$. Therefore, we may neglect the probability of two particles occupying the same state. The number of different ways to arrange the particles in the states in this case is

$$\Omega = \frac{N!}{P!\,(N-P)!}$$

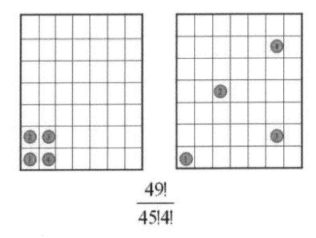

$$\frac{49!}{45!4!}$$

Figure 12: Two possible ways for arranging 4 particles in 49 boxes.

The first particle can be placed in any of the 49 boxes. The second particle can be placed in one of only 48 boxes; therefore it is possible to place two particles in 49 × 48 ways. However, since the particles are identical, the number of different configurations must be divided by 2. The third particle can be in any of 47 different boxes, and the number of identical configuration is 2 × 3, so the number of different ways will be $\frac{49 \times 48 \times 47}{2 \times 3}$, and so on. In mathematics, we define n factorial as $n! \equiv n \times (n - 1) \times ... \times 2 \times 1$. Therefore, the number of different ways to put 4 particles into 49 boxes is $\frac{49 \times 48 \times 47 \times 46}{4 \times 3 \times 2} = \frac{49!}{4!(49-4)!}$.

Each different way to distribute P particles over N states is called a configuration. In statistical thermodynamics it is called a microstate.

A microstate is one arrangement of a system that can be distinguished from any other arrangement of that system. The total number of the microstates is designated Ω, and Boltzmann assumed that each microstate in a system in equilibrium has an equal probability.

Let us now calculate the relation between entropy and the number of microstates. We use the extensivity (additive) property of entropy, and assume that the system's entropy, S, is related to the number of microstates, Ω , such that $S = f(\Omega)$. We want to find the function f. To do so, we take a vessel, A, similar to the one described in figure 12. Now, we put another vessel, B, next to vessel A. The particles cannot transfer between the vessels. Total entropy will be

$$S = S_A + S_B = f(\Omega_A) + f(\Omega_B).$$

Since each microstate of vessel A can coexist with all the microstates of vessel B, the total number of the microstates is $\Omega = \Omega_A \times \Omega_B$. Therefore,

$$f(\Omega_A \times \Omega_B) = f(\Omega_A) + f(\Omega_B).$$

This equation is a simple mathematical problem. The function that solves it is the logarithmic function multiplied by a constant k:

$$S = k \ln\Omega.$$

The value of constant k, known today as Boltzmann's constant, was calculated empirically using the gas laws, and is one of the important constants of nature. This expression of entropy is an essential tool in calculating the distributions of statistical systems (such as ideal gases, see Appendix A-4.)

Appendix A-3

Gibbs's Entropy

As we saw in the appendix A-2, the Boltzmann entropy is based on two assumptions: first, that the entropy of two adjacent vessels is the sum of the entropies of both vessels, and second, that the total number of the microstates of the two vessels is the product of the number of microstates of each of them.

We obtained entropy as $S = k \ln\Omega$, were k is Boltzmann's constant and Ω is the number of microstates. Gibbs's question was, what will be the entropy of a single microstate? The entropy value of a single microstate depends on the number of microstates. If a system has Ω microstates, the probability of the system, in equilibrium, to be in a single microstate will be

$$p = \frac{1}{\Omega}.$$

If the number of microstates is greater than 1, there is some uncertainty, which increases the entropy. Since the entropy of a microstate is proportional to the logarithm of the probability, p, the entropy of a microstate is proportional to $\ln p \equiv \ln\frac{1}{\Omega}$.

The sum of the entropies of all the microstates should yield Boltzmann's entropy. Assuming that the entropy of a single microstate is $\phi \ln p$, ϕ is an unknown function that we seek to find. If all the microstates have equal probabilities, and since $\ln\frac{1}{\Omega} = -\ln\Omega$ by definition, then

$$S = k\ln\Omega = \Omega\phi\ln\frac{1}{\Omega}.$$

This means that $\phi = -k\frac{1}{\Omega} = -kp$ or the entropy of each microstate is $-kp \ln p$. If we allow each microstate have a different probability, p_i, than we obtain the expression known as Gibbs's entropy:

$$S = -k \sum_{i=1}^{\Omega} p_i \ln p_i.$$

The main advantage of Gibbs's entropy is our ability to assign a different probability to each microstate, and therefore to describe systems not in equilibrium. Perhaps it would be better to call this quantity – as Boltzmann and Shannon did – H; however, this expression is today called Gibbs's entropy. We discussed this point in the chapter on Shannon entropy and file compression.

Appendix A-4

Exponential Energy Decay and the Maxwell-Boltzmann Distribution

How is energy distributed among particles? All microstates, by definition, have equal energy. Also, in equilibrium, all microstates have the same probabilities and entropy is at a maximum. What we want is to calculate the distribution of energy among particles such that entropy will be at a maximum. First we express the entropy in terms of the probabilities of the particles in the various states. In a case where the number of particles is much smaller than the number of possible states, the number of microstates is

$$\Omega = \frac{N!}{P!\,(N-P)!}.$$

We can use Stirling's approximation, $\ln N! \cong N \ln N - N$. Let the probability of a particle being in a given state be $= \frac{P}{N}$. Then, Boltzmann's entropy is

$$S = k \ln \Omega \cong -Nk\{p\ln p + (1-p)\ln(1-p)\}.$$

One should not confuse the probability p in this equation, which is the probability of a state, with the microstate probability of Gibbs's entropy. To avoid confusion, let us use the index j for states:

$$S = -k \sum_{j=1}^{N} \{p_j \ln p_j + (1-p_j)\ln(1-p_j)\}.$$

Normally, when we want to find the minimum or maximum of a function, we determine where the slope with respect to a variable vanishes, namely, where

$$\frac{\partial f(p)}{\partial p} = 0.$$

The reason is because the slope of a function at its minimum or maximum is zero.

However, here we have to consider an additional point: we have a fixed amount of energy, Q, to distribute among the particles. Therefore we have to find the maximum S, taking into account that

$$Q = \sum_{j=1}^{N} p_j \varepsilon_j,$$

where ε_j is the energy of the state j or,

$$Q - \sum_{j=1}^{N} p_j \varepsilon_j = 0.$$

The last equation is called a constraint. We want to find the maximum of S under the constraint that the total energy in all the states is Q. Problems like this are usually solved using a technique called Lagrange multipliers, namely, by defining a function as follows:

$$f(p_j) = S(p_j) + \beta(Q - p_j \varepsilon_j).$$

This function is identical to the entropy since the second term is null. However, now the derivation contains another variable, β, called the Lagrange multiplier, which is related to the energy of the system.[23]

---

[23] In fact, one can also subtract the constraint. However the result thus obtained is not physically sound.

The derivation $\frac{\partial f(p_j)}{\partial p_j} = 0$ yields $\frac{p_j}{1-p_j} = e^{-\beta \varepsilon_j}$.

When $p_j \ll 1$, we obtain the so-called "normal distribution," namely,

$$p_j = e^{-\beta \varepsilon_j}.$$

Since all the microstates have the same energy, it is easy to see from the gas laws that $\beta = \frac{1}{kT}$.

Usually, we are interested in the relative energy of the state $\rho(\varepsilon_j)$. Therefore, we shall divide the probability of the energy ε_j by the total sum of states $Z = \sum_{j=1}^{N} p_j$.

The function Z, is called the partition function. Therefore,

$$\rho(\varepsilon_j) = \frac{e^{-\beta \varepsilon_j}}{Z} = \frac{e^{-\frac{\varepsilon_j}{kT}}}{Z}.$$

We see that as the energy of a state rises, its probability decreases exponentially. This is a typical behavior that is seen in many distributions in nature. In this case, the distribution of speeds of the gas particles is "Gaussian" (bell-like). The reason for this is that the speed of a particle (we are dealing with "billiard balls" particles) is related to its energy according to $\varepsilon = \frac{1}{2}mv^2$. When we add energy to the gas, it tends to flow to the colder particles. Only a very few particles can hold a lot of energy. The result is that exponential decay prefers average-energy particles, with just a few energy-rich ones. As we shall see later, this is not the only common distribution in nature.

Appendix A-5

The Temperature of an Oscillator

The molecules of an ideal gas exchange energy among them only by elastic collisions. The energy can be stored in the particles as translational energy, which changes the spatial location of the particles. It can also be stored in the rotational motion of the particles and in the vibrations of molecules along chemical bonds. Any movement that is independent of any other movement is called "a degree of freedom." For example, a particle in space has three translational degrees of freedom: up and down, left and right, and forwards and backwards. A degree of freedom is a microstate; therefore, in equilibrium, each microstate will have the same amount of energy as all other microstates.

If we take a single-atom ideal gas such as helium or neon, we shall see that in order to raise the average temperature by one kelvin, it is necessary to heat it by $\frac{3k}{2}$ joules per atom. If the molecule of a gas has two atoms, such as oxygen, nitrogen, or hydrogen, it is necessary to heat each molecule by $\frac{7k}{2}$ joules in order to raise the temperature by one kelvin. The conclusion is that each degree of freedom holds $\frac{kT}{2}$ Joules.

Why? A single-atom gas has three degrees of freedoms; therefore, its energy is $\frac{3k}{2}$ joules per kelvin, or $\frac{3kT}{2}$ joules in total. In a diatomic molecule there are, in addition, two rotational degrees of freedom. The third one, along the axis of the chemical bond, is negligible, as the atom's angular momentum is infinitely small because it is a point mass. Diatomic molecules have, in addition, vibration, and this vibration (this can be checked using polyatomic molecules) has kT energy. This is because the vibration contains both potential and kinetic energy, and each one of them contributes

$kT/2$ energy. We shall soon see that this result has important thermodynamical consequences. Moreover, it is also a result of Planck's black body equation.

Since thermodynamic considerations are universal, the result for a harmonic oscillator, $E = kT$, must always hold true. To demonstrate this, we can show that a harmonic oscillator – for example a mechanical pendulum – is a Carnot machine.

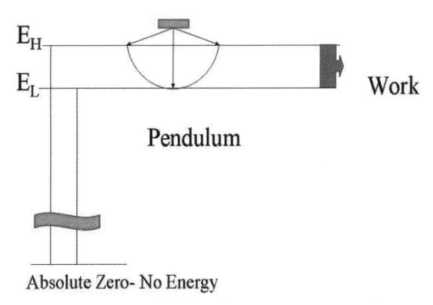

Absolute Zero- No Energy

Figure 13· A bob hanging by a rod moves from the point of maximum energy, E_H, to the point of minimum energy allowed by the rod, E_L, converting the energy difference, $E_H - E_L$, into mechanical movement (work) over and over. This is a periodic Carnot machine.

Pushing the bob by applying work, W, it will move up to its maximum height, which is

$$h = \frac{W}{mg},$$

where g is the gravitational force per unit mass that the earth applies at the altitude where the pendulum is placed. The bob also carries energy when it is at rest. This is a purely potential energy, due to the gravitational force. Part of the energy can be extracted by increasing the length of the rod: an operation equivalent to reducing the temperature of the colder reservoir in a classic Carnot machine.

The energy balance of the bob is $E_H = E_L + W$. It is possible to convert the movement of the bob into work by letting it collide with a mechanical gear or a wheel. The work obtained is $\leq E_H - E_L$. Since in any harmonic oscillator $E = kT$, we obtain

$$\frac{W}{E_H} \leq \frac{T_H - T_L}{T_H},$$

which is Carnot's efficiency. This derivation explains the analogy between the production of work by a waterfall, which interested Carnot's father, and Carnot's heat engine.

Figure 14: It is possible to produce work from a waterfall in an amount equal to the difference in the water's energy between the higher point, h_H, and the lower point, h_L. This analogy was known to Carnot and was pointed out in his book.

Appendix A-6

Energy Distribution in Oscillators

Planck was well versed in thermodynamics. He was the first to use both Boltzmann's entropy and Clausius's entropy in his solution for one of the most important problems in science, concerning black body radiation, namely, the distribution of the radiation energy among the radiation modes. Planck first assumed that the energy of the radiation is quantized, and then he asked how many microstates are possible if we have P quanta (today called photons) in N states (radiation modes). The answer is:

$$\Omega = \frac{(N + P - 1)!}{(N - 1)!\,P!}$$

$$\frac{(7+9-1)!}{(7-1)!\,9!}$$

Figure 15: Planck's distribution.

Contrary to the Maxwell-Boltzmann gas statistics, in which two atoms cannot be in the same state, Planck's statistics allows for several particles (photons) in the same state (radiation mode). Therefore, the number of permutations is the number of states plus the number of particles minus 1 factorial and not like in Maxwell-Boltzmann case the number of states factorial. Why? In the Maxwell-Boltzmann statistics, the first particle can be in N states, the second in $N - 1$ states, etc. In Planck's statistics, on the other hand, every particle can be in all N states. Therefore, every state can be identified also by the number of particles in it. That means that we can have $N + P$ different microstates, less one. This can be illustrated by an example: Suppose we have 1 state and 9 particles. If we do not subtract the 1, we obtain 10 microstates, instead of 1 which is the correct answer (there is obviously only one possible way to put 9 particles in one state).

For simplicity's sake, we shall not follow Planck's original calculations, but rather derive Planck's distribution using the Lagrange multipliers technique, as we did for the Maxwell-Boltzmann energy distribution derivation. We denote

$$n = \frac{P}{N}.$$

Here, n is the number of photons in a state (radiation mode). In the Maxwell-Boltzmann distribution, we called the same ratio p, from the word probability (as it was always smaller than 1). However, here it can be as large as P. Using Stirling's approximation, as before, we get

$$S = k \ln \frac{(N+P-1)!}{(N-1)!\,P!} \cong kN\{(n+1)\ln(n+1) - n\ln n\}.$$

Again, we can write this expression as a sum of the radiation modes:

$$S = k \sum_{j=1}^{N} \left\{ (n_j + 1)\ln(n_j + 1) - n_j \ln n_j \right\},$$

and again use the constraint regarding the fixed amount of energy,

$$Q = \sum_{j=1}^{N} n_j \, \mathcal{E}_j.$$

We define the function

$$f(n) = k\{(n+1)\ln(n+1) - n\ln n\} + \beta(Q - n\mathcal{E}),$$

find the maximum,

$$\frac{\partial f(n)}{\partial n} = 0,$$

and obtain

$$n(\mathcal{E}, \beta) = \frac{1}{e^{\beta \mathcal{E}} - 1}.$$

Planck then assumed that the energy of a particle of electromagnetic radiation is proportional to its frequency, ν, namely $\mathcal{E} = h\nu$, where h is a constant today called Planck's constant. Recall that $\beta = \frac{1}{kT}$. Therefore, we can write this highly important result:

$$n(\nu, T) = \frac{1}{e^{\frac{h\nu}{kT}} - 1}.$$

Thus, the equation for the spectral radiation energy emission of a black body is given by

$$Q(\nu, T) = n(\nu, T)Nh\nu.$$

From this equation, and based on Wien's displacement radiation law, Planck derived the value of h, and quantum mechanics took off.

When n is very large, the amount of energy that the photon carries is much smaller than the average energy of the radiation mode, kT, and one obtains

$$Q(v, T) = NkT,$$

which is the Rayleigh-Jeans law. When n is very small, one obtains the Maxwell-Boltzmann law,

$$Q(v, T) = Nhve^{-\frac{hv}{kT}}.$$

This calculation that Planck made was one of the most important calculations of science, so it deserves a verbal explanation too. Planck made two separate assumptions: (a) that energy is quantized and therefore it is possible to calculate entropy by maximizing the number of microstates; and (b) that the amount of energy in a quantum is proportional to its frequency. As we shall see later, a similar calculation can explain many social phenomena in our life.

Appendix B-1

File Compression

Let us examine a few examples of file compression.

Suppose Bob sends Alice a text file. Texts files are not random collections of words. In every language there are words that appear more frequently than others (as described by Zipf's law, discussed in Chapter 5 and in Appendix B-3). For example, in most texts, the probability of finding the word "if" is much larger than the probability of finding the word "epistemology." Bob knows the content of the file that he wants to send, and therefore he can calculate the minimum amount of bits required to transmit this content by composing a lookup table to compress the file. For example, if Bob wants to convey to Alice the day of his visit, he can construct a table in which Sunday=000, Monday=001, Thursday=011, etc. and send her a three-bit file.

Practically, file compression is not done this way. In order for Alice to decompress any file she receives, she needs some kind of universal tool. Moreover, for obvious practical reasons, it should be done transparently (without user intervention). Bob too does not wish to prepare and transmit an ad hoc lookup table every time he wants to send a message to Alice. This is the reason why most people use a multipurpose compression algorithm that works automatically on files of the same kind. For example, we use a ZIP algorithm to compress a text file and a JPG algorithm to compress picture files. JPG compression carries less content than that of the original file because our brain does not need all the details that appear in a raw image taken by a camera to comprehend a picture. In text transmission we have to compress the file in such a way that all its content will be fully preserved.

Not everyone is aware of the fact that when we talk over the telephone our voice is digitized and compressed in the handset; it is than transmitted to the listener, uncompressed in his handset, and the membrane in the handset vibrates then using the decompressed data in a way that mimics the vibrations of our original voice. All these operations are done transparently and automatically. File compression is very important in engineering because it saves money, and many engineers working in information technology are dealing with it. However, further discussion of this area is beyond the scope of this book.

There are three stages in any compression algorithms:

Bob goes through the file looking for redundant structures.

The file is rewritten as a random file such that the redundant structures will be much shorter than their original length. For example, if we have a file whose content is one million "1" digits, the file will be written as "1 × 1,000,000," and then sent to Alice.

Alice receives the compressed file, decompresses it using her table and thus reconstructs the original file.

Obviously, Bob and Alice must have the appropriate matching software. If Bob and Alice are conventional users, they can buy commercial software. Or Bob and Alice may prefer to program the software themselves in order to achieve higher compression efficiency for specific data or for the transmission of classified information.

When Alice receives an N-bit file, she obtains N bits of information, even if the file can be compressed into M bits. The reason is that she has no *a priori* knowledge about the file's content. Indeed, that is the connection between information theory and entropy: entropy is a quantitative expression of the lack of knowledge (uncertainty) that an observer of a physical system has, or equivalently, it is the lack of information that the receiver of a communication has. Bob, on the other hand, knows the content of the file and, if he wishes, he can compress it and send Alice an M-bit file.

For example, let us assume that Bob has a file that contains P "1"bits and $N - P$ "0" bits. The number of possible different files is:

$$\Omega = \frac{N!}{(N - P)!\,P!}.$$

By how much can this file be compressed into a random file, M bits in length, in which $\Omega = 2^M$?

We can find M from this equation:

$$2^M = \frac{N!}{(N-P)!\,P!}.$$

Using the Stirling formula, as we did in previous appendices, we obtain:

$$M \cong -\frac{N}{\ln 2}\{p\ln p + (1-p)\ln(1-p)\},$$

where $p = \frac{P}{N}$ is the fraction of the 1's in the file. If we use harmonic oscillators for transmission, we obtain that the entropy of the compressed file is $S = kM\ln 2$, where k is the Boltzmann constant.

Obviously, if p is not ½, then $M < N$, where M is the Shannon limit.

So, by taking an uncompressed file of length N and compressing it to the Shannon limit, we received a shorter file of length M, which is in thermodynamic equilibrium. When Alice receives an uncompressed file, all she knows is that its entropy, S, is $kN\ln 2$. However, in fact the file carries only $kM\ln 2$ entropy. Since in general $N \geq M$, we can write,

$$S \geq kM\ln 2,$$

which is Clausius's inequality.

Let us examine a numerical example: Alice is in the USA studying global warming. Bob, in Israel, is asked to send Alice the deviations from the average of the maximum daily temperatures in Tel Aviv in August. Since Bob and Alice know that the average daily maximum temperature in Tel Aviv in August is 30°C, they agree that Bob will send "1" when the temperature is higher than or equal to 30°C, or "0" if it is lower. Since there are 31 days in August, Bob transmits to Alice a 31-bit file with 31 bits of information.

What happens if Alice asks Bob to send her a file in which "1" represents the hottest day in August, and "0" for any other day in this month? Alice will again receive a 31-bit file that contains 31 bits of information. However, if we assume that there is only one "hottest" day in August, it is clear that Bob and Alice know that the file has less information, and therefore it can be compressed. The compression can be done in many ways. For instance, they can agree that Bob will send only the date of the hottest day. How many bits are required for sending the date? This can be found from $2^M = 31$, which means that they need 5 bits. The theoretical limit can be found in the expression for M that appears above, namely,

$$M \cong -\frac{31}{\ln 2}\left\{\left(\frac{1}{31}\right)\ln\left(\frac{1}{31}\right) + \left(1 - \frac{1}{31}\right)\ln\left(1 - \frac{1}{31}\right)\right\} \approx 4.9.$$

Practically, it is impossible to send fractions of bits, so Bob must send a 5-bit file, which is the intuitive result we got earlier.

This example demonstrates the confusion that the concept of entropy can cause. In the first case, Bob sent a 31-bit file. There was no *a priori* knowledge whether the maximum temperature in a certain day was above or below 30°C. Therefore, the file was in a state of equilibrium even if only one day (or no day!) had a temperature higher than 30°C.

In the second case, we did have *a priori* knowledge that only one day could have a maximum temperature. Therefore, the amount of uncertainty was smaller. The file was not in equilibrium and could be compressed to a 5-bit file in which every bit has an equal probability of being either 1 or 0.

Appendix B-2

Distribution of Digits in Decimal Files – Benford's Law

Let us calculate the distribution of digits in a decimal file that maximizes Shannon's entropy (i.e., the number of microstates). We shall calculate the distribution of P oscillators in N sequences, where a sequence is a digit, and the number of oscillators in it is the value of the digit. According to Planck, the number of microstates is,

$$\Omega = \frac{(N + P - 1)!}{(N - 1)! \, P!} .$$

Shannon's entropy is $S = \ln \Omega$. The number of oscillators in a sequence is $= \frac{P}{N}$, where n can be any integer from 1 to 9 (we are not interested in empty sequences). From the Stirling formula we obtain that

$$S \cong \sum_{n=1}^{9} \{(n + 1) \ln(n + 1) - n \ln n\} .$$

This equation is similar to Planck's equation. We designate $\varphi(n)$ as the number of digits having n oscillators (which is the number of digits, n, in the decimal file). We have a constraint on the total number of oscillators in the file, namely,

$$P = \sum_{n=1}^{9} n \varphi(n).$$

Therefore, the Lagrange equation will be

$$f(n) = S + \beta \left\{ P - \sum_{n=1}^{9} n\varphi(n) \right\}.$$

The extremum with respect to n is $\partial f(n)/\partial n = 0$, or

$$\varphi(n) = \frac{1}{\beta}\ln(1 + \frac{1}{n}).$$

In order to find the relative distribution of digits regardless of the length N of a file, we divide $\varphi(n)$ by the total number of digits:

$$N = \sum_{n=1}^{9} \varphi(n) = \frac{1}{\beta}\left\{ \ln\left(\frac{2}{1}\right) + \ln\left(\frac{3}{2}\right) + \cdots + \ln\left(\frac{10}{9}\right) \right\} = \frac{1}{\beta}\ln 10 \,.$$

In Appendix A-4 we divided the probability p_j of the particles having energy ε_j that we got from the Lagrange equation by the partition function $Z = \sum_j p_j$ to obtain the normalized distribution, $\rho(\varepsilon_i) = \dfrac{e^{-\beta\varepsilon_j}}{Z}$. The normalization here is analogous to the Maxwell-Boltzmann distribution, $(n) = \dfrac{\varphi(n)}{N}$.

In the present case, β, which is so important in classical thermodynamics ($\beta = \dfrac{1}{kT}$) disappears, and we obtain

$$\rho(n) = \log_{10}\left(1 + \frac{1}{n}\right).$$

This is Benford's law.

Appendix B-3

Planck-Benford Distribution – Zipf's law

According to Planck, the number of possible ways to distribute P links among N nodes is

$$\Omega = \frac{(N + P - 1)!}{(N - 1)! P!}.$$

Shannon's entropy is $S = \ln\Omega$. Since the numbers of links in a node is given as an integer, $n = \frac{P}{N}$, we can write the Lagrange equation as in Appendix B-2, namely,

$$f(n) = S + \beta \left\{ P - \sum_{n=1}^{N} n\varphi(n) \right\},$$

where $\varphi(n)$ is the number of nodes having n links, and the total number of links in the net is

$$P = \sum_{n=1}^{N} n\varphi(n).$$

The net includes only nodes that have at least one link (otherwise they would not be in it). The extremum of the Lagrange equation with respect to n is identical to the one obtained in Appendix B-2, namely,

$$\varphi(n) = \frac{1}{\beta} \ln(1 + \frac{1}{n}).$$

We shall count the total number of nodes as a function of n and β, namely $N = \sum_{n=1}^{N} \varphi(n)$:

$$N = \sum_{n=1}^{N} \varphi(n) = \frac{1}{\beta}\left\{\ln\left(\frac{2}{1}\right) + \ln\left(\frac{3}{2}\right) + \cdots + \ln\left(\frac{N+1}{N}\right)\right\} = \frac{1}{\beta}\ln(N+1),$$

and obtain the normalized distribution

$$\rho(n) = \frac{\ln\left(1 + \frac{1}{n}\right)}{\ln(N+1)}.$$

This extremely important expression is worth some discussion. It means that in an optimal network, the number of nodes with many links is lower than the number of nodes with fewer links. Or in other words, only a few nodes will have many links, whereas many nodes will have to make do with a few links. This is the equation responsible for all inequality in life: wealth, social networks, and hierarchical organizations such as armies, corporations, and companies, to name a few.

This derivation yields Zipf's law, which states that in many languages the most frequent word appears twice as often as the second most frequent one, and the second most frequent one will appear twice as often as the fourth most frequent one, etc. The expression $\varphi(n)$ may be rewritten as

$$n = \frac{1}{e^{\beta\varphi(n)} - 1}.$$

In the classical limit $n \gg 1$, $\beta\varphi(n) \ll 1$. In this case the equation above can be approximated as

$$n\varphi(n) \cong \frac{1}{\beta},$$

which means that the product of the number of links and the number of nodes (or in general, the number of particles multiplied by the number of boxes where there are many more particles than boxes) obeys the rule

$$\frac{\varphi(1)}{\varphi(2)} = \frac{\varphi(2)}{\varphi(4)} = \frac{\varphi(4)}{\varphi(8)} = \cdots = 2 .$$

This rule is known as Zipf's law.

Biographical Sketches

Frank Albert Benford (1887– 1948)

American electrical engineer and physicist. Graduate of the University of Michigan. Benford worked his entire life at General Electric; his main expertise was in optic metrology. In 1937 he developed an instrument to measure the refractive index of glass. He wrote more than 100 papers and had about 20 patents to his credit. Benford is mainly known for the law that bears his name, concerning the unequal distribution of digits in random lists of numerical data, which was first discovered by Newcomb by observing the wear and tear of logarithmic tables. Benford tried, unsuccessfully, to derive the law that now bears his name.

Dietrich Braess (1938 –)

German mathematician, professor at Ruhr University in Bochum, Germany. In 1986 he observed that in an optimal user-network, the addition of a link changes its equilibrium and reduces the efficiency of the network. A famous example: when a section of 42nd Street in New York City was closed, instead of the traffic congestion predicted by experts, the traffic flow actually improved. Similarly, when a new road was built in Stuttgart, Germany, traffic conditions worsened, and improved only after the road was closed to traffic. This phenomenon is now called "Braess's Paradox."

Anton Josef Bruckner (1824–1896)

Austrian musician, considered one of the most important post-romantic composers. He worked for a few years as an assistant teacher, gave private music lessons (Boltzmann was one of his students), and in the evenings, played the violin in village dances. He studied with Simon Schechter and Otto Kitzler until the age of forty. Only in his mid-forties was his talent recognized, and he achieved fame only in his mid-sixties. He composed symphonies and sacred choral works.

Henry Andrews Bumstead (1870-1920)

American physicist who worked in the field of electromagnetism. A student of Gibbs, he penned Gibbs's eulogy based on his personal acquaintance with him. He was a professor of physics at Yale University, and the director of its Sloane Physics Laboratory.

Robert Bunsen (1811–1899)

German chemist who worked at the University of Göttingen and conducted research into the emission spectra of heated elements. Along with Gustav Kirchhoff, he used spectroscopic methods to discover the elements cesium and rubidium. He developed analytic methods for studying gases, and was one of the pioneers of photochemistry. With technician Peter Desaga, he developed the Bunsen burner that is used in laboratories all over the world to this very today. The Bunsen burner produced hotter, clearer flame than any previous gas burner. Bunsen also developed the most effective antidote against arsenic poisoning. This research almost led to his own death from arsenic poisoning and he lost the use of one of his eyes.

Lazare Hippolyte Carnot (1801–1888)

French educator and politician, Sadi Carnot's younger brother. From 1815 (Napoleon's final defeat) until 1823, he lived with his father in exile in Magdeburg, Germany. His early interests lay in literature and philosophy, until he entered politics. In 1839, 1842, and again in 1846, he was elected to the Chamber of Deputies as deputy for Paris, representing the radical left wing. In 1848 he was appointed Minister of Education, and set out to organize the system of primary education. He proposed a bill calling for free compulsory education, but was forced to resign a short time later on a point of principle – he refused to hold any position which required taking an oath of allegiance to Emperor Louis Napoleon. From 1864 to 1869 he was a member of the republican opposition. He died three months after his son, Marie François Sadi Carnot, was elected to the presidency of the Republic. Among his writings was a two-volume memoire about his father, Lazare Nicolas Marguerite Carnot.

Anders Celsius (1701–1744)

 Swedish astronomer, professor at Uppsala University. His father and grandfather had both been professors of astronomy and mathematics. Celsius studied at Uppsala University, where his father taught; in 1730 he too began teaching there, and remained there till his death from tuberculosis in 1744, at the age of only forty two. Celsius is widely known for the metric temperature scale used in most of the world (with the notable exception of the United States, where the Fahrenheit scale is still used). His outstanding contribution was assigning the freezing and boiling points of water as the benchmark points of the scale (0° C and 100° C, respectively), after a series of meticulous experiments demonstrated that the freezing point of water is independent of latitude or atmospheric pressure, whereas the boiling point was dependent on atmospheric pressure. The results he obtained were amazingly accurate, even to modern day standards. In addition, Celsius formulated a rule for determining the boiling point of water when the barometric pressure deviated from the standard of one atmosphere. Actually, when Celsius proposed his temperature scale in 1742, it was upside down to today's scale : 0° was the boiling point of water, and 100° the freezing point. In 1745, one year after his death, his scale was reversed and became the current Celsius scale. It is worth noting that in 1730, Réaumur suggested another scale, based on the freezing and boiling points of water and divided into eighty degrees. There is evidence that in 1740 the Réaumur scale was divided into 100 degrees and was called centigrade, as it is called today; nevertheless, Réaumur's name was largely forgotten. In 1948, the General Conference on Weights and Measures adopted the Celsius scale as the standard, yet in 1956, it changed the standard to the Kelvin scale, in which 0° K is the absolute zero, but each unit (called kelvin) is still equivalent to a degree of the Celsius scale.

Carlo Cercignani (1939-2010)

Italian professor of theoretical mechanics at the Polytechnic Institute of Milan. A member of the Italian Academy (*Accademia dei Lincei*) and a foreign member of the French Academy of Sciences in Paris. The chairman of a number of international companies and committees in the field of mathematics, mechanics and space research. Won two medals for his achievements in mathematics, and an honorary doctorate from the Université Pierre et Marie Curie. He wrote and edited scientific texts, among them a book on Boltzmann entitled *The Man Who Trusted Atoms*.

Benoît Paul Émile Clapeyron (1799–1864)

French road and bridge engineer and an expert in the design of steam engines, who initiated and built the first railway line between Paris and Saint-Germaine. His work led him to take interest in the efficiency of the steam engines and Carnot's work. In his papers, he presented Carnot's work in a straightforward, graphic manner, while further developing the reversibility principle. His main contribution to thermodynamics was introducing Carnot's work, and thus giving a huge push to the development of the field. He also served as a professor in the Académie des Sciences in Paris.

Gabriel Daniel Fahrenheit (1686–1736)

Dutch inventor. Born in Poland to a well-to-do a merchant, but lived most of his life in the Dutch Republic. At the age of fifteen, after both his parents had died, he became an apprentice to a merchant in Amsterdam. Four years later he began working as a glassblower, and by 1714 had invented the first scientific thermometer, which contained alcohol. At some point, he decided to replace the alcohol with mercury. The scale that was later named after him was defined only ten years later, spanning 0 to 212 degrees. The 0° degree was the temperature of a brine solution, 32° was the temperature of a mixture of ice and water, and 100° was the human body's temperature, measured under the arm. He died, still a bachelor, in The Hague, Netherlands.

James David Forbes (1809-1868)

Scottish physicist and glaciologist who worked in the areas of heat conduction, seismology and the study of glaciers. He graduated from the University of Edinburgh, eventually becoming a professor there from 1833 to 1859, when he became president of the United College of St. Andrews. Already at the age of nineteen he had become a fellow of the Royal Society of Edinburgh, and four years later was elected to the Royal Society of London. His research on glaciers began in 1840, and after many observations in Switzerland and Norway, he surmised that a glacier is an imperfect liquid or a viscous body, that is pushed along the slopes as a result of the mutual pressure of its parts. During his expeditions, he also measured the boiling point of water at various altitudes. His data, published in 1857, is known in statistics as "the Forbes data."

Günther Hermann Grassmann (1809–1877)

German mathematician and physicist, known at the time mainly as a linguist, but today more appreciated as a mathematician. A paper on the theory of tides that he presented in 1840 included the first mention ever of what is known today as linear algebra, as well as the concept of vector space. In 1844 he published his masterpiece, a book on the foundations of linear algebra. In 1853 he published his theory on color mixing – the law of three colors – that is today named after him. In 1861 he presented the first axiomatic formalism of arithmetics using induction. Because his mathematical work did not earn any recognition in his lifetime, the disappointed Grassmann turned to linguistics. He published a dictionary, a collection of folk songs, translations, and more, and indeed was renown in this area. Only after his death were his mathematic methods slowly adopted, among others, by Gibbs.

Fritz Haber (1868–1934)

Jewish-German chemist, the 1918 Nobel laureate in Chemistry for his work on the synthesis of ammonia from its components. The importance of his work to the chemical fertilizer industry and to agriculture on the one hand, and to explosives and poison gases on the other, made him one of the greatest chemists of his time. From 1886 to 1891 he was a student of Bunsen's. Before Hitler's rise to power, Haber, a staunch German patriot, was at the forefront of his nation's science.

He was called "the father of chemical warfare" for his work on the development of chlorine and other poison gasses during World

War I. His wife, Clara Immerwahr, also a Ph.D. in chemistry, could not reconcile herself to his obsession for chemical warfare and committed suicide in the garden of their home the day Haber left for the Eastern Front to oversee the use of gas against the Russians. For the services to his country, he was greatly honored. In the 1920s, scientists at his institution had developed the insecticide Zyklon A which was later upgraded to Zyklon B, the gas used by the Nazis in their extermination camps. With Hitler's rise to power, Haber was stripped of all his rights and forced to leave Germany. He worked in Cambridge, England, for a short time and was considering a position at the Weizmann Institute in Israel, but could not find his place at either. One year after leaving Germany, in 1934, Haber died in exile from a heart attack. He did not live long enough to witness the use to which his invention was put to exterminate his own people, among them members of his immediate family.

Otto Hahn (1879–1968)

German chemist, the 1944 Nobel laureate in chemistry for his work on the fission of the atomic nucleus. He worked in close collaboration with Lise Meitner, a converted Jewess. Their professional collaboration began in 1907 and went on for thirty years; and their friendship lasted a lifetime. During the First World War, Hahn served until 1916 in Haber's special unit for chemical warfare, which developed, tested and produced poison gas for military purposes. In 1921 Hahn discovered a material that he named "uranium z" (the element protactinium) whose significance in nuclear physics became clear later. In 1924 Hahn was elected a full member of the Prussian Academy of Sciences. In 1938 he and Fritz Strassman published results of radiochemical experiments that indicated the presence of lighter elements among the products of the bombardment of uranium nuclei by slow neutrons. He sent these baffling results to Lise Meitner, who had escaped to Sweden from Nazi persecution, and she correctly interpreted them as nuclear fission. Otto Hahn opposed the Nazi dictatorship and assisted many others of his colleagues to flee Germany. He tried unsuccessfully to persuade Planck to enlist well-known professors to protest publicly the attitude of the Nazi regime towards Jewish scientists. As early as 1934, he resigned from the University of Berlin in protest over the dismissal of his Jewish colleagues Lise Meitner, Fritz Haber, and James Franck, yet remained on as the director of the Kaiser-Wilhelm Institute for Chemistry in Berlin (where he served from 1928 until 1946). In 1944 he was captured by the British, who suspected him of collaborating on the German nuclear bomb project, even though he had had no part in it. In November 1945, while he was still detained in England, he read in a newspaper that he had won the 1944 Nobel Prize in Chemistry. Hahn later returned to the then West Germany, where he again directed the Max Planck Institute for Chemistry (as the Kaiser-Wilhelm Society had been renamed) from 1948 to 1960. After World War II he became a relentless protester against the proliferation of nuclear weapons.

Sir William Rowan Hamilton (1805–1865)

Irish-English physicist, astronomer, and mathematician, who made many contributions to classical mechanics, optics and algebra. His greatest contribution was a reformulation of Newtonian mechanics, known today as Hamiltonian mechanics, which is central to electromagnetism and quantum mechanics. In mathematics, he is best known for discovering quaternions. Dublin-born Hamilton showed a rare aptitude for languages and at the age of thirteen already read Hebrew, classical and modern European languages, as well as Persian, Arabic, Hindustani, Sanskrit and Malay. When he was sixteen, he read Euclid's *Elements* and Newton's *Principia*. At the age of seventeen he began studying at Trinity College, Dublin, specializing in mathematics. There, in 1827 – when he was barely

22 – and had not yet graduated, he was appointed Professor of Astronomy. That same year he presented a theory of a single function, known as a "Hamiltonian" that unified and combined components of mechanics, optics and mathematics and is the basis of wave theory. In mathematics, he developed a maximization technique that, ironically, is now called Lagrange multipliers, extensively used in the appendices to this book. In 1837 he was knighted. He presented his quaternion (an expansion of complex numbers into four dimensions) in 1852. Many opposed his idea, but it was adopted by Tait, and Gibbs also made use of it. Today, quaternions are used in computer graphics, cybernetics and signal processing.

Werner Karl Heisenberg (1901–1976)

German physicist, the 1932 Nobel laureate in physics for his contribution to quantum mechanics. Alongside Niels Bohr, Paul Dirac and Erwin Schrödinger, he is considered one of the founding fathers of that field. He is especially known for his uncertainty principle in quantum theory. In addition, he contributed to nuclear physics, the quantum field theory and particle physics. With the rise of the Nazis to power, he was interrogated by the SS following criticism from members of the German physicists community, but his name was later cleared. He was one of the directors of the German atomic bomb project, which fortunately was never realized, and no one took seriously his claim after the war that he had deliberately sabotaged the project. He was arrested at the end of the Second World War and detained in England from 1945 to 1946. Upon his return to Germany, he became director of the Kaiser-Wilhelm Institute for Physics, which had been renamed later the Max Planck Institute for Physics and Astrophysics. Heisenberg directed the institute until 1970. He died of cancer in 1976.

Herman von Helmholtz (1821–1894)

German physician and physicist who made significant contributions to the fields of physiology and physics. In physiology, he calculated the mathematics of the eye and formulated theories on vision, on visual spatial perception and on color vision. In physics, he is well known for his law of the conservation of energy, and for his contributions to both electrodynamics and chemical thermodynamics. His work on conservation of energy in 1847 stemmed from his observations of the muscle's metabolism: he sought to show that energy was not lost during the movement of a muscle. Based upon the early works of Sadi Carnot, Émile Clapeyron and James Joule, he calculated the relationships between work, heat, light energy, electrical energy and magnetic energy, and treated them all uniformly. He became famous in 1851 for his invention of the ophthalmoscope, an instrument for examining the eye's interior. He also wrote about auditory perception and invented the Helmholtz resonator, which measures the intensity of various sounds. As a philosopher, he explored the philosophy of science, writing about the relation between the laws of perception and the laws of nature, on aesthetics, and on the civilizing power of science. In 1858 he was appointed Professor of Anatomy and Physiology at the University of Heidelberg. He continued, over the years, to probe deeper into physics, and in 1871 he left Heidelberg to receive the chair of physics at the University of Berlin. In 1888 he was appointed the first director of the Physico-Technical Institute in Berlin, where he stayed until his death.

Sir James Hopwood Jeans (1877–1945)

British mathematician, physicist and astronomer, one of the fathers of statistical mechanics and radiation theory. He was a partner in formulating the Rayleigh-Jeans Law which is the classic approximation of black body radiation. Despite this, when Planck published his full solution to black body radiation, Jeans did not accept it. One of his most important discoveries is called the Jeans length – the critical radius of an interstellar cloud, which depends on the temperature and density of the cloud and the mass of its particles. A cloud smaller than the Jeans length will not have sufficient gravity to overcome the pressure of the gas and will not collapse into a star, whereas a cloud that is larger than the Jeans length will collapse. Apart from his scientific books, upon his retirement he also wrote popular science books.

James Prescott Joule (1818–1889)

An English physicist, the son of a brewer. He studied arithmetic and geometry at the Manchester Literary and Philosophical Society, where he became interested in electricity. He managed the brewery that he inherited from his father for a number of years until he sold it in 1854. During this time he had regarded his dabbling in science as a hobby, and in 1838 had already published his first paper on electricity. In 1840 he discovered the law that bears his name today, which calculates the amount of heat produced by an electrical current passing through a resistor. Despite his achievements, it was difficult for him to find a place for himself in the scientific community, where he was perceived as a parochial dilettante. In 1843 he published the results of his research on heat, including his findings on the equivalency of heat and mechanical work. This led him to the idea of conservation of energy, which then led him on to the first law of thermodynamics. A short time later, in Germany, Helmholtz acknowledged Joule's work. Helmholtz's conclusive statement in 1847 of the law of conservation of energy brought about a widespread recognition of Joule's contribution. In 1847, at Oxford University, Joule presented his theory to Michael Faraday and Lord Kelvin, yet they remained skeptic. Some time has passed before Kelvin accepted Joule's authority and collaborated with him, among other things, on the development of a scale of absolute temperature. His collaboration with Kelvin eventually led to the discovery of what is known now as the Joule-Thomson effect, a modification in the behavior of an ideal gas due to inter-molecular forces in gases. The publication of these results contributed to the acceptance of Joule's achievements as well as the establishment of the kinetic theory of gases. The metric unit of energy was named after him.

Joseph M. Juran (1904–2008)

Romanian management consultant, whose main contribution was in the area of quality control; indeed, he was known as "the father of quality." In 1937 Juran extrapolated the Pareto Principle (20:80 rule) in such a way that allowed managers to distinguish between "the vital few" and "the useful many" in their operations. He was also the first to call this principle "Pareto's Rule." From 1951 until his death in 2008, he kept busy with improving the performance and quality of goods and services, and wrote extensively about it. He is mainly remembered as the one who added the human element to quality control. In 1979 he founded the Juran Institute for the purpose of doing research and providing practical solutions to quality control issues in industrial organizations.

Daniel Kahneman (1934–)

Israeli-born American psychologist, the 2002 Nobel laureate in economics. Born in Tel Aviv, he lived in France, mainly on the run during World War II, and then emigrated to Israel. He studied for his PhD in psychology at the University of California in Berkeley. In 1961 he joined the faculty of psychology department at the Hebrew University in Jerusalem. His research with Amos Tversky on judgment and decision-making under uncertainty earned him the Nobel Prize (Tversky had died earlier, but the Nobel Committee saw fit to note his contribution). In their research, they demonstrated that – contrary to the most basic assumption of economic analysis, namely, that decision-making is a rational process – a disproportionately large amount of weight is attached to small risks, in comparison with the weight given to potential profits; that the presence or absence of alternatives can change priorities; and that the way in which alternatives are semantically and mathematically framed has an irrational influence on decision makers. In 1978 he took a position at the University of British Columbia, Canada; in 1986, at the University of California, Berkeley; and in 1993, at Princeton University, where he works at present. Since 2000, he has also been a member of the Center for the Study of Rationality at the Hebrew University in Jerusalem.

William Thomson, Lord Kelvin (1824–1907)

British mathematical physicist and engineer. Born in Belfast, he moved to Glasgow when his father was appointed to the Department of Mathematics at the University of Glasgow. He received his education in mathematics from his father. He began his studies at the University of Glasgow, and later studied at Cambridge. His first paper, dealing with Fourier's analysis, was published in 1841. In 1846, at the age of only twenty-two, he was appointed Professor of Natural Philosophy at the University of

Glasgow, where he worked on the mathematical analysis of electricity and on thermodynamics. In 1848 he proposed an absolute temperature scale based on Carnot's theory, used today as the standard scientific temperature scale. Between 1849 and 1852 he published three influential papers on heat theory; however it appears that he overlooked the connection between Joule's findings and Carnot's principle, whereas Clausius did incorporate it in his studies on the same subject. In 1852 he read Joule's work, but it took him many years to accept it. In 1856 he published a paper on electricity and magnetism that helped lead Maxwell to his monumental theory of electromagnetism. Surprisingly, Kelvin did not support Maxwell's ideas, and his search for a unifying theory only served to distance him from Maxwell's ideas. Some say that in the first half of his career, Kelvin could not be wrong, and in the second half, he seemed incapable of being right! Among others, he dismissed atomic theory, opposed Darwin's theory of evolution (due to an erroneous calculation concerning the age of the Earth), and rejected Rutherford's ideas about radioactivity. In 1860 he coauthored a book with Peter Guthrie Tait, *Treatise on Natural Philosophy*. Thomson made important contributions to the laying of the first transatlantic telegraph cable between Ireland and Newfoundland, Canada, for which he was awarded knighthood from Queen Victoria in 1866, becoming Sir William Thomson, and in 1892 he was dubbed Baron Kelvin of Largs. His patents for measuring transmitted signals over cables (the mirror galvanometer) and consultancy services to various companies made him wealthy. He published 600 papers, was elected to the Royal Society in 1851, and was its president three times. The unit of the absolute temperature scale was named after him; the kelvin is equivalent to 1° Centigrade.

Gustav Kirchhoff (1824–1887)

German physicist, one of the fathers of electrical circuit theory as well as spectroscopy, and one of the first scientists to investigate black body radiation (in fact, it was he who in 1862 coined the term "black body radiation"). Four different sets of physical laws are named after him, in the fields of electric circuit theory, thermal emission, spectroscopy, and thermochemistry. He formulated his circuit laws as a seminar exercise presented in 1845 when still an undergraduate student; this later developed into his PhD dissertation. In 1859 he proposed the law of thermal radiation, and in 1861 he proved it. Beginning in 1854 he worked at the University of Heidelberg, in collaboration with Robert Bunsen, with whom he developed spectroscopy and discovered the elements cesium and rubidium. He was part of the academic and social circle that surrounded Helmholtz. At the same time, Kirchhoff discovered (simultaneously with but independently of Wilhelm Weber) that the speed of an electric current in a wire conductor is independent of the substance of the wire, and is almost identical to the speed of light. They both interpreted this similarity as a coincidence, instead of taking the next step, as Maxwell did five years later, when he deduced that light was an electromagnetic phenomenon. In 1854 he received the chair of theoretical physics at Heidelberg. Kirchhoff was physically disabled, and most of his life used crutches or a wheelchair. Even though he received many offers from a number of universities, he rejected them because he was content at Heidelberg. Nevertheless, as the years progressed, his experimental work, from which he derived much satisfaction, became wearisome due to his disability, and therefore he accepted in 1875 an offer from the Department of Mathematical Physics at Berlin.

Leo Koenigsberger (1837–1921)

German mathematician and a historian of science. Known mainly for his extensive biography of Hermann von Helmholtz, which he wrote from 1902-1903. He was born in Posen (today Poznań, Poland), the son of an affluent merchant. Studied at the University of Berlin, and taught in Greifswald, Heidelberg, Dresden and Vienna before settling back in Dresden, where he taught from 1884 to 1914. Koeningsberger's main interests lay in elliptical functions and differential equations.

Gottfried Wilhelm Leibniz (1646–1716)

German mathematician and philosopher. Despite his enormous contributions to mathematics, philosophy and many fields of science, he was never part of any academic institution, perhaps because his attempts to combine different disciplines were ahead of his time. While in Paris in the 1670s, he developed the basis of calculus. After publishing a number of papers on the subject, Isaac Newton claimed that Leibniz stole from him the basic ideas of this important branch of mathematics, and a bitter quarrel erupted between them. The basic facts are that Newton had indeed developed calculus before Leibniz did, but published his findings only decades later. Today it is accepted that the two worked entirely independently on the development of calculus; nevertheless, the mathematical notation used today are Leibniz's, not Newton's. Leibniz traveled widely in Europe and was made a member of both the French Academy of Science and the British Royal Society. But as a protégée of the Duke of Brunswick in

Hanover, he had to return there, serving as court Counselor for many years. His intellectual achievements are too many to relate here, and it is possible that a great many of them are still not known (presumably buried in the cellars of the Royal Library in Hanover). In mathematics, aside from his work on calculus, Leibniz contributed to the theory of probability and improved mechanical calculators. In physics, he studied the subject of kinetic energy, potential energy and momentum. In theology, he published a book called *Théodicée*, in which he grappled with the question of why the world, the creation of a perfect God, is not perfect. He also contributed to biology, geology, medicine, psychology, linguistics and the social sciences, which were then in their infancy. Among all those other things, he was also the first European to take an interest in the teachings of Confucius. Leibniz took an active part in the struggle of the Duke of Hanover to assume the English crown, but when the Duke became King George I, he showed no gratitude (actually, he joined Newton's supporters in the bitter priority dispute over calculus), and Leibniz was forgotten by all by the time he died. Not one of the distinguished people with whom he had been associated during his life took the trouble to attend his funeral in 1716. The Berlin Academy, which he founded and of which was the first president, the Royal Society of London and the French Academy of Science all ignored his death. Today he is considered one of the greatest thinkers of all times.

Hendrik Antoon Lorentz (1853–1928)

Dutch physicist, the 1902 Nobel laureate in Physics, together with Pieter Zeeman, for the discovery and theoretical explanation of the Zeeman Effect (the splitting of a spectral line in the presence of a magnetic field). Zeeman, Lorentz's student, discovered the effect in 1896, and Lorentz provided the theoretical explanation. Lorentz is mainly remembered for his mathematical transformation that appears in the special theory of relativity. Indeed, Einstein and Poincaré called the equations of special relativity "the Lorentz Transformations," and the special theory of relativity was initially called the Lorentz-Einstein Theory.

Josef Loschmidt (1821–1895)

Austrian-Bohemian physicist and chemist, son of farmer. Thanks to a priest who persuaded his parents to send him to high school, he went on to study at Prague's Karl Ferdinand University. His first paper, in 1861, received little attention from the chemistry community. At the age of 44, while still a high school teacher, he calculate the size of a molecule, solving one of the most important problems of his time. To do so he used the kinetic theory of gases innovatively to derive a value for the diameter of a molecule (which then made possible the calculation of Avogadro's number). His work was done during a period when the kinetic theory and the existence of molecules were still controversial. The calculation of Avogadro's number (or, as it was called in German-speaking countries, Loschmidt's number) finally won him recognition. In 1866, thanks to Josef Stefan, Loschmidt was given a post at the University of Vienna, and in 1872 he became a full professor. James Clerk Maxwell used Loschmidt's data to calculate the diameters of various gas molecules. Even though he was a close friend of Boltzmann, Loschmidt questioned his colleague's attempt to derive the second law of thermodynamics from kinetic theory, that eventually led to Boltzmann's statistical expression of entropy. The leading chemists of his time rejected or ignored his pioneering work on chemical structure, but Stefan, Boltzmann, Maxwell and other leading physicists accepted his ideas and used them. In Boltzmann's opinion, Loschmidt's excessive modesty was the reason that he did not receive the appreciation and honor he deserved.

Ernst Mach (1838–1916)

Austrian-Bohemian physicist and philosopher. One of the fathers of fluid mechanics, whose name is familiar today mainly because the unit for the speed of sound was named after him. His father, a graduate of the University of Prague, was a high school teacher. Until age 15, Mach was taught by his parents, then he went to a gymnasium, and subsequently to the University of Vienna, where he studied mathematics, physics and philosophy. In 1860 he received his PhD, and in 1864 he was appointed Professor of Mathematics at the University of Graz. In 1867 he was appointed professor of experimental physics at Karl Ferdinand University in Prague, where he remained for 28 years. In 1901 he retired from the university because of his ill health. His work focused mainly on interferometry, refraction, polarization and reflection of light (the Mach-Zehnder interferometer is still in use today in various fields). This led him to studies on supersonic velocities, and he published a paper on this subject in 1877. He also developed a highly influential branch of philosophy of science, which was known later as logical positivism.

Lise Meitner (1878–1968)

Austrian physicist. Born into a Jewish family, she converted to Lutheranism as an adult. She specialized in nuclear physics and radioactivity and worked for thirty years with Otto Hahn, the chemist and 1944 Nobel laureate, on research that led to nuclear fission. Even though she was a longstanding, active partner in Hahn's research and contributed the theoretical calculations proving that the nucleus of the atom indeed splits under certain conditions, the Nobel Committee decided not to award her the prize together with Hahn. Until 1934 Meitner held a senior position on the faculty of sciences in the University of Berlin, then she was dismissed because of her Jewish origin; yet as an Austrian citizen, she was allowed to continue her work with Hahn at the Kaiser-Wilhelm Society. But when Austria was annexed to Germany she was forced to escape and moved to Stockholm. Hahn maintained his correspondence with her, and while in Sweden, she was the first to interpret the data he sent her as evidence of nuclear fission. In 1949 she received Swedish citizenship, and later moved to the United States, but had no success finding a suitable academic position and retired from research. In 1997, element 109, meitnerium, was named in her honor.

Stanley Milgram (1933–1984)

American social psychologist. In the 1950s he published the "six degrees of separation" study, which deals with the necessary number of links required to connect two persons who do not know each other. He also earned publicity for his psychological studies that tested the readiness of individuals to abuse others while following the orders of an authoritative figure (the motivation for these experiments was his desire understand the behavior of individual Nazis during the Holocaust). Milgram studied political science at Queens College, New York, and then went on to study for his Ph.D. at the Department of Social Psychology at Harvard University. He received his doctorate in 1960. His controversial studies raised many ethical issues, in part because his experiments generated highly stressful conditions that sometimes turned out to have been traumatic for his subjects. At the same time, there is no dispute about the importance of his findings. Between 1963 and 1967 he was a lecturer at Harvard, but never received tenure because of the controversy surrounding his research. From 1967 to 1984 he taught at New York University. He also conducted research on violence in television, urban psychology and more. Milgram died of a heart attack at the age of 51.

Walther Nernst (1864–1941)

German physicist and chemist, the 1920 Nobel laureate in chemistry for his pre-WWI work on thermodynamics and photochemistry, in which he formulated the third law of thermodynamics. He was one of the first scientists involved in chemical warfare research during World War I. He joined Ostwald in Leipzig, where he did important work. In 1894 he decided to accept an offer from Göttingen, where he founded and served as director of the Institute of Physical Chemistry and Electrochemistry. In 1905 he was appointed Professor of Chemistry, and later of physics, at the University of Berlin. He advocated for the military advantage to be gained from chemical weaponry and suggested introducing certain compounds, for example tear gas, into bullets in ordinary use. The experiment was a failure, and he left chemical weaponry and returned to his laboratory in Berlin. In 1924 he was appointed director of the Institute for Physics and Chemistry in Berlin and remained there until his retirement in 1933. Both his sons were killed in the First World War. He spoke warmly of the open atmosphere that Boltzmann created in Graz, and the time he was willing to spend with outstanding students.

Simon Newcomb (1835–1909)

Canadian-American astronomer and mathematician, who contributed much to economics, statistics, and even to science fiction literature. As a child he received no formal education, and learned mainly from his father, who was a teacher. When he moved to the United States in 1854, he worked for a few years as a teacher, and in his spare time studied a wide range of topics, in particular mathematics and astronomy. In 1857 he went to the Lawrence Scientific School at Harvard University, graduating with a B.Sc. in 1858. In 1861 he was appointed Professor of Mathematics and Astronomy at the United States Naval Observatory, Washington D.C. Following that, he took the post of professor of mathematics and astronomy at Johns Hopkins University. His astronomical measurements from that time came to be international standards. Between 1878 and 1883 he worked on measuring the speed of light (part of the time with Abraham Michelson, who was Helmholtz's student, and who received the Nobel Prize for his work in the field in 1907). In 1881 he discovered the statistical law of the uneven distribution of digits known today as Benford's law. He died of bladder cancer.

William Nicol (1768–1851)

Scottish physicist and geologist who, in 1828, invented the first device to polarize light, today called the Nicol Prism. Not much is known about him, other than the fact he lectured in natural philosophy at the University of Edinburgh and later retired and lived in isolation in Edinburgh. He conducted numerous studies on fluid inclusions in crystals and on the microscopic structure of fossil wood, but until 1826, he had not published anything. The prism he invented allowed him to extend his research on the refraction and polarization of light, and was later used to study the optical activity of organic compounds, but again, the late publication of his discoveries delayed their use by about forty years. In 1815 he developed a method for preparing especially thin sections of rocks and crystals, that allowed for the first time the observation of the internal structure of the minerals using transmitted light, instead of reflected light. The Dorsum Nicol ridge on the moon was named after him.

Wilhelm Ostwald (1853–1932)

German chemist, born in Riga, the 1909 Nobel laureate in Chemistry for his work on the catalysis, reactions' rate and chemical equilibrium. He is considered the father of physical chemistry, and among other achievements, he coined around 1900 the term "mole" (the molecular weight of a substance expressed in grams). Along with Ernst Mach and others, he opposed atomic theory, although Ironically, the concept of "mole" was directly related to it (a mole of any substance has exactly the same number of molecules). In addition to chemistry, he engaged in philosophy and painting, and was very interested in the theory of colors. He was also an active member in the World Esperanto Association. Between 1875 and 1881 he worked at the University of Tartu, Estonia, and from 1881 to 1887 at the Riga Polytechnicum. In 1877 he moved to Leipzig, where he worked until his death.

Jules Henri Poincaré (1854–1912)

French mathematician and theoretical physicist who made substantial and fundamental contributions to pure and applied mathematics, including topology, and mathematical physics. One of the fathers of topology, he formulated one of the most famous problems in this field, on the collapse of spherical universes – the Poincaré conjecture, that was proven in 2002 by the Russian-Jewish mathematician Grigori Perelman. Poincaré was the first to describe a chaotic deterministic system, and thus laid the foundation for modern chaos theory. He presented the modern principle of relativity, and was the first to formulate the Lorentz transformations in their modern symmetrical form. He discovered velocity transformations pertaining to the theory of relativity which are still in use. The Poincaré group, used in mathematics and physics, was named after him. Poincaré studied mathematics at the École Polytechnique (founded by Lazare Carnot), then went on to study mathematics and mine engineering at École des Mines, after which he became a mining inspector and a lecturer in mathematics at Caen University, where he taught for two years, but did not earn any praise for his teaching style. His PhD thesis was in the field of differential equations. In 1881 he joined the faculty of the Sorbonne, where he stayed for the rest of his career, holding the chairs of Physical and Experimental Mechanics, Mathematical Physics and Theory of Probability, and Celestial Mechanics and Astronomy. In 1887, at the age of 32, Poincaré was elected to the French Academy of Sciences, whose president he became in 1906. Already in 1888 he won a mathematical competition held by the Oscar II, King of Sweden, for a partial solution to the problem of how stable is the solar system (the famous three-body problem). He never left the realm of mining, becoming the chief engineer of French mines in 1893, and later on national chief inspector. Other than his numerous contributions to many and varied subjects, he wrote popular books on mathematics and physics. In contrast with Bertrand Russell, who was convinced that mathematics was a branch of logics, Poincaré believed that intuition was at the heart of mathematics. He would solve problems in his head, and only later write the solutions down on paper. In 1912, at the age of 58, he died after prostate surgery.

John William Strutt, Lord Rayleigh (1842–1919)

English physicist, the 1904 Nobel laureate in physics for his discovery of the element argon. His initial work was concerned with oscillators and optics. Later on he worked in many field in physics: sound, wave theory, color perception, electrodynamics, electromagnetics, the scattering of light, flow, hydrodynamics, gas density, viscosity, capillary action, elasticity and photography. His accurate experimental data led him to determine standards for electrical resistance, electric currents and electromotive forces. His final efforts focused on electrical and magnetic problems. He explained the phenomenon of light scattering as a function of wavelength, now called the Rayleigh scattering. A mathematical method for calculating frequencies is also name after him, as are two craters, one on the moon and one on Mars. He inherited the title of baron in 1873 upon the death of his father. Between 1879 and 1884 he was the Cavendish Professor of Physics at Cambridge, taking up the post after Maxwell vacated it. In 1884 he left Cambridge and continued his experimental work at his estate in Essex. From 1887 to 1905 he was Professor of Natural Philosophy at the Royal Institution of Great Britain, as Tyndall's successor. Between 1905 and 1908 he served as president of the Royal Society.

Georg Friedrich Bernhard Riemann (1826–1866)

German mathematician who made many important contributions to analytic and differential geometry, some of which paved the way for the development of the general theory of relativity. His father was a Lutheran pastor. From a very young age Riemann showed great interest in mathematics, and while in high school he read a huge volume by Legendre (900 pages) in six days. In 1846, when he was 19, he began studying philology and theology at Göttingen University, with an aim to help his family's finances, but already in that first year he obtained his father's approval to study mathematics. He studied elementary mathematics courses with Gauss, and later did his PhD under him. He was also much influenced by Weber during the year and a half he worked as his teaching assistant. He also spent two years in Berlin, where he studied under Jacobi and Dirichlet. As part of his obligations as a lecturer, he had to give three lectures, which went on to become the foundations for modern geometry – Riemannian geometry – which was to provide, as mentioned above, the basis for the general theory of relativity. In 1859 he became chairman of the mathematics department in Göttingen. Riemann was the first to propose the use of more than three or four dimensions to describe physical reality. Throughout his life he spent time on efforts tried to prove mathematically the truth of the Scriptures. He died in 1866 from tuberculosis, survived by his wife and daughter. The housekeeper, upon hearing about his death, threw away all his papers; it is possible that she thus destroyed the proof for what is today called the Riemann hypothesis on the source of prime numbers. To this day, nobody has been able to prove it, and it is considered one of the most important unsolved problems in mathematics.

Arthur Schopenhauer (1788–1860)

German philosopher, known for his pessimism, pacifism and cosmopolitan outlook. The son of an affluent merchant family, he became financially independent at age 21, having inherited his father's fortune. In 1809 he went to study medicine at Göttingen University, but after two years left to study philosophy in Berlin. He received his Ph.D. from Jena University. In 1820 he became professor at University of Berlin. He adamantly opposed Hegel's philosophy, and deliberately scheduled his lectures to coincide with Hegel's. He did not have much of an audience. He never married, and had no contact with his mother. He was prone to anxiety, and some claim that this influenced his pessimistic outlook. Schopenhauer claimed that the Will is the essence of things, coined the term "unconscious" and claimed that the sex drive was the basic expression of the Will. His ideas influenced Freud. He admired genius, because he saw in it a release from involvement in the world, from passion and from interests. He believed that Nature was the highest aristocrat, and that the differences in social status that nature proscribes are much greater than that of the society of any nation based on birthright, title, means or status.

Erwin Schrödinger (1887–1961)

Austrian theoretical physicist, the 1933 Nobel Prize laureate in physics for the equation named after him, which is considered one of the greatest achievements of 20th century science. One of the fathers of quantum mechanics (whose basic concept, the quantum, was a result of black body radiation research). Schrödinger's equation revolutionized quantum mechanics, and consequently chemistry and physics. In 1927 Schrödinger succeeded Planck at the University of Berlin, but in 1933, disgusted with the Nazi regime, he decided to leave Germany. He became a Fellow of Magdalene College at Oxford University, and a short while later won the Nobel prize (along with Paul Dirac). He did not fit in at Oxford, partly because of his unconventional lifestyle (he lived in a *ménage à troi*). In 1934 he visited Princeton University, and although offered a permanent position, he did not accept it, again, perhaps, because of his lifestyle. He finally accepted an offer in 1936 from the University of Graz in Austria. After the *Anschluss* in 1938, Schrödinger published a statement recanting his previous letter of opposition to the Nazi regime. He later regretted this, and even personally apologized to Einstein. Nevertheless, he was eventually fired from the university for his "political unreliability" and left the Third Reich. In 1940 he accepted the position of Director of the School for Theoretical Physics in Dublin, Ireland, where he remained for 17 years. He continued his wild lifestyle, including involvement with female students, and fathered two children to two Irishwomen. In 1944 he wrote one of the first books on the origin of life, *What is Life?*, which included a discussion of negative entropy and greatly influenced the discoverers of the structure of DNA, Francis Crick and James Watson. Schrödinger retired in 1955, returned to Vienna in 1956, and died there from tuberculosis in 1961.

Arnold Sommerfeld (1868–1951)

German theoretical physicist, one of the pioneers of atomic and quantum physics. He studied mathematics and physics in Königsberg, East Prussia, and remained there after receiving his PhD in 1891. Felix Klein, his doctoral advisor, persuaded him to concentrate on applied mathematics. In 1897 he took over Wilhelm Wien's post at the Clausthal-Zellerfeld Academy. At Klein's request, he undertook to edit the fifth volume of his *Encyklopädie der mathematischen Wissenschaften mit Einschluss ihre Anwendungen,* an effort that would consume some 28 years. From 1906 on, he was professor of physics and Director of the Theoretical Physics Institute at the University of Munich. He had a special ability to discover potential talents, and many of his students –Wolfgang Pauli, Werner Heisenberg, Hans Bethe, Peter Debye, Linus Pauling, and Isidor I. Rabi – became Nobel laureates. He had warm, informal relationships with his students, and encouraged open, productive scientific discussions. Sommerfeld's mathematical contribution to Einstein's special theory of relativity helped it win over skeptics. One of his best-known accomplishments was a model of a stable atom that he developed with Niels Bohr. Despite being nominated for the Nobel Prize a grand total of 81 times (an achievement in itself), he never won one. Sommerfeld died in 1951 in Munich from injuries suffered in a traffic accident while walking with his grandchildren.

Johannes Stark (1874–1957)

German physicist, the 1919 Nobel laureate in physics for his discovery of the Stark effect – the splitting of spectral lines in electric fields (similar to the Zeeman effect, which was explained by Lorenz). He studied physics, mathematics, chemistry and crystallography at the University of Munich and finished his PhD studies in 1897. He worked in a number of universities (Hanover, Aachen, and Greifswald). He focused on three main areas: electric currents in gases, analytic spectroscopy, and chemical valance. From 1933 until his retirement in 1939, he was the president of the Physical-Technical Society of Berlin. He was a member of the "German Physics" movement – a Nazi-inspired group of scientists that utterly rejected theoretical physics in general and the "Jewish" theory of relativity in particular – even though previously, in 1907, as an editor of the *Radioactive and Electronic Annual,* he had written a glowing review of Einstein's (barely known then) paper on the principle of relativity. Under the Nazi regime, his goal was to become the Führer of German physics. He came out strongly against Einstein and other Jewish scientists, and even against Werner Heisenberg – who was not a Jew, and participated in Hitler's atomic program, but had "sinned" in his defense of Einstein's theory of relativity, and was thus regarded as a "white Jew." Stark also threatened Max von Laue, and demanded that he toe the party line "or else." As he saw things, only pure-blooded Arians could hold scientific positions in Germany, because Jewish scientists lacked the attitude and the creativity necessary for work in the natural sciences. After the war he did research in his private laboratory in his country home in Upper Bavaria.

Joseph Stefan (1835–1893)

Austrian physicist, mathematician and poet. Both his parents were Slovenians of the lower middle class: his father was a miller and baker, and his mother a maidservant; both were illiterate, and married only when he was 11 years old so that their son would be allowed to study at the gymnasium (illegitimate children could not attend school). His talents were apparent already as a boy, and his teachers recommended he continue his studies. He finished first in his class, and considered joining the Benedictine order, but his interest in mathematics and physics prevailed. In 1857 he graduated in mathematics and physics from the University of Vienna. During that time he also published a number of poems in Slovene, but abandoned that endeavor after his work was harshly criticized. He taught physics at the University of Vienna, became director of the Physical Institute in 1866, and was elected Vice-President of the Vienna Academy of Sciences. He is mainly remembered for discovering the relation between the intensity of black body radiation and its temperature. Stefan derived his law from experimental measurements made by Irish physicist John Tyndall. In 1884 Boltzmann, one of Stefan's students, derived the law theoretically. This is known today as the Stefan-Boltzmann law. Using his law, Stefan was the first to calculate the temperature of the sun's surface. Stefan devoted his life to science, often sleeping in his laboratory, and even though it did not leave him much time for a social life, he was much admired by his students, regarded as a scientist who was easy to talk to, pleasant and encouraging. He married when he was 56, but died of a heart attack one year later.

Sir George Gabriel Stokes (1819–1903)

Irish mathematician and physicist who made many important contributions to fluid dynamics (the Navier-Stokes equations), optics and mathematical physics (Stokes's theorem). He was secretary, and later president, of the Royal Society. Stokes was born in Ireland and pursued his academic studies at Cambridge. He graduated in 1837, and began publishing significant work already in 1840. Stokes had a rare combination of rich mathematical knowledge and experimental skill, both of which he made much use of. Most of his work was concerned with waves and the transformations imposed on them during passage through different media. He investigated fluorescence, among other phenomena, and in one of his experiments discovered that ultraviolet light can pass through quartz (although not through glass). In other experiments, he helped determine the composition of chlorophyll. His broad outlook allowed him to understand and appreciate contributions of other physicists, such as Joules, before the scientific community had accepted their theories. It may be noted that much of his research, for example in spectroscopy, was not published in his lifetime. Due to his fame he was asked to investigate the notorious train accident known as the Dee bridge disaster in 1847. He discovered that the reason for the accident was the use of cast lead for the supporting beam, which collapsed under pressure. As a result of this discovery, many bridges in Britain were demolished and then rebuilt. For his work and public activity he was awarded many honors, including the title of baronet.

Peter Guthrie Tait (1831–1901)

Scottish physicist; classmate and good friend of James Clerk Maxwell. He is known mainly for the physics book he wrote with Kelvin in 1860. He was one of the pioneers of thermodynamics, and in 1865 wrote a book on the history of this science.

Sir Joseph John Thomson (1856–1940)

British physicist, the 1906 Nobel laureate in physics for discovering the electron and his work on the conduction of electricity in gases. Born in Scotland, he studied engineering at Manchester and in 1876 moved to Trinity College, Cambridge. By 1884 he had already replaced Lord Rayleigh as the Cavendish Professor of Physics. In the same year he was elected to the Royal Society and later served as its director (1916–1920). He was a gifted instructor and seven of his assistants, and also his son, were themselves Nobel laureates. Thomson's earthshaking discovery of the electron was published in 1897. He was knighted in 1908, and later became the Master of Trinity College until his death in 1940. In 1913 he discovered the existence of isotopes of stable elements and paved the way for the development of the field of mass spectroscopy. He is buried in Westminster Abbey, the resting place of many a great Briton, including Sir Isaac Newton.

Robert Henry Thurston (1839–1903)

American engineer, inventor and lecturer. One of the first graduates of Brown University's School of Engineering. In 1885, when he was 46, he took over as director of Sibley College of mechanical engineering at Cornell University, turning it into the best engineering college in the United States. Today he is mainly known for his translation of Carnot's paper on the motive power of heat.

August Toepler (1836–1912)

German physicist, known for his experiments in electrostatics. Graduated in chemistry in 1860 and later turned to experimental physics. After teaching at the Poppelsdorf Academy and at the Polytechnic Institute of Riga, he was appointed a professor at the University of Graz in 1868, where he established a new physics institute. In 1876, when he left Graz to become director of the Physics Institute at the Dresden Technical University, his former position was given to Boltzmann, who accepted it eagerly, since he could now teach physics instead of mathematics. Toepler remained in Dresden until his retirement in 1900. In 1865 Toepler applied Foucault's knife-edge test, initially developed to examine lenses, to telescope mirrors and to the examination of the flow of liquids or gases. The method is called today schlieren photography, or the schlieren technique. Using this technique, he was the first successfully to make acoustic waves "visible." This method is important in high-speed cinematography and in wind tunnels, and is used to even today. Toepler invented other instruments, including a mercury pump that bears his name.

Amos Tversky (1937–1996)

Israel-born American psychologist, one of the pioneers of research in the field of cognitive bias, in collaboration with Daniel Kahneman. His father was a veterinarian and his mother was a member of the Israeli parliament. During his service in the Israel army, he was decorated for saving the life of a comrade. After receiving his doctorate from the University of Michigan, he returned to Israel in 1965, taking a position at Hebrew University in Jerusalem. In 1978 he moved to Stanford University in California, where he married a professor of psychology at the same university. After Tversky's death, Kahneman, along with Vernon Smith, was awarded the Nobel Prize in Economics in 2002, to a large extent for the research that had been done with Tversky. Tversky did not receive the prize, as it is not awarded posthumously. Yet exceptionally, his name was mentioned by the Nobel Committee as Kahneman's partner in the prize-winning work on judgment and decision-making under uncertainty. Their paper, "The Framing of Decisions and the Psychology of Choice," was a major breakthrough. In 1982 they published a book (along with Paul Slovik), *Judgment Under Uncertainty*. Tversky made major contributions in other areas of psychology. He died of a metastatic melanoma.

Max von Laue (1879–1960)

German physicist and the 1914 Nobel laureate in physics for the discovery of the diffraction of x-rays in crystals. He also contributed to the fields of optics crystallography, quantum theory, superconductivity, and the theory of relativity. He was instrumental in re-establishing science in Germany after World War II. Von Laue studied under Planck and was friends with Einstein. In Berlin, he worked on entropy in radiation and on the thermodynamic significance of the coherence of light waves. During Hitler's reign, he secretly helped Jewish scientists emigrate from Germany, and openly opposed the regime's policies. At a physics convention in 1933 he compared dubbing the theory of relativity as "Jewish physics" to the persecution of Galileo; he blocked the membership of Nazi physicist Johannes Stark (the 1919 Nobel laureate in physics) to the Prussian Academy of Science; he compared Fritz Haber's exile to Themistocles' expulsion from Athens; and more. When the Nazis invaded Denmark, Hungarian chemist George de Hevesy dissolved von Laue's and James Franck's Nobel Prize gold medals to prevent the Nazis from stealing them. At the end of the war, the Nobel Society recast the medals from the original gold.

Julius Robert von Mayer (1814–1878)

German physicist and physician, one of the fathers of thermodynamics. In 1841 he formulated the law of conservation of energy (known today as the first law of thermodynamics: energy can neither be created nor destroyed.) Upon the publication of Joule's paper on the conversion of mechanical energy into heat in 1843, von Mayer claimed to have discovered this phenomenon first. And indeed, wrote a paper on the conversion of mechanical work into heat in 1842 and sent it to *Annalen de Physik*, which was turned down. He rewrote the paper (adding, among other things, claims that plants convert light into chemical energy) and published it in a different journal – in the field of chemistry and pharmacology. The scientific establishment, including Helmholtz and Joules, were wary of his discoveries. When Joules claimed priority, and after two of his children had died one after the other in 1848, Mayer threw himself out of his third-floor window in 1850 and was hospitalized for a time in an asylum for the insane. Only in 1862 did he finally win the recognition he deserved, when physicist John Tyndall presented his work at the Royal London Institution. In 1867, he was awarded personal nobility in Germany, adding the prefix "von" to his name. He died of tuberculosis in 1878.

John von Neumann (1903–1957)

One of the greatest mathematicians of the twentieth century, the son of a Jewish family in Hungary, where he received his education in chemistry at the University of Budapest. In 1930, upon the death of his father, he immigrated to the United States. He made significant contributions to many areas of science and engineering. Besides originating the idea of computer memory, he and Oscar Morgenstern introduced game theory. In addition, he was the father of the operator theory in quantum mechanics, and also contributed to the development of the nuclear bomb; unlike many of his Manhattan Project colleagues, he went on to work on "super" – the thermonuclear bomb. Already at the age six he could divide an eight-digit numbers in his head. After completing his studies at the University of Budapest, he got a degree in chemical engineering in Zurich and in Berlin. He wrote his PhD dissertation in mathematics in 1928. By the age of 25, he had already published ten important papers. In 1930 he was invited to visit Princeton, and in 1933 he was one of the first four members, with Einstein and Gödel, at the Institute of Advanced Study there, where he remained until his death. Between 1936 and 1938 Alan Turing was a student at the Department of Mathematics in Princeton; von Neumann invited him to stay on as his research assistant, but Turing chose to return to Cambridge. During the war, his vast knowledge in hydrodynamics, ballistics, metallurgy, game theory, and statistics contributed to the development of mechanical devices for computation. Throughout the war years, he worked as a consultant to a number of national committees. Afterwards he focused on developing the computer at the Institute of Advanced Study. He continued working with the Los Alamos Group, and further developed computer capabilities for the solution of the problems involved in building the hydrogen bomb. Since he was dissatisfied with the computers of his time, he reorganized the logical structure of the computer and added to it internal memory. In 1955 he developed either bone or pancreatic cancer, probably due to exposure to radiation from the atomic bomb test during the war, and died a year and half later. On his deathbed, to the astonishment of his friends, he asked for a catholic priest.

Wilhelm Eduard Weber (1804–1891)

German physicist who made important contributions in the fields of magnetism and electricity. His PhD dissertation, presented to the University of Halle in 1826, dealt with the acoustic theory of reed organ pipes. He became a lecturer at Halle and remained there until 1831, when, upon the recommendation of Gauss, he was appointed professor of physics at the University of Göttingen. In his work with Gauss, he prepared sensitive magnetometers and other instruments to measure both direct and alternate current. In 1833 he preceded Samuel Morse in the construction of an electrical telegraph 3,000 meters long that connected his physics laboratory to Gauss's observatory; this was the world's first working telegraph. He invented the electrometer and precisely defined the unit of electrical resistance. Two of his brothers, Ernst Heinrich (who formulated Weber's Law in psychology that deals with physiological sensitivity to perceived changes in stimuli) and Eduard Frederic, were well-known scientists in their own right in the fields of anatomy and physiology. In 1837, with six of his colleagues, he was dismissed from Göttingen University for signing a petition protesting the abolition of the liberal constitution by the Duke of Hanover. He continued to do research at Göttingen, without a formal position, but then he was appointed professor of physics at Leipzig in 1843.

In 1849, he returned to his former position in Göttingen. In 1871 he suggested that atoms are comprised of positive charges surrounded by negative charges, and that the application of an electric potential on a conductor will cause the negatively charged particles to move from one atom to the next. He gave similar explanations for thermal conductivity and thermo-electricity. At the time, most scientists did not believe in the existence of atoms. The unit of magnetic flux, the weber (Wb), was named after him.

Hermann Weyl (1885–1955)

German mathematician who made his mark in the fields of symmetry, logic and numbers theory, one of the most influential mathematicians of the 20th century. Among other achievements, he was one of the first who connected the ideas of general relativity with Maxwell's electromagnetic laws. He got his PhD at the University of Göttingen under the supervision of David Hilbert. He was in Zürich when Einstein began working on his general theory of relativity, and under Einstein's influence, Weyl became enthralled by mathematical physics. There he also met Schrödinger, and they became close friends. In 1930 he left Zürich to succeed Hilbert at Göttingen, but with the rise of Nazism in 1933, he left (his wife was Jewish) for the Institute for Advanced Study in Princeton. He worked there until his retirement in 1951. At Princeton, he began to develop his ideas on information theory and efficient information systems.

Wilhelm Wien (1864–1928)

German physicist, the 1911 Nobel laureate in physics for his contribution to the understanding of black body radiation. He worked in Helmholtz's laboratory from 1883 to 1885, and later moved to the University of Berlin and worked with Max Planck. In 1893 he discovered that as the temperature of an emitting body rises, so does the maximum energy frequency (in other words, he identified the relationship between the maximum emission frequency of a black body to its temperature). In 1896 he formulated this discovery as the emission law bears his name, on which Planck based his quantum theory in 1901. Additionally, Wien laid the foundations of mass spectroscopy.

Ernst Zermelo (1871–1953)

German mathematician whose work had major implications for the foundations of mathematics and philosophy. He studied mathematics, physics and philosophy in Berlin. After his graduation in 1889, he remained in Berlin as research assistant to Planck, and under his guidance began studying hydrodynamics. From 1897 to 1910 he was in Göttingen, at that time the leading center for mathematical research in the world. From 1910 to 1916 he worked at Zurich University. In 1926 he was appointed to an honorary chair at the University of Freiberg, but his abhorrence of Hitler's regime made him resign in 1935. After the war he was reinstated, at his request, to his position. In 1904 he wrote a paper in which he proved that any finite numerical set could be well-ordered. The paper was a response to the challenge proposed by David Hilbert to the participants of the International Congress of Mathematicians in 1900: to find the solution to 23 unsolved fundamental questions during the coming century. His publication earned him fame and the position of Professor in Göttingen in 1905. Among other things, he wrote a paper questioning the correctness of Boltzmann's H-theorem.

George Kingsley Zipf (1902–1950)

 American linguist who studied the statistical distributions of words in various languages, searching for universal relationships revealed in texts regardless of the language itself. He worked at Harvard University, specializing in Chinese languages. The law named after him states that people use a few words frequently and many words seldom. The most-used word in any given language will appear in any sufficiently long text twice as often as the second-most-used word, which will appear twice as often as the fourth-most-used word, and so on. Zipf also showed that in many languages, such as English, there is an inverse relation between the frequency of a word and its length. That is, the most common words are also the shortest. He described this as an aspect of the principle of least effort. His obsession with this idea, along with some of his political views regarding Hitler's Germany, gave him a reputation of being somewhat eccentric, if not outrightly insane. Zipf discovered that his law could also be applied to the distribution of urban populations or other communities, and added that the distribution of income as a function of social standing also behaved according to his law (this observation was made by Pareto, before him).

Oded Kafri and Hava Kafri

Bibliography

"Anders Celsius," Wikipedia,
http://en.wikipedia.org/wiki/Anders_Celsius"

Angrist, S. W. and Helper, L. G., *Order and Chaos – Laws of Energy and Entropy* (New York: Basic Books, 1967)

Bader, A. and Parker, L., "Joseph Loschmidt, Physicist and Chemist," *Physics Today* Vol. 54(3) (March 2001): 45

Barabashi, A.L., *Links, the New Science of Networks* (Tel-Aviv: Yediot Ahronot and Hemed Books, 2004)

Beaudry, P., "Lazare Carnot: Organizer of Victory – How the 'Calculus of Enthusiasm' Saved France," *American Almanac* (July 21, 1997)

Bellis, M., "Outline of Railroad History,"
http://inventors.about.com/library/inventors/blrailroad.htm

——, "What is Thermometer,"
http://inventors.about.com/b/2004/11/16/the-history-behind-the-thermometer.htm

Benford, F., "The law of anomalous numbers," *Proceedings of the American Mathematical Soc*iety, 78 (1938): 551-572

Bogomolny, A., "Benford's Law and Zipf's Law," http://www.cut-the-knot.org/do_you_know/zipfLaw.shtml

Boltzmann, R., *Vorlesungen über Gastheorie* (2 vols., Leipzig: J. A. Barth, 1896-1898)

——, *Vorlesungen über Maxwells Theorie der Elektrizität und des Lichtes* (2 vols., Leipzig: J. A. Barth, 1891, 1893)

——, *Vorlesungen über Die Prinzipe Der Mechanik* (2 vols., Leipzig: J. A. Barth, 1897, 1904)

L. Boltzmann, "Weitere Studien über das Wärmegleichgewicht unter Gasmolekülen", *Sitzungsberichte Akademie der Wissenschaften* 66 (1872): 275-370, in *idem.*, *Wissenschaftliche Abhandlungen*, Vol. 1, 1909, pp. 316-402.

Braess, D. von, "Über ein Paradoxon aus der Verkehrsplanung," *Unternehmensforschung* (1969), **12**: 258–268

Braess's Paradox (Counter Intuitive Theory being used by World's Major Cities), http://expertvoices.nsdl.org/cornell-info204/2010/04/13/braess-paradox-counter-intuitive-theory-being-used-by-worlds-major-cities/

Bumstead, H. A., "Josiah Willard Gibbs," *American Journal of Science*, Ser. 4, Vol. XVI (September 1903): 187-202

Campbell, L. and Garnett, W., *The Life of James Clerk Maxwell* (London: Macmilian and Co., 1882)

Carnot, S., Réflexions sur la puissance motrice du feu et sur les machines propres à développer cette puissance (Paris: Bachelier, 1824); Trans., ed., intr. R. Fox, Sadi Carnot – Reflections on the Motive Power of Heat and on Machines Fitted to Develop that Power (Manchester: Manchester University Press, 1986); also idem, Reflections on the

Motive Power of Heat, Trans., ed., intr., Thurston, R. H.
(New York: John Wiley & Sons, 1897)

Cercignani, C., *Ludwig Boltzmann: The Man Who Trusted Atoms*
(New York: Oxford University Press, 1998)

"Claude Elwood Shannon," Wikipedia,
http://en.wikipedia.org/wiki/Claude_Shannon

Clausius, R., *Abhandlungen über die mechanische Wärmetheorie,
Zweite Abteilung* (Braunschweig: Friedrich Vieweg und
Sohn,1867); *Trans.* W. R. Browne, *The Mechanical Theory
of Heat* (London: John van Voorst, 1879)

——, "Über verschiedene für die Anwendung bequeme Formen der
Hauptgleichungen der mechanischen Wärmetheorie,"
Annalen der Physik und Chemie, 125 (1865): 353; trans.,
excrp. in William Francis Magie, *A Source Book in Physics*
(New York: McGraw-Hill, 1935)

——, *Memoires: Mechanical Theory of Heat, 1850-1865* (London,
May 1867); in
http://www.humanthermodynamics.com/Clausius.html

Cohen, E. G. D., "Boltzmann and Statistical Mechanics in
Boltzmann's Legacy 150 years After His Birth," *Atti dei
Convengni Lincei* (Accademia Nazionale dei Lincei, Roma)
131 (1996): 9-23; in http://xxx.lanl.gov/abs/cond-
mat/9608054

——, "Entropy, Probability and Dynamics,"
http://arxiv.org/PS_cache/arxiv/pdf/0807/0807.1268v2.pdf
(10 July 2008)

Cohen, D. and Talbot, K., "Prime numbers and the first digit
phenomenon," *J. Number Theory* 18 (1984): 261-268.

Crease, R. P., "Science as Drama,"
physicsworld.com/cws/article/print/25726 (Sept. 1, 2006)

Crowther, J. G., *Famous American Men of Science* (New York:
Freeport, 1969)

Dawkins, R., *The Selfish Gene* (New York: Oxford University
Press, 1989)

Drake, S., *Galileo at Work: His scientific biography.* (Mineola,
NY: Courier Dover, 2003)

Dyson, F. J. 11-16 Nov. 2007. "Why is Maxwell Theory so hard
to understand," The Second European Conference on
Antennas and Propagation, 2007. *EuCAP 2007*; in
http://www.clerkmaxwellfoundation.org/DysonFreemanArt
icle.pdf

Everitt, F., "James Clerk Maxwell: a force for physics," *Physics
World* (Dec. 1, 2006): 1-12

Erlichson, H. "Sadi Carnot, Founder of the Second Law of
Thermodynamics," *European Journal of Phys*ics 20 (1999):
183-192

"Ernst Mach," Wikipedia,
http://en.wikipedia.org/wiki/Ernst_Mach"

Flamm, D., "Ludwig Boltzmann – A pioneer of Modern Physics" in http://arxiv.org/abs/physics/9710007 (7 Oct. 1997)

——, "Boltzmann: A disordered genius," in physicsworld.com/cws/article/print/2481

Ferris, T., *Coming of Age in the Milky Way,* (new York: New York, Perennial, 2003)

Forfar, D. O., "Origins of the Clerk (Maxwell) Genuis," *Bulletin of the Institution of Mathematics and its Application,* Vol. 28, No. 1/2 (January-February 1992): 4-16

Forfar, D. O., "James Clerk Maxwell: his qualities of mind and personality as judged by his contemporaries," *Mathematics Today,* Vol 38, No. 3, (June 2002): 83

"Gabriel Daniel Farenheit," http://www.answers.com/topic/fahrenheit

Garber, E. S. G. *et al.* (eds.), *Maxwell on Heat and Statistical Mechanics* (Bethlehem: Lehigh University Press, 1995)

Gibbs, J. W., Elementary Principles in Statistical Mechanics with Special Reference to Thermodynamics (New York: Dover, 1902)

——, *The Scientific Papers of J. Willard Gibbs*, Bumstead, H. A., and Van Name, R. G., eds. (New York: Dover, 1961)

Goldstine, H. H., *The Computer from Pascal to Von Neumann* (Princeton: Princeton University Press, 1980)

Harman, P. M. (ed.), *The Scientific Letters and Papers of James Clerk Maxwell 1846-1862* Vol. 1, 197 (Cambridge: Cambridge University Press, 1990)

Hawking, S., *A Brief History of Time*, (New York: New York, Bantam, 1966)

Heilbron, J. L., The Dilemmas of an Upright Man: Max Planck and the Fortunes of German Science (Cambridge: Harvard University Press, 2000)

The History of Economic Thought Website, "Vilfredo Pareto, 1848-1923," http://cepa.newschool.edu/het/profiles/pareto.htm

Hutchinson, I.. "James Clerk Maxwell and the Christian Proposition," *MIT IAP Seminar: The Faith of Great Scientists* (Jan. 1998, 2006): 3-20

"James Clerk Maxwell," Wikipediahttp://en.wikipedia.org/wiki/James_Clerk_Maxwell"

"James Prescott Joule (1818-1889), http://www. corrosion-doctors.org/Biographies/JouleBio.htm

"Josiah Willard Gibbs (1839-1903)," http://www.corrosion-doctors.org/Biographies/GibbsBio.htm

"Josiah Willard Gibbs 1839-1903," http://www.aip.org/history/gap/Gibbs/Gibbs.html

"Josiah Willard Gibbs," http://www.answers.com/topic/willard-gibbs (2006)

Jurgan, J. M. (ed), *Quality Control Handbook* (New York: McGraw-Hill, 1951)

Kahneman D. and co-authors (2005) *Rationality, Fairness, Happiness.* Selected Writings, Edited by Maya Bar-Hillel (Hebrew).

Kossovsky, A. E., "Towards a better understanding of the leading digits phenomena," arXiv:math/0612627

Lightman, A. P. (2005). "The discoveries: great breakthroughs in twentieth-century science, including the original papers", (Toronto: Alfred A. Knopf Canada, 2005)

Lewis, Gilbert N. and Merle Randall, *Thermodynamics and the Free Energies of Chemical Substances* (New York: McGraw-Hill, 1923)

Lienhard, J. H., "Lazare & Sadi Carnot," in http://www.uh.edu/engines/epi1958.htm

Lindley, D., Boltzmann's Atom – The Great Debate That Launched a Revolution in Physics (New York: The Free Press, 2001)

Longair, M., "James Clerk Maxwell: Scotland's Greatest Physicist," *The Scotman* (15 April 2006): 4-16

"Ludwig Boltzmann (1844-1906)," http://corrosion-doctors.org/Biographies/BoltzmannBio.htm"

"Ludwig Edward Boltzmann," http://www.answers.com/topic/ludwig-boltzmann

McCartney, M., "William Thomson: king of Victorian physics," http://www.physicsworld.com/cws/article/print/16484, Dec 1, 2002

Magie, William Francis, *A Source Book in Physics* (New York: McGraw-Hill, 1935).

"Max Planck", Britannica Concise Encyclopedia (2006)

"Max Planck," Wikipedia, http://en.wikipedia.org/wiki/Max_Planck

Max Planck Institute, "Max Planck - His Life, Work, and Personality," http://www.max-planck.mpg.de/framset_e.htm

Maxwell Foundation, "The Impact of Maxwell's Work," http://www.clerkmaxwellfoundation.org/html/further_max well'simpact.html"

Maxwell Foundation, "Who Was James Clerk Maxwell?" http://www.clerkmaxwellfoundation.org/html/who_was_m axwell_.html

Maxwell, J. C., "On the description of oval curves, and those having a plurality of foci," *Proceedings of the Royal Society of Edinburgh*, Vol. II (1846)

Maxwell, J. C., "A Dynamical Theory of the Electromagnetic Field," *Philosophical Transactions of the Royal Society of London* 155 (1865): 459-512

Maxwell, J. C., *A Treatise on Electricity and Magnetism* (Oxford: Clarendon Press, 1873)

Miller, G. A. and Newman, E. B., "Tests of a statistical explanation of the rank-frequency relation for words in written English," *American Journal of Psychology*, 71 (1958): 209-218.

Moffatt, K. *Homage to Clerk Maxwell*, http://www.clerkmaxwellfoundation.org/html/further_docu ments.html.

Nash, J., "Non-Cooperative Games," *The Annals of Mathematics* 54(2), 1951: 286-295

Newman, M. E., "Power-law, Pareto Distribution and Zipf's law," *Contemporary Physics* Vol. 46, No. 5 (29 May 2006): 323-351.

Newcomb, S., "Note on the Frequency of Use of the Different Digits in Natural Numbers," *Ameican Journal of Math*ematics 4 (1881): 39-40

"Nicolas Leonard Sadi Carnot," Wikipedia, http://en.wikipedia.org/wiki/Nicolas_L%C3%A9onard_Sad i_Carnot"

Nigrini, M., "A Taxpayer Compliance Application of Benford's Law," *Journal of the American Taxation Assoc*iation 18 (1996): 72-91

Nobel Web, "Max Planck, The Noble Prize in Chemestry 1909," http://www.nobelprize.org/nobel_prizes/chemistry/laureate s/1909/planck-bio.html (2008)

Nobel Web, "Wilhelm Ostwald, The Nobel Prize in Chemistry 1909," http://www.nobelprize.org/nobel_prizes/chemistry/laureates/1909/ostwald-bio.htm

O'Connor, J. J. and Robertson, E. F., "Claude Elwood Shannon," in http://www-history.mcs.stand.ac.uk/Mathematicians/Shannon.html (October 2003)

——, "Historic topics: A visit to James Clerk Maxwell's house," in http://www-history.mcs.st-and.ac.uk/HistTopics/Maxwell_House.html (November 1997)

——, "James Clerk Maxwell", in http://www-history.mcs.st-and.ac.uk/Mathematicians/Maxwell.html (November 1997)

——, "John William Strutt (Lord Rayleigh)" in http://www-history.mcs.st-and.ac.uk/Mathematicians/Rayleigh.html (October 2003)

——, "Josiah Willard Gibbs," http://www-history.mcs.st-and.ac.uk/Mathematicians/Gibbs.html (February 1997)

——, "Lazare Nicolas Marguérite Carnot," in http://www-history.mcs.st-and.ac.uk/Biographies/Carnot.html (December 1996)

——, "Ludwig Boltzmann," in http://www-history.mcs.st-and.ac.uk/Mathematicians/Boltzmann.html (September 1998)

——, "Max Karl Ernst Ludwig Planck". http://www-history.mcs.st-and.ac.uk/Mathematicians/Planck.html (October 2003)

——, "Nicolas Léonard Sadi Carnot," in http://www-history.mcs.st-and.ac.uk/Mathematicians/Carnot_Sadi.html (October 1998)

——, "Rudolf Juluis Emmanuel Clausius," in http://www-history.mcs.st-and.ac.uk/Mathematicians/Clausius.html (December 2000)

——, "William Thomson (Lord Kelvin)," in http://www-history.mcs.st-and.ac.uk/Mathematicians/Thomson.html (October 2003)

Pais, A., Subtle is the Lord... (Oxford: Oxford University press, 1982)

"Pareto Principle – The 80-20 Rule – Complete Information," http://www.gassner.co.il/pareto

Pareto, V. *Cours d'économie politique* (Lausanne et Paris: Rouge, 1897)

Pareto, V., "Un applicazione di teorie sociologiche," *Revista Italiana di sociologia*, 1901, pp. 402-456

Pareto, V., *Trattato Di Sociologia Generale* (4 vols.), (Firenze: Barbèra, 1916)

"Peter Guthrie Tait," Wikipedia, http://en.wikipedia.org/wiki/Peter_Guthrie_Tait

Planck, M., *Scientific Autobiography and Other Papers*, trans. F. Gaynor (New York: Philosophical Library, 1949)

"Rail Transport," Wikipedia,

 http://en.wikipedia.org/wiki/Rail_transport, 2008

Rautio, J. C., "Maxwell's Legacy," *IEEE microwave magazine*

 (June 2005): 46-53

"Revolution and the growth of industrial society, 1789–1914,

 Encyclopedia Britannica,

 http://www.britannica.com/EBchecked/topic/195896/histor

 y-of-Europe/58403/Revolution-and-the-growth-of-

 industrial-society-1789-1914

"Rudolf Clausius," Wikipedia,

 http://en.wikipedia.org/wiki/Rudolf_Clausius

Schopenhauer, A., *Über die Freiheit des menschlichen Willens,*

 1839; *Trans.* K. Kolenda, *On the Freedom of the Will*

 (Oxford: *Basil Blackwell*, 1985)

"Shannon explaining why he named his uncertainty function

 'entropy'," *Scientific American* Vol. 225, No 3 (1971): 180

Shannon, C. E., "A mathematical theory of communication," *Bell*

 System Technical Journal Vol. 27 (July and October,

 1948): 379-423, 23-656 respectively

Shannon, C. E. et al. (eds.)., *Claude Elwood Shannon: Collected*

 Papers (New York: IEEE Press, 1993)

Slepian, D. (ed.), Key Papers in the Development of Information

 Theory (New York: IEEE Press, 1974)

Srinivasan, J., "Sadi Carnot and the Second Law of

 Thermodynamics," *Resonance* (Nov. 2001): 42-48

Stanford Encyclopedia of Philosophy (2004), "Boltzmann's work in Statistical Physics"

Stearns, P. N. (ed), *The Encyclopedia of World History*, Vol. V, *The Modern Period, 1789-1914* (New York: Houghton Mifflin, 2001)

Tversky, A. and Kahenman D.,"Loss aversion in riskless choice: A reference-dependent model", *Quarterly Journal of Economics* 106 (1991): 1039-1061

University of Cambridge, Biographical Information, *James Clerk Maxwell, 1831-1879, Professor of Experimental Physics* http://www.nahste.ac.uk/isaar/GB_0237_NAHSTE_P1314. html

"Vilfredo Pareto," Wikipedia, http://en.wikipedia.org/wiki/Vilfredo_Pareto

Weaver W., and Shannon C. E., *The Mathematical Theory of Communication* (Urbana, Illinois: University of Illinois Press, 1949)

"Wilhelm Wein," Wikipedia, http://en.wikipedia.org/wiki/Wilhelm_Wien

"William Thomson, 1st Baron Kelvin," Wikipedia, http://en.wikipedia.org/wiki/William_Thomson,_1st_Baron _Kelvin"

Zipf, G. K., Human Behavior and the Principle of Least-Effort (New York: Addison-Wesley,1949)

Endnotes

Prologue

[1] Angrist and Helper (1967), p. 215.

Chapter 1

[2] Stearns (2001), pp. 424-427.

[3] Bellis, M., http://inventors.about.com/library/inventors/blrailroad.htm.

[4] Carnot (1824), ed. Thurston (1897), pp. 37-41.

[5] Ibid., p. 48.

[6] Beaudry (1997); see also Lienhard, in
http://www.uh.edu/engines/epi1958.htm.

[7] Carnot (1824), ed. Thurston (1897), p. 28.

[8] Ibid., pp. 35-36.

[9] Crease (2006), Act III, Scene 2, physicsworld.com/cws/article/print/25726.

[10] Helmholtz: (1847).

[11] Carnot (1824), ed. Thurston (1897), Introduction, p. 6.

[12] Clausius (1867), p. 365.

[13] E. E. Daub, cited in O'Connor and Robertson (Dec. 2000), http://www-history.mcs.st-and.ac.uk/Mathematicians/Clausius.html.

[14] Clausius (1850), in Magie (1935), pp. 79, 368-97, 500-24.

[15] Clausius (1865).

[16] Ibid., p. 125.

[17] http://en.wikipedia.org/wiki/History_of_entropy#cite_ref-Clausius_6-0.

Chapter 2

[18] Quoted in D. O. Forfar, "James Clerk Maxwell" (1992).

[19] Lindley (2001), p. 47.

[20] Boltzmann (1872).

[21] Flamm, D., April 9, 1999, physicsworld.com/cws/article/print/2481.

[22] Lindley (2001), p. 56.

[23] Boltzmann (1891, 1893).

[24] Quoted in O'Connor and Robertson, "Ludwig Boltzmann", http://www-history.mcs.st- and.ac.uk/Mathematicians/.html.

[25] Ibid.

[26] Lindley (2001), p. 146.

[27] Boltzmann (1896, 1898).

[28] Boltzmann (1897, 1904).

[29] Pais (1982), p. 65.

[30] *Columbia Encyclopedia*, "Gibbs, Josiah Willard".

[31] "Graphical Methods in the Thermodynamics of Fluids", in Gibbs (1961).

[32] "A Method of Geometrical Representation of the Thermodynamic Properties of Substances by Means of Surfaces," in *ibid.*

[33] O'Connor and Robertson, http://www-history.mcs.st- and.ac.uk/Mathematicians/Gibbs.html.

[34] "On the Equilibrium of Heterogeneous Substances," in Gibbs (1961).

[35] Gibbs (1902).

[36] Lindley (2001), p. 155.

[37] Crowther (1969), "Gibbs".

[38] Bumstead (1903).

[39] Lewis and Randall (1923).

[40] Harman (1990), Vol. 1, p. 197.

[41] Maxwell Foundation: Who was James Clerk Maxwell?
http://www.clerkmaxwellfoundation.org/html/who_was_maxwell_.html.

[42] Maxwell (1846).

[43] Campbell and Garnett (1882), p. 80.

[44] Harman (1990), Vol. I, p. 197.

[45] Maxwell Foundation, "Who was James Clerk Maxwell?"

[46] Maxwell (1865); Quoted in: Maxwell Foundation, "Who Was James Clerk Maxwell?"

[47] Maxwell (1873).

[48] Ibid., p. xi.

Chapter 3

[49] Drake (2003), pp. 20–21.

[50] Ferris (2003), p. 204.

[51] Hawking (1996), p. 10.

[52] Planck (1950), p. 33.

[53] Lightman (2005), p. 8.

[54] Max Planck; http://en.wikipedia.org/wiki/Max_Planck.

[55] Ibid..

[56] Ibid..

[57] Heilbron (2000), p. 150.

[58] Ibid., p. 151.

[59] Max Planck Institute; Worldview, www.max-planck.mpg.de/framset_e.htm.

[60] M. Planck, (1901), 4: 553.

Chapter 4

[61] *Scientific American* (1971), Vol. 225, p. 180.

[62] Goldstine (1980), p. 119.

[63] C. E. Shannon (1948), pp. 379-423 and 623-656.

[64] Weaver and Shannon (1949), p. 121.

Chapter 5

[65] Dawkins (1989).

[66] Schopenhauer (1985).

[67] Milgram, (1967), Vol. 2, 60-67

[68] http://expertvoices.nsdl.org/cornell-info204/2010/04/13.

[69] Braess (1969).

[70] Nash (1951).

[71] Pareto (1897).

[72] Pareto (1901), pp. 402-456.

[73] Pareto (1916).

Conclusion

[74] Tversky and Kahneman (1991), pp.1039-1061.

Made in the USA
San Bernardino, CA
11 February 2020